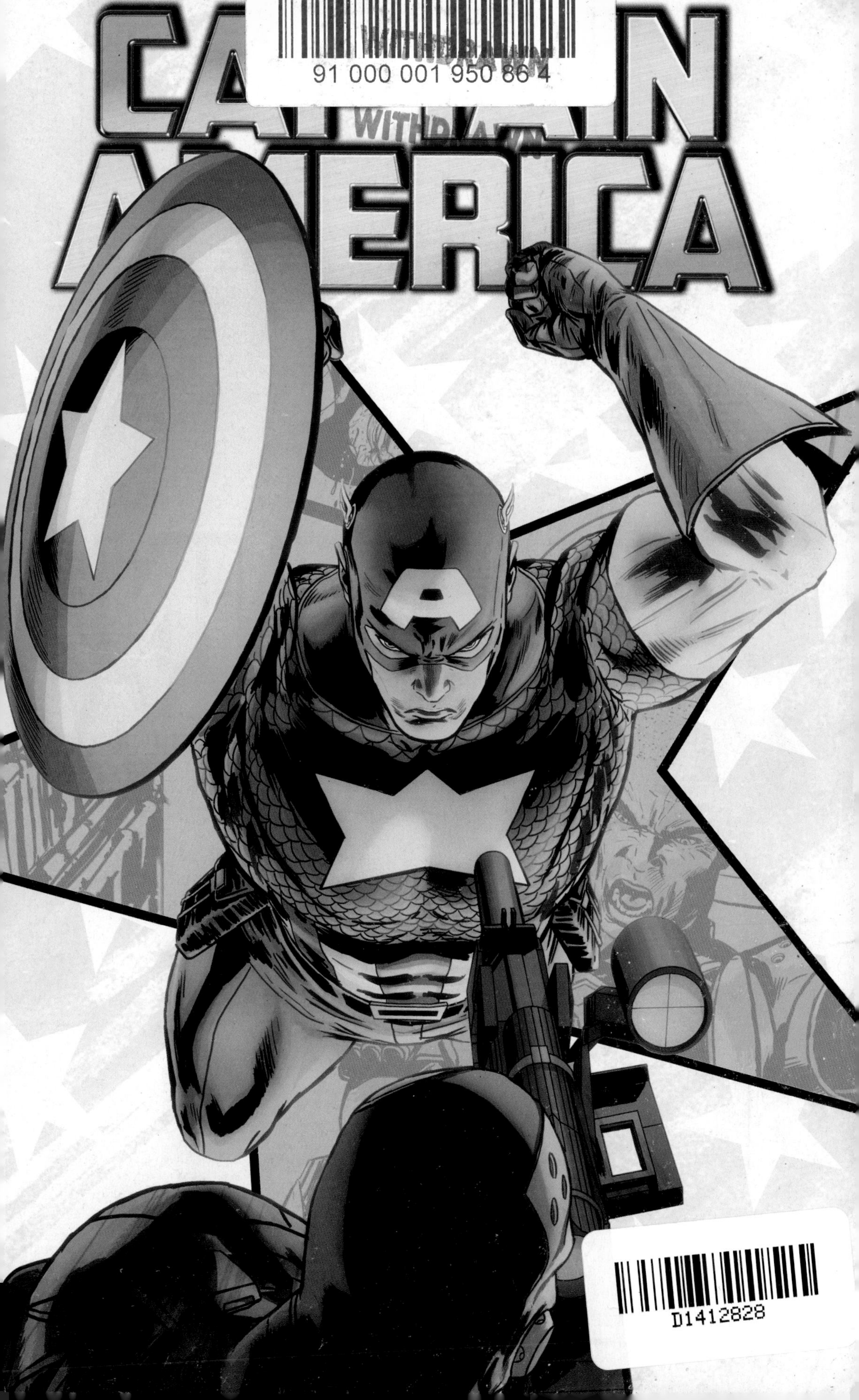

CAPTAIN AMERICA

CAPTAIN AMERICA BY ED BRUBAKER VOL. 3. Contains material originally published in magazine form as CAPTAIN AMERICA (2011) #11-14 and CAPTAIN AMERICA (1968) #328. First printing 2012. Hardcover ISBN# 978-0-7851-6075-5. Softcover ISBN# 978-0-7851-6076-2. Published by MARVEL WORLDWIDE, INC., a subsidiary of MARVEL ENTERTAINMENT, LLC. OFFICE OF PUBLICATION: 135 West 50th Street, New York, NY 10020. Copyright © 1987, 2012 and 2013 Marvel Characters, Inc. All rights reserved. Hardcover: $24.99 per copy in the U.S. and $27.99 in Canada (GST #R127032852). Softcover: $19.99 per copy in the U.S. and $21.99 in Canada (GST #R127032852). Canadian Agreement #40668537. All characters featured in this issue and the distinctive names and likenesses thereof, and all related indicia are trademarks of Marvel Characters, Inc. No similarity between any of the names, characters, persons, and/or institutions in this magazine with those of any living or dead person or institution is intended, and any such similarity which may exist is purely coincidental. **Printed in the U.S.A.** ALAN FINE, EVP - Office of the President, Marvel Worldwide, Inc. and EVP & CMO Marvel Characters B.V.; DAN BUCKLEY, Publisher & President - Print, Animation & Digital Divisions; JOE QUESADA, Chief Creative Officer; TOM BREVOORT, SVP of Publishing; DAVID BOGART, SVP of Operations & Procurement, Publishing; RUWAN JAYATILLEKE, SVP & Associate Publisher, Publishing; C.B. CEBULSKI, SVP of Creator & Content Development; DAVID GABRIEL, SVP of Publishing Sales & Circulation; MICHAEL PASCIULLO, SVP of Brand Planning & Communications; JIM O'KEEFE, VP of Operations & Logistics; DAN CARR, Executive Director of Publishing Technology; SUSAN CRESPI, Editorial Operations Manager; ALEX MORALES, Publishing Operations Manager; STAN LEE, Chairman Emeritus. For information regarding advertising in Marvel Comics or on Marvel.com, please contact Niza Disla, Director of Marvel Partnerships, at ndisla@marvel.com. For Marvel subscription inquiries, please call 800-217-9158. **Manufactured between 8/13/2012 and 9/24/2012 (hardcover), and 8/13/2012 and 3/25/2013 (softcover), by R.R. DONNELLEY, INC., SALEM, VA, USA.**

10 9 8 7 6 5 4 3 2 1

TOWER HAMLETS
LIBRARIES

91000001950864	
Bertrams	30/05/2013
GRA	£14.99
THISCH	TH13000044

WRITER
ED BRUBAKER
ARTIST
PATCH ZIRCHER
WITH **MIKE DEODATO** (#14)
COLOR ARTIST
PAUL MOUNTS
LETTERER
VC'S JOE CARAMAGNA
COVER ART
**PATCH ZIRCHER &
MATT HOLLINGSWORTH**
ASSISTANT EDITORS
**JOHN DENNING
& JAKE THOMAS**
ASSOCIATE EDITOR
LAUREN SANKOVITCH
EDITOR
TOM BREVOORT

CAPTAIN AMERICA #328 (1987)

WRITER
MARK GRUENWALD
ART
PAUL NEARY & VINCE COLLETTA
COLORS
KEN FEDUNIEWICZ
LETTERS
DIANA ALBERS
EDITOR
DON DALEY

CAPTAIN AMERICA CREATED BY
JOE SIMON & JACK KIRBY

COLLECTION EDITOR
JENNIFER GRÜNWALD
ASSISTANT EDITORS
ALEX STARBUCK & NELSON RIBEIRO
EDITOR, SPECIAL PROJECTS
MARK D. BEAZLEY
SENIOR EDITOR, SPECIAL PROJECTS
JEFF YOUNGQUIST
SENIOR VICE PRESIDENT OF SALES
DAVID GABRIEL
SVP OF BRAND PLANNING & COMMUNICATIONS
MICHAEL PASCIULLO
BOOK DESIGN
JEFF POWELL

EDITOR IN CHIEF
AXEL ALONSO
CHIEF CREATIVE OFFICER
JOE QUESADA
PUBLISHER
DAN BUCKLEY
EXECUTIVE PRODUCER
ALAN FINE

DURING THE DARK DAYS OF THE EARLY 1940S, A COVERT MILITARY EXPERIMENT TURNED STEVE ROGERS INTO AMERICA'S FIRST SUPER-SOLDIER, CAPTAIN AMERICA. THROUGHOUT THE WAR, CAP AND HIS PARTNER BUCKY FOUGHT ALONGSIDE OUR INFANTRY AND WITH A GROUP OF HEROES KNOWN AS THE INVADERS. IN THE CLOSING MONTHS OF WWII, CAPTAIN AMERICA AND BUCKY WERE BOTH PRESUMED DEAD IN AN EXPLOSION OVER THE ENGLISH CHANNEL.

DECADES LATER, A FIGURE WAS FOUND TRAPPED IN ICE, AND CAPTAIN AMERICA WAS REVIVED. HAVING SLEPT THROUGH THE MAJORITY OF THE 20TH CENTURY, STEVE ROGERS AWAKENED TO A WORLD HE NEVER IMAGINED, A WORLD WHERE WAR HAD MOVED FROM THE BATTLEFIELD TO THE CITY STREETS... A WORLD IN DIRE NEED OF...

CAPTAIN AMERICA

THE TERRORIST ORGANIZATION HYDRA HAS BEEN EXPANDING, LED BY A NEW QUEEN HYDRA AND THE FORMER ALLIED OPERATIVE CODENAME BRAVO. IN THEIR INVESTIGATIONS OF HYDRA'S PLANS, CAPTAIN AMERICA'S TEAM GAINED INTEL FROM THE EX-SERPENT SQUAD CRIMINAL KNOWN AS VIPER IN EXCHANGE FOR WITNESS PROTECTION AND A NEW LIFE.

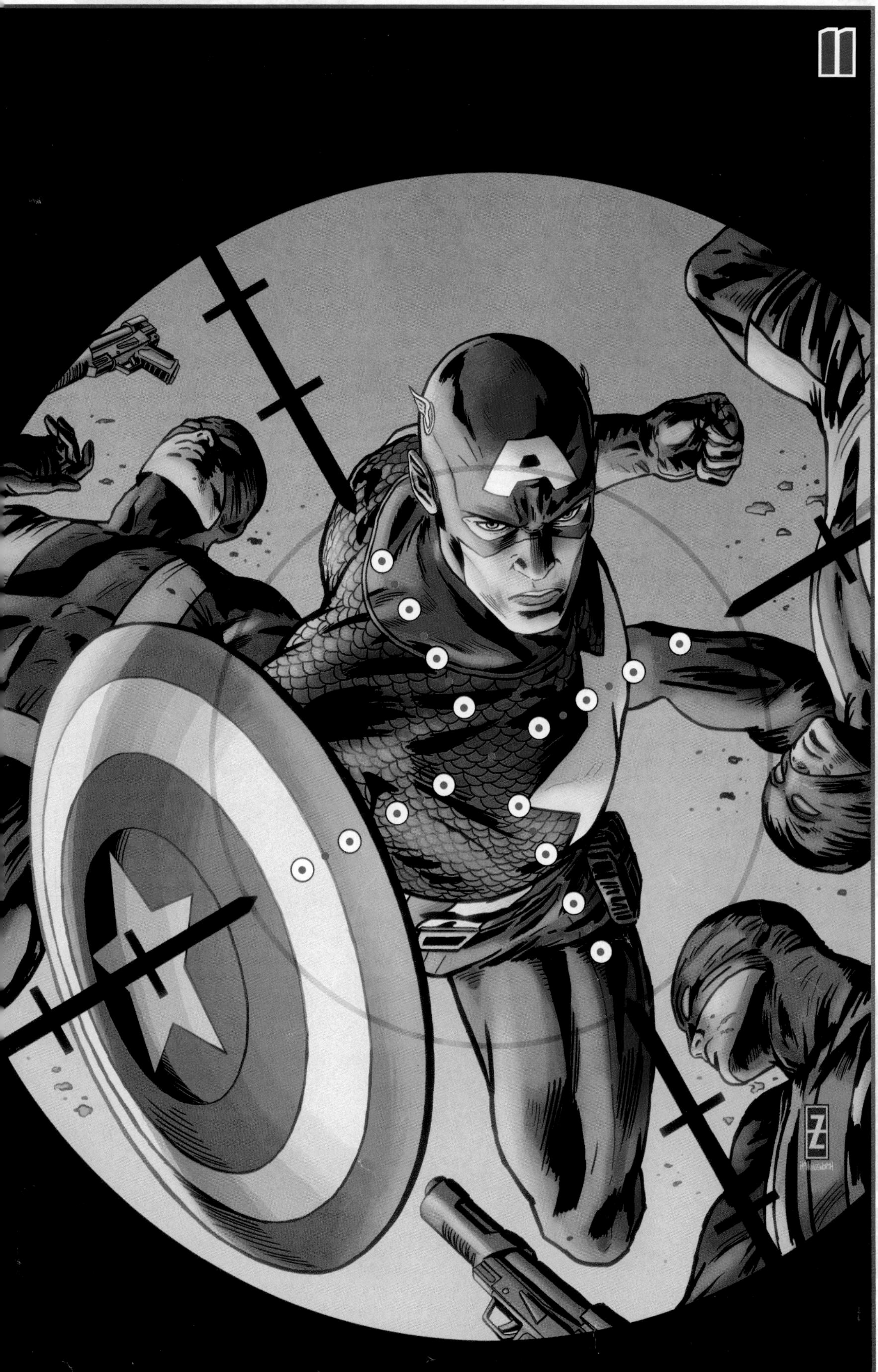
11

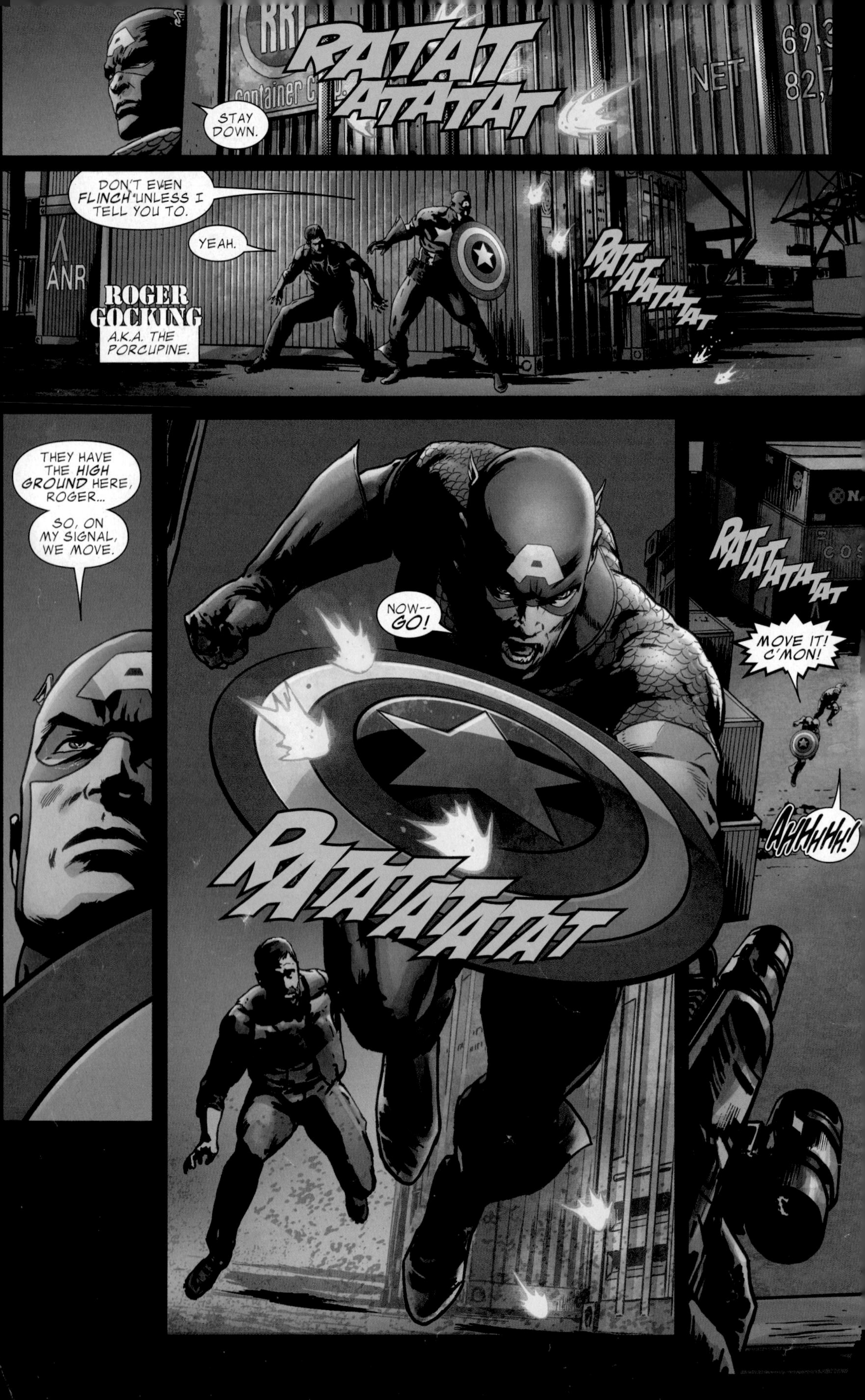

RATAT ATATAT
STAY DOWN.
DON'T EVEN FLINCH UNLESS I TELL YOU TO.
YEAH.
RATATATATATAT
ROGER GOCKING
A.K.A. THE PORCUPINE.
THEY HAVE THE HIGH GROUND HERE, ROGER...
SO, ON MY SIGNAL, WE MOVE.
NOW-- GO!
RATATATATATAT
RATATATATATAT
MOVE IT! C'MON!
AHHHHH!

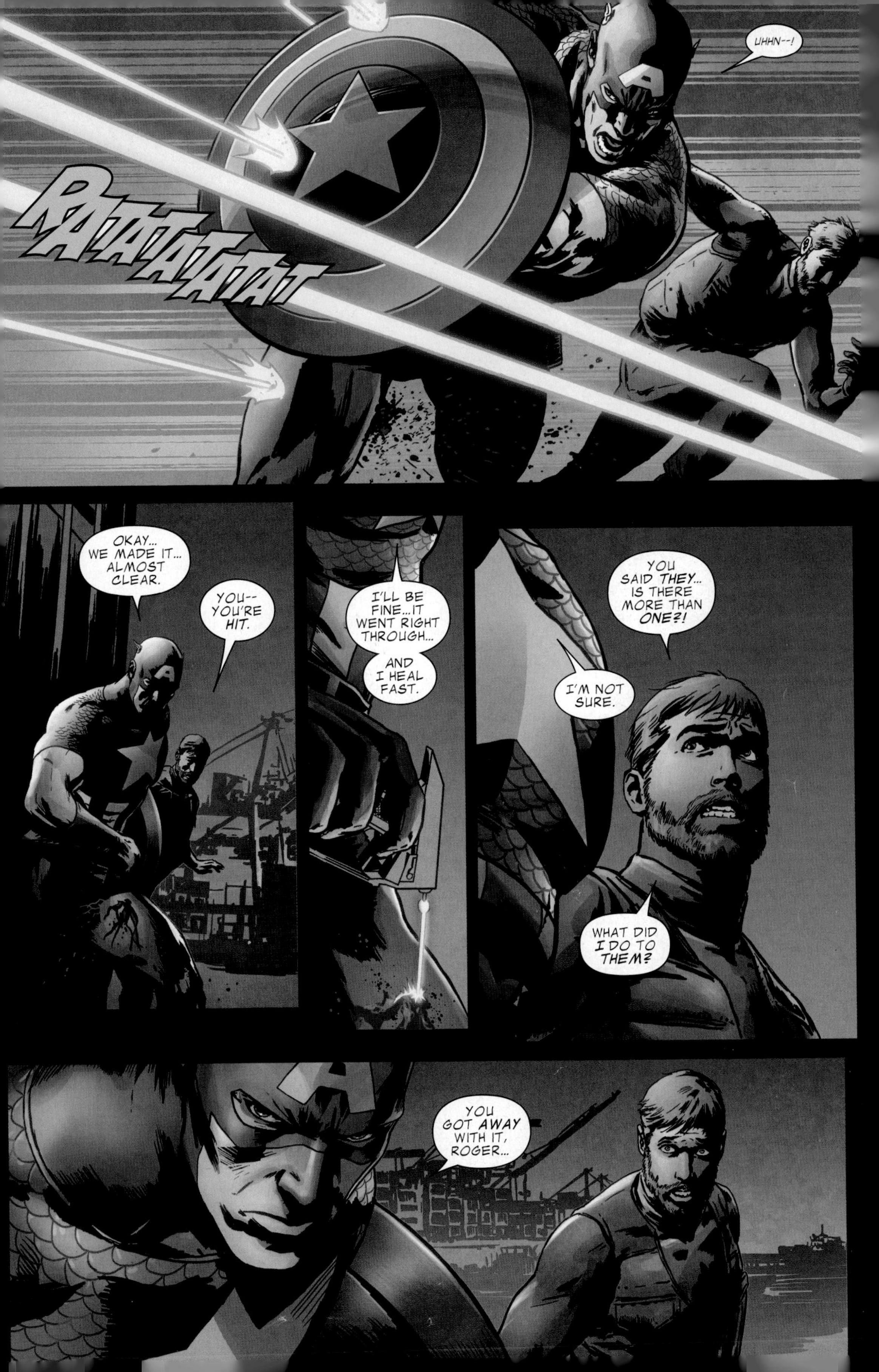
RATATATATATAT
UHHN--!
OKAY... WE MADE IT... ALMOST CLEAR.
YOU-- YOU'RE HIT.
I'LL BE FINE...IT WENT RIGHT THROUGH...
AND I HEAL FAST.
YOU SAID THEY... IS THERE MORE THAN ONE?!
I'M NOT SURE.
WHAT DID I DO TO THEM?
YOU GOT AWAY WITH IT, ROGER...

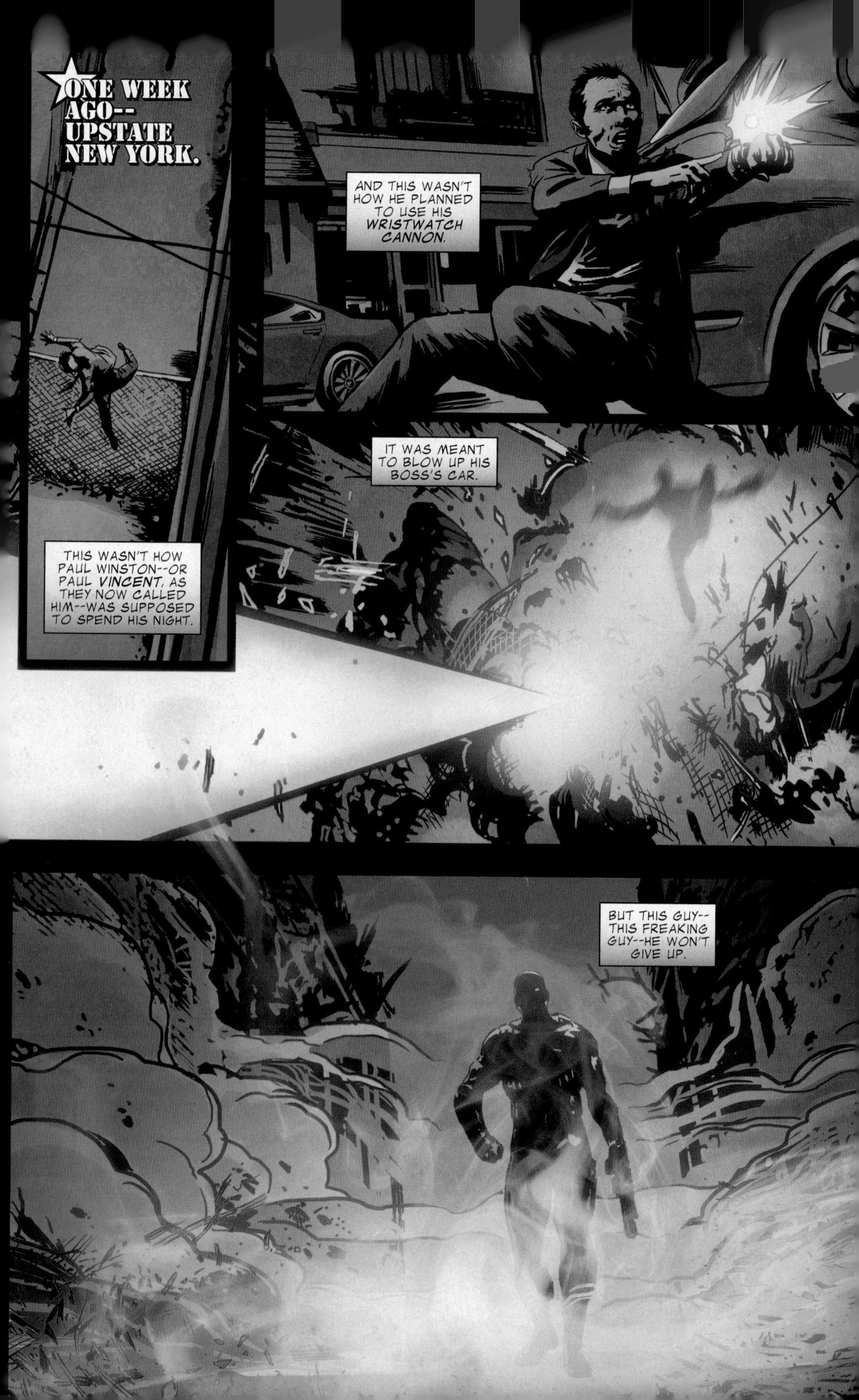
ONE WEEK AGO-- UPSTATE NEW YORK.
THIS WASN'T HOW PAUL WINSTON--OR PAUL VINCENT, AS THEY NOW CALLED HIM--WAS SUPPOSED TO SPEND HIS NIGHT.
AND THIS WASN'T HOW HE PLANNED TO USE HIS WRISTWATCH CANNON.
IT WAS MEANT TO BLOW UP HIS BOSS'S CAR.
BUT THIS GUY-- THIS FREAKING GUY--HE WON'T GIVE UP.

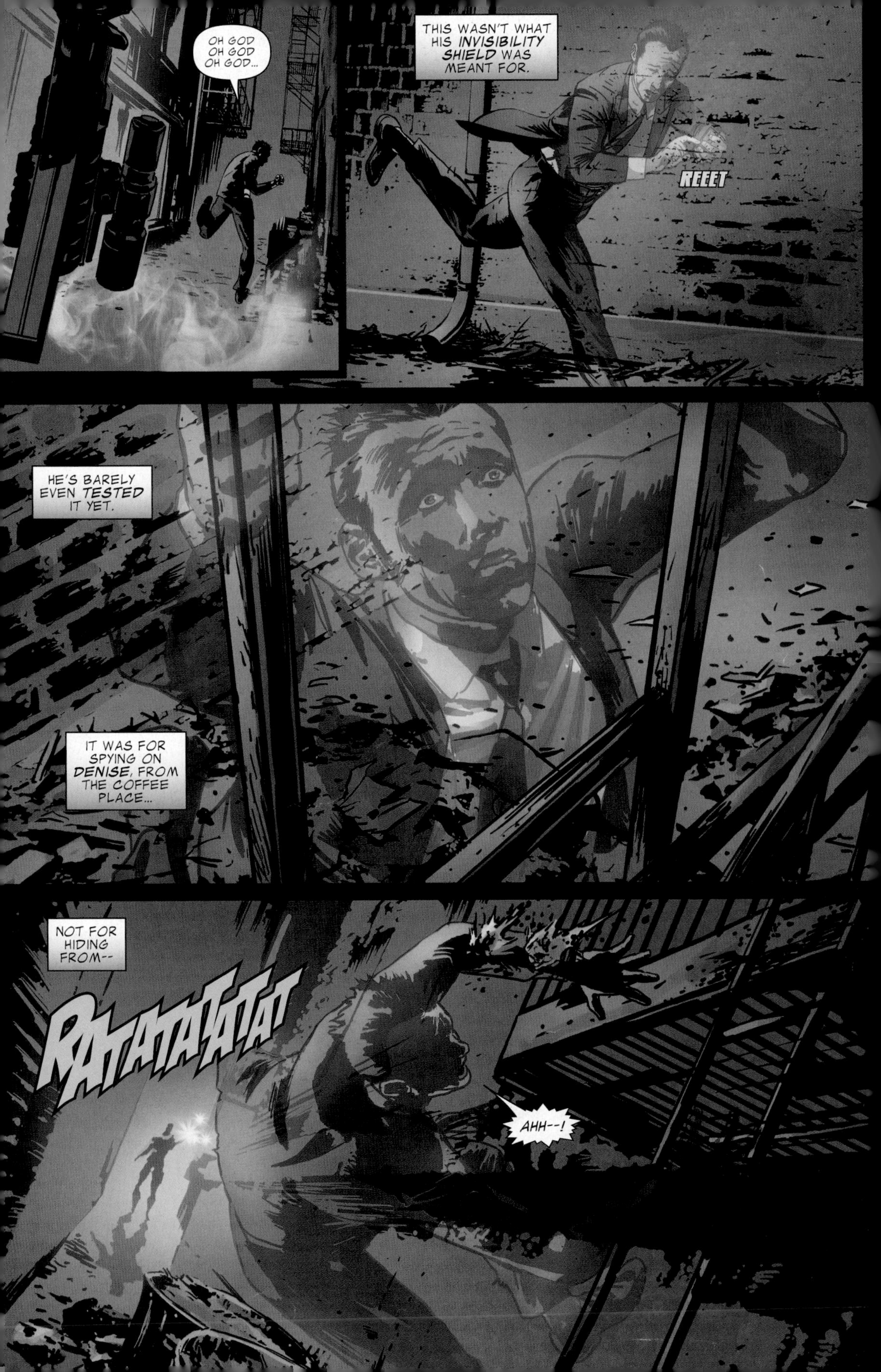
OH GOD
OH GOD
OH GOD...
THIS WASN'T WHAT HIS INVISIBILITY SHIELD WAS MEANT FOR.
REEET
HE'S BARELY EVEN TESTED IT YET.
IT WAS FOR SPYING ON DENISE, FROM THE COFFEE PLACE...
NOT FOR HIDING FROM--
RATATATATAT
AHH--!

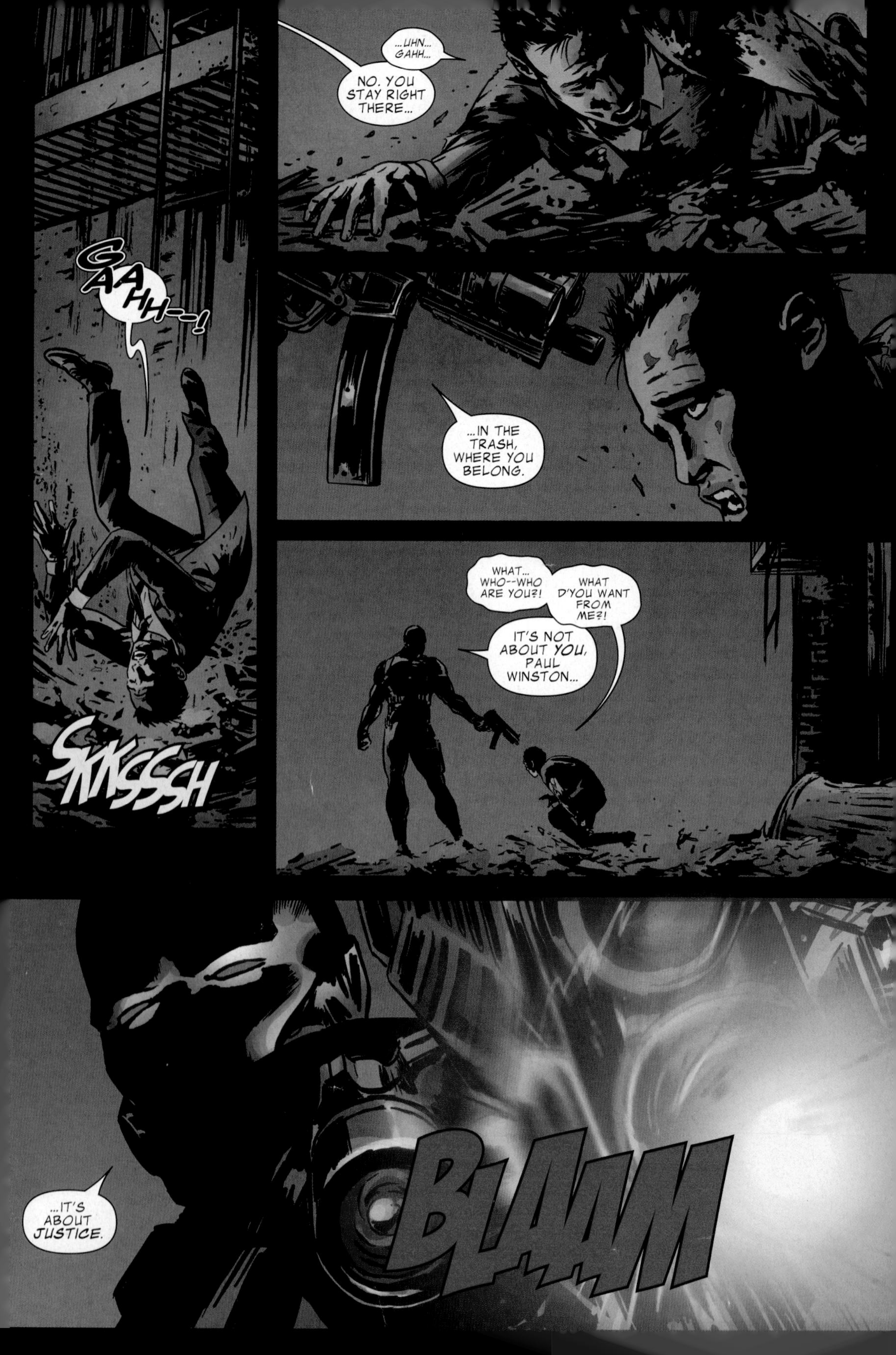
...UHN... GAHH...
NO. YOU STAY RIGHT THERE...
GAHH--!
SKKSSSH
...IN THE TRASH, WHERE YOU BELONG.
WHAT... WHO--WHO ARE YOU?!
WHAT D'YOU WANT FROM ME?!
IT'S NOT ABOUT YOU, PAUL WINSTON...
...IT'S ABOUT JUSTICE.
BLAAM

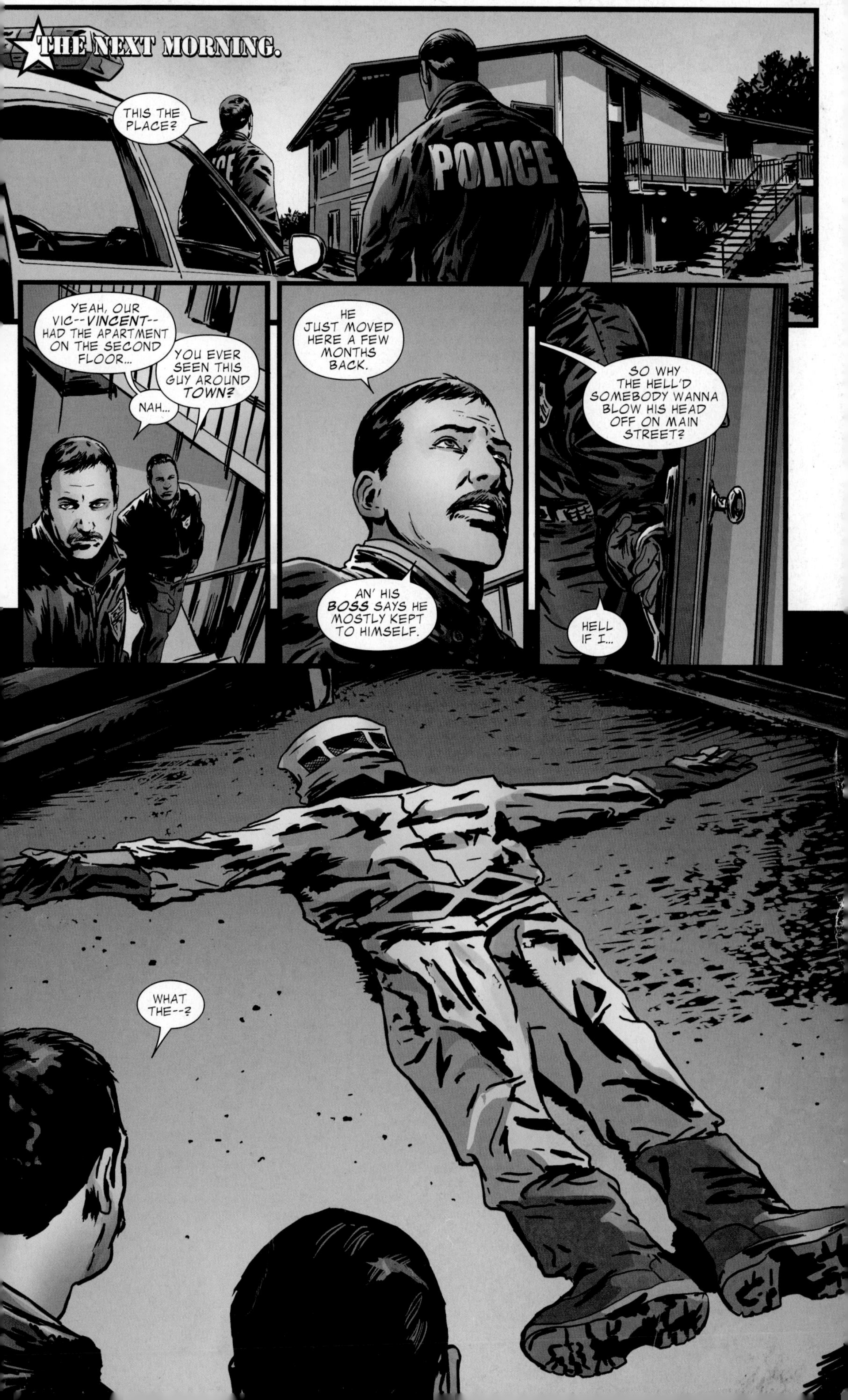
THE NEXT MORNING.
THIS THE PLACE?
POLICE
YEAH, OUR VIC--VINCENT--HAD THE APARTMENT ON THE SECOND FLOOR...
YOU EVER SEEN THIS GUY AROUND TOWN?
NAH...
HE JUST MOVED HERE A FEW MONTHS BACK.
AN' HIS BOSS SAYS HE MOSTLY KEPT TO HIMSELF.
SO WHY THE HELL'D SOMEBODY WANNA BLOW HIS HEAD OFF ON MAIN STREET?
HELL IF I...
WHAT THE--?

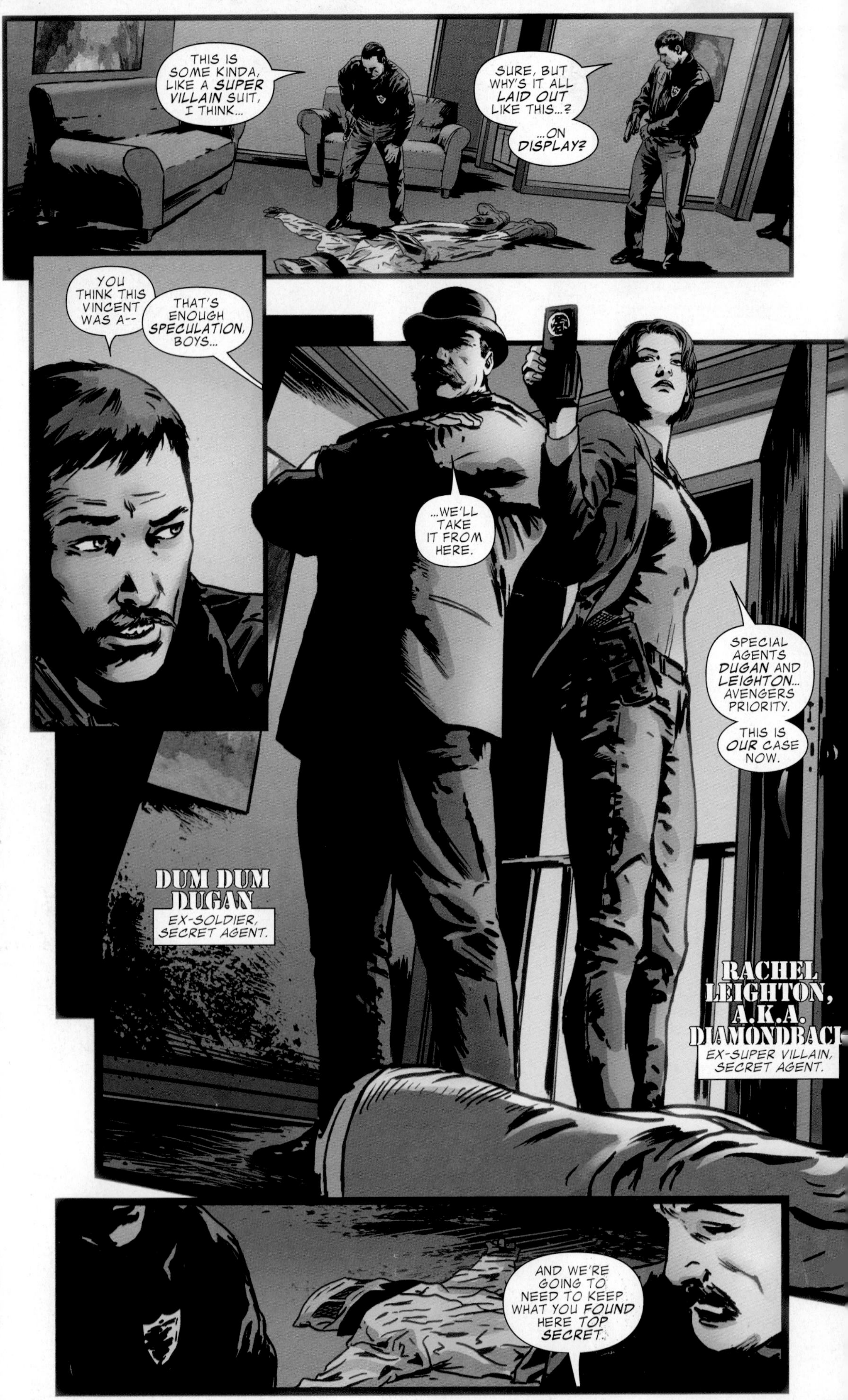
THIS IS SOME KINDA, LIKE A SUPER VILLAIN SUIT, I THINK...
SURE, BUT WHY'S IT ALL LAID OUT LIKE THIS...?
...ON DISPLAY?
YOU THINK THIS VINCENT WAS A--
THAT'S ENOUGH SPECULATION, BOYS...
...WE'LL TAKE IT FROM HERE.
SPECIAL AGENTS DUGAN AND LEIGHTON... AVENGERS PRIORITY.
THIS IS OUR CASE NOW.
DUM DUM DUGAN
EX-SOLDIER, SECRET AGENT.
RACHEL LEIGHTON, A.K.A. DIAMONDBACK
EX-SUPER VILLAIN, SECRET AGENT.
AND WE'RE GOING TO NEED TO KEEP WHAT YOU FOUND HERE TOP SECRET.

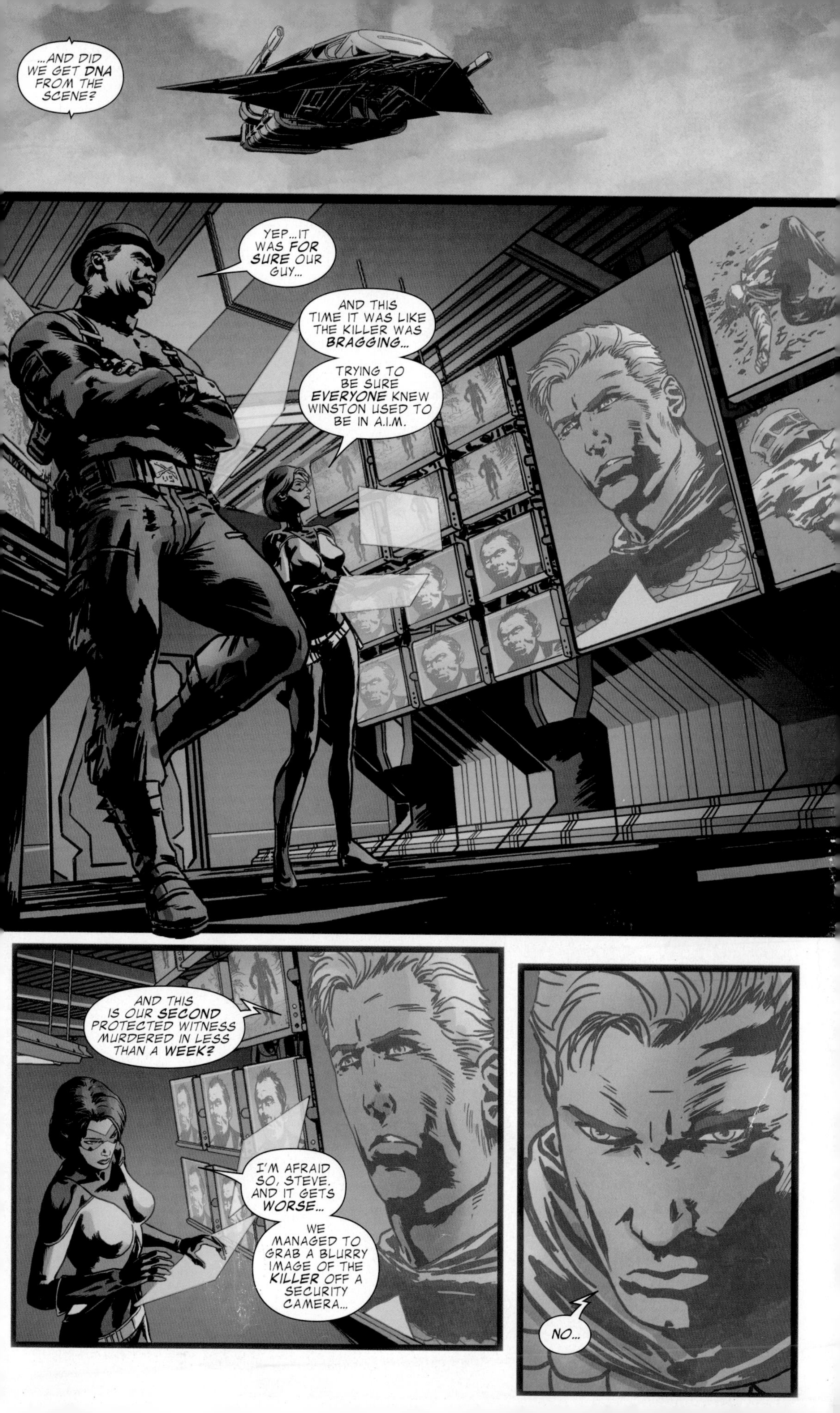
...AND DID WE GET DNA FROM THE SCENE?
YEP...IT WAS FOR SURE OUR GUY...
AND THIS TIME IT WAS LIKE THE KILLER WAS BRAGGING...
TRYING TO BE SURE EVERYONE KNEW WINSTON USED TO BE IN A.I.M.
AND THIS IS OUR SECOND PROTECTED WITNESS MURDERED IN LESS THAN A WEEK?
I'M AFRAID SO, STEVE. AND IT GETS WORSE...
WE MANAGED TO GRAB A BLURRY IMAGE OF THE KILLER OFF A SECURITY CAMERA...
NO...

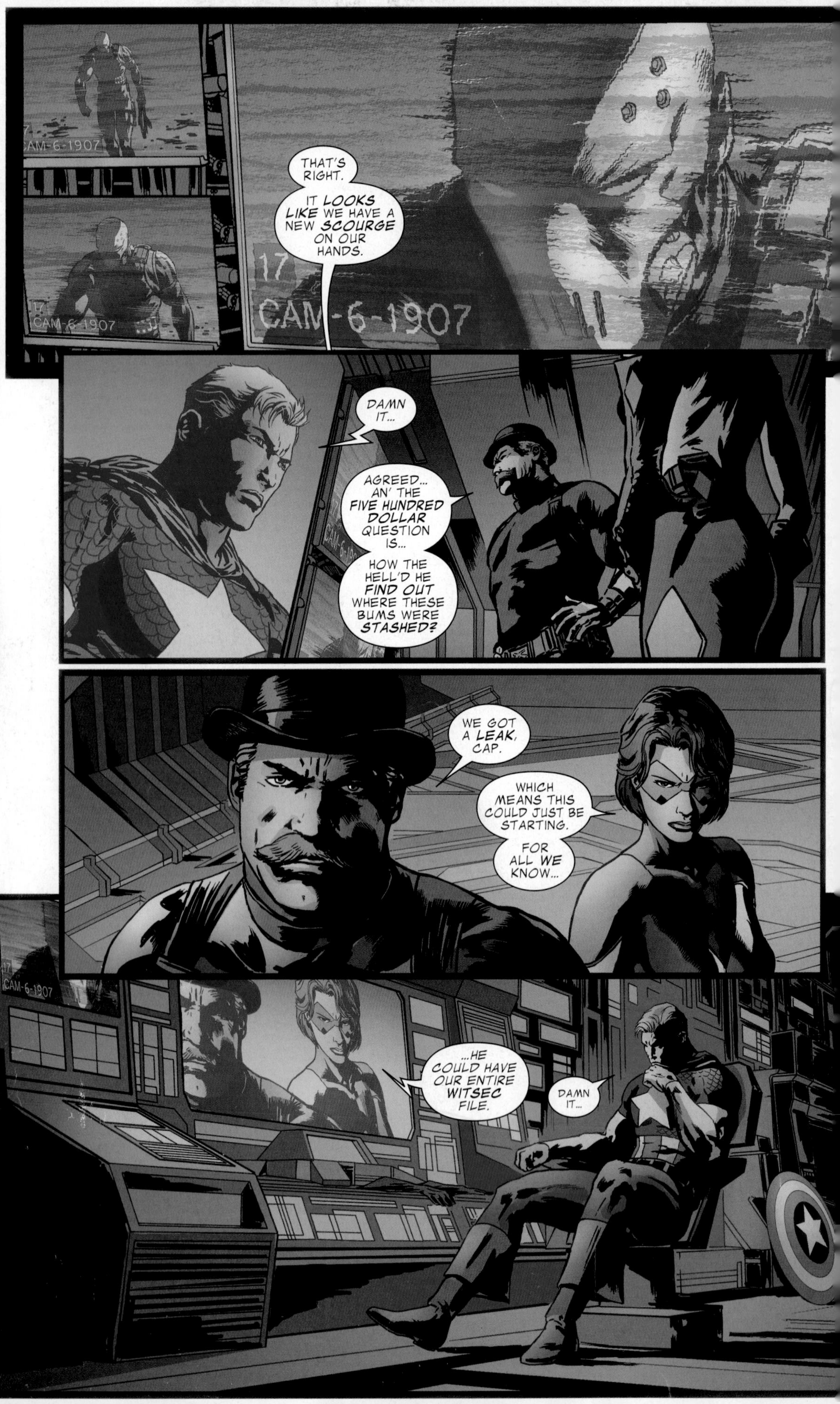
17
CAM-6-1907
17
CAM-6-1907
17
CAM-6-1907
THAT'S RIGHT.
IT LOOKS LIKE WE HAVE A NEW SCOURGE ON OUR HANDS.
DAMN IT...
AGREED... AN' THE FIVE HUNDRED DOLLAR QUESTION IS...
HOW THE HELL'D HE FIND OUT WHERE THESE BUMS WERE STASHED?
WE GOT A LEAK, CAP.
WHICH MEANS THIS COULD JUST BE STARTING.
FOR ALL WE KNOW...
17
CAM-6-1907
...HE COULD HAVE OUR ENTIRE WITSEC FILE.
DAMN IT...

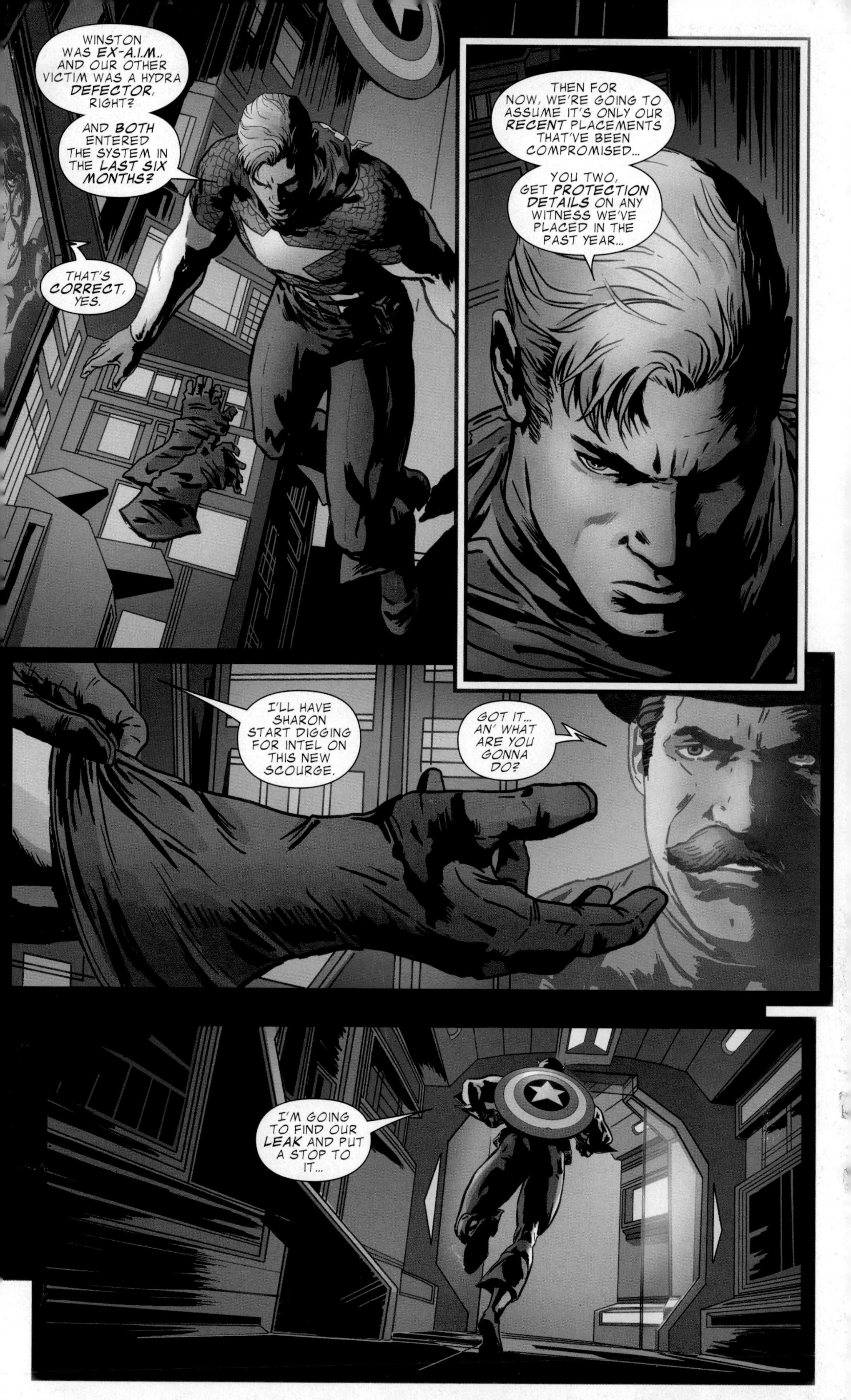

WINSTON WAS EX-A.I.M., AND OUR OTHER VICTIM WAS A HYDRA DEFECTOR, RIGHT?
AND BOTH ENTERED THE SYSTEM IN THE LAST SIX MONTHS?
THAT'S CORRECT, YES.
THEN FOR NOW, WE'RE GOING TO ASSUME IT'S ONLY OUR RECENT PLACEMENTS THAT'VE BEEN COMPROMISED...
YOU TWO, GET PROTECTION DETAILS ON ANY WITNESS WE'VE PLACED IN THE PAST YEAR...
I'LL HAVE SHARON START DIGGING FOR INTEL ON THIS NEW SCOURGE.
GOT IT... AN' WHAT ARE YOU GONNA DO?
I'M GOING TO FIND OUR LEAK AND PUT A STOP TO IT...

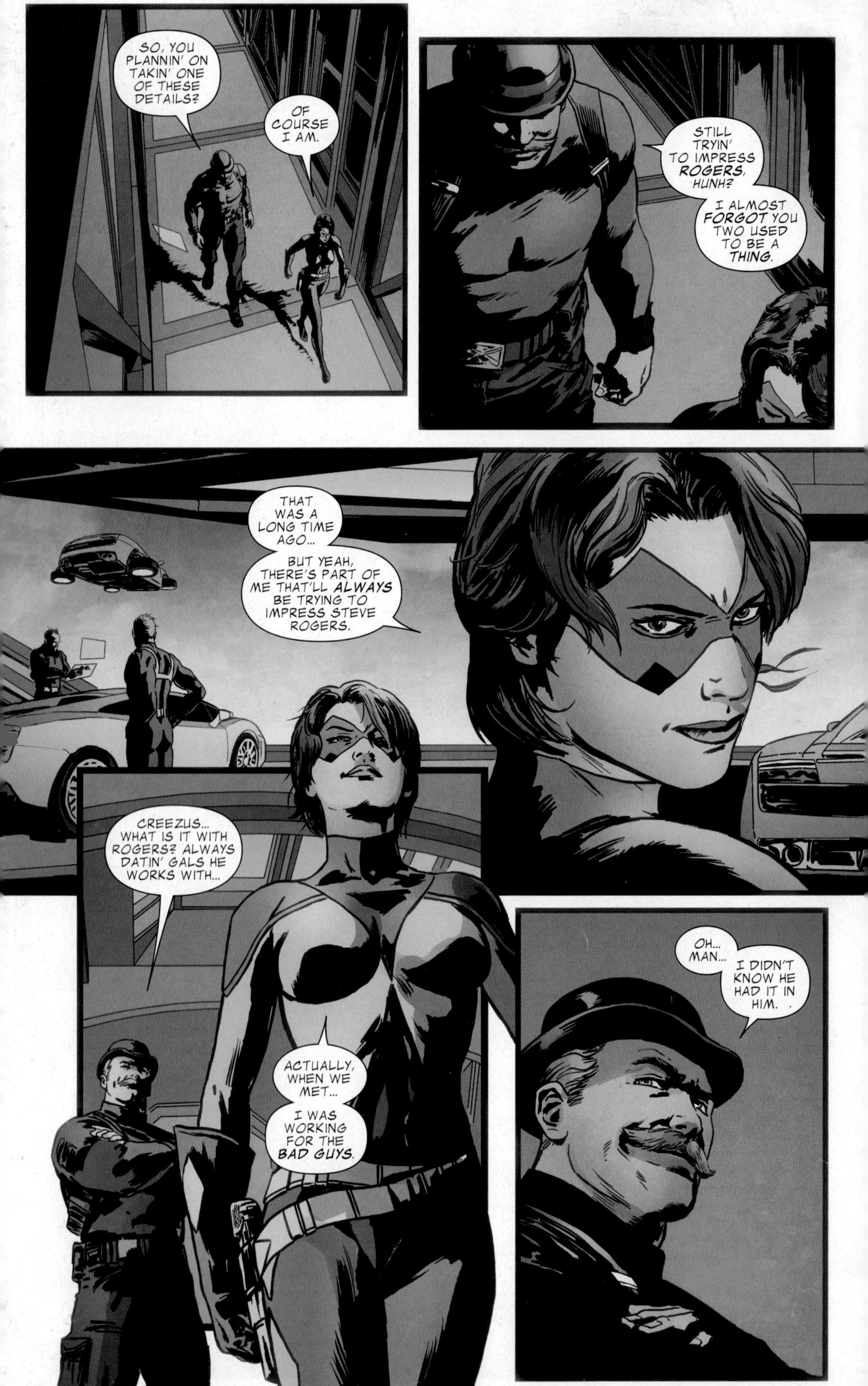
SO, YOU PLANNIN' ON TAKIN' ONE OF THESE DETAILS?
OF COURSE I AM.
STILL TRYIN' TO IMPRESS ROGERS, HUNH?
I ALMOST FORGOT YOU TWO USED TO BE A THING.
THAT WAS A LONG TIME AGO...
BUT YEAH, THERE'S PART OF ME THAT'LL ALWAYS BE TRYING TO IMPRESS STEVE ROGERS.
CREEZUS... WHAT IS IT WITH ROGERS? ALWAYS DATIN' GALS HE WORKS WITH...
ACTUALLY, WHEN WE MET...
I WAS WORKING FOR THE BAD GUYS.
OH... MAN...
I DIDN'T KNOW HE HAD IT IN HIM.

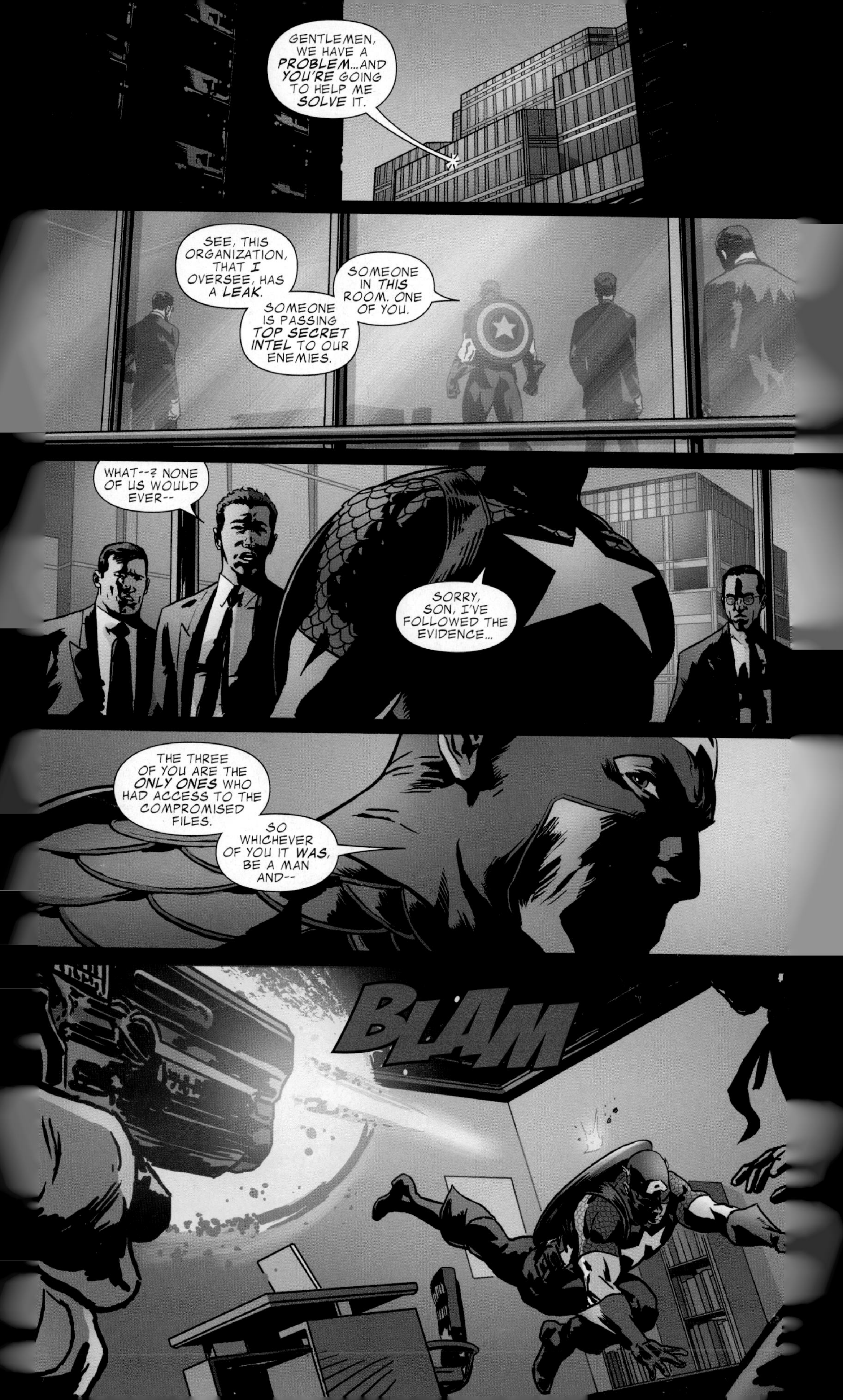
GENTLEMEN, WE HAVE A PROBLEM...AND YOU'RE GOING TO HELP ME SOLVE IT.
SEE, THIS ORGANIZATION, THAT I OVERSEE, HAS A LEAK.
SOMEONE IS PASSING TOP SECRET INTEL TO OUR ENEMIES.
SOMEONE IN THIS ROOM. ONE OF YOU.
WHAT--? NONE OF US WOULD EVER--
SORRY, SON, I'VE FOLLOWED THE EVIDENCE...
THE THREE OF YOU ARE THE ONLY ONES WHO HAD ACCESS TO THE COMPROMISED FILES.
SO WHICHEVER OF YOU IT WAS, BE A MAN AND--
BLAM

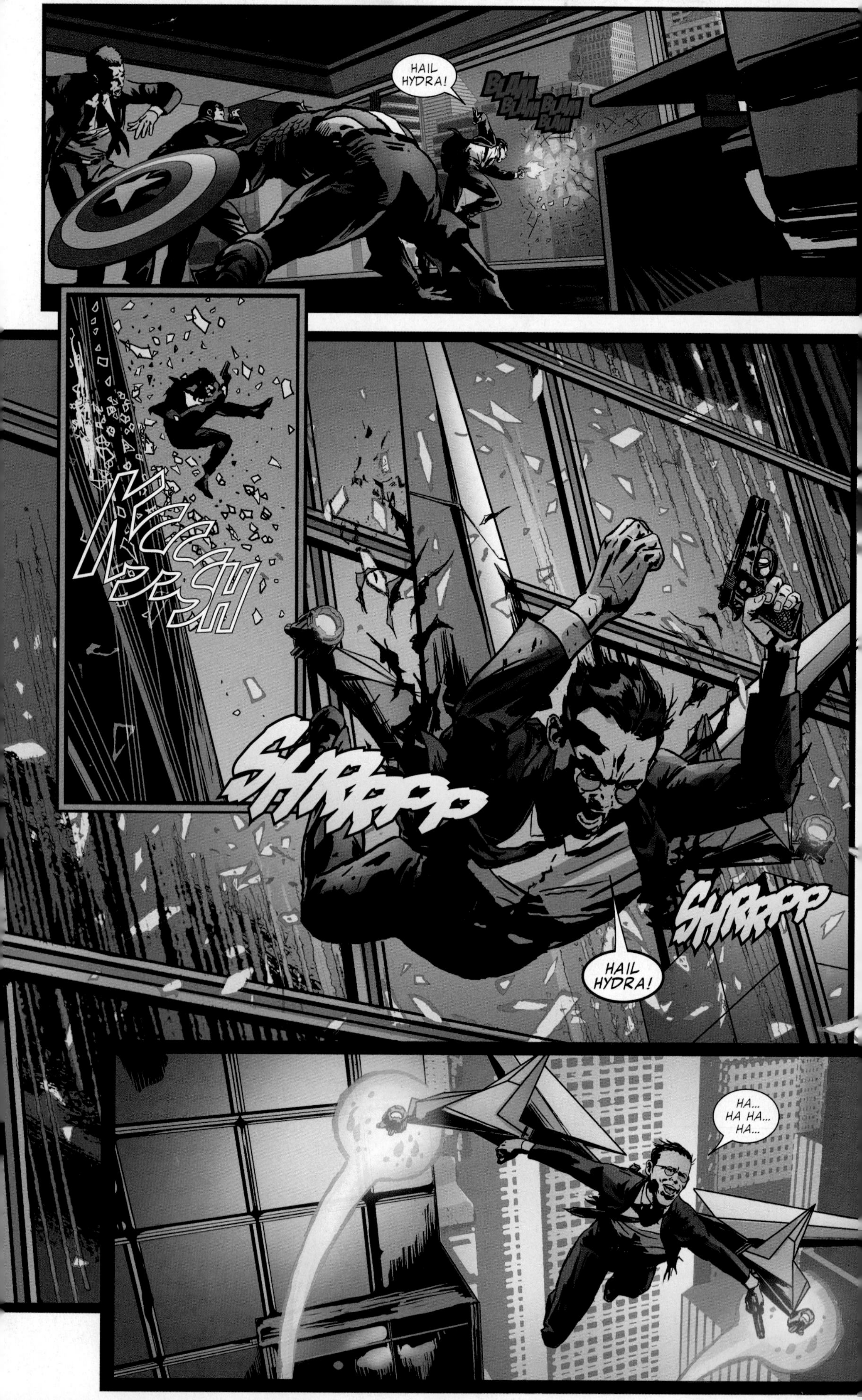
HAIL HYDRA!
BLAM BLAM BLAM BLAM
KSSSH
SHRRPP
SHRRPP
HAIL HYDRA!
HA... HA HA... HA...

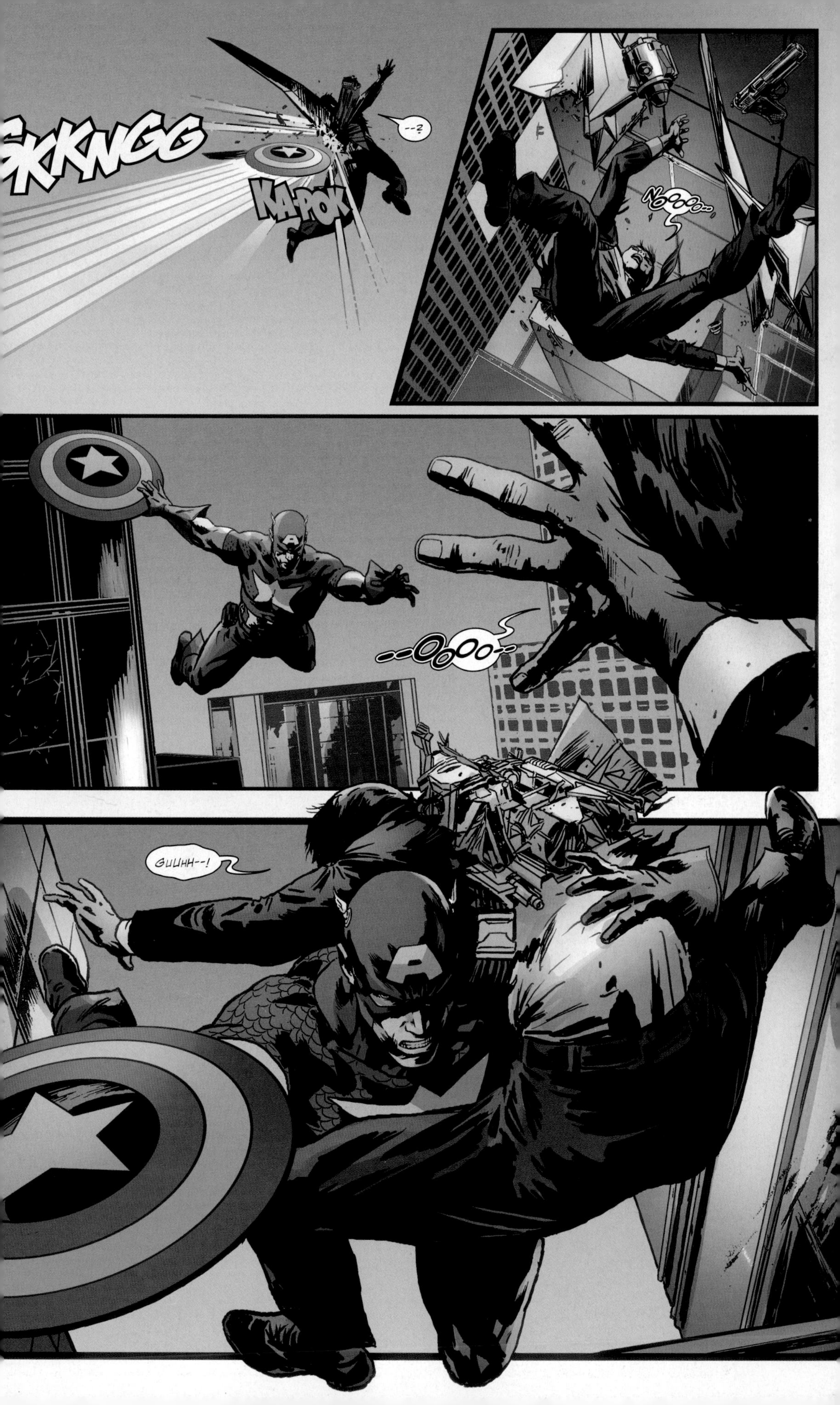

SKKNGG
--?
KA-POK
NOOOO--
--OOOOO--
GUUHH--!

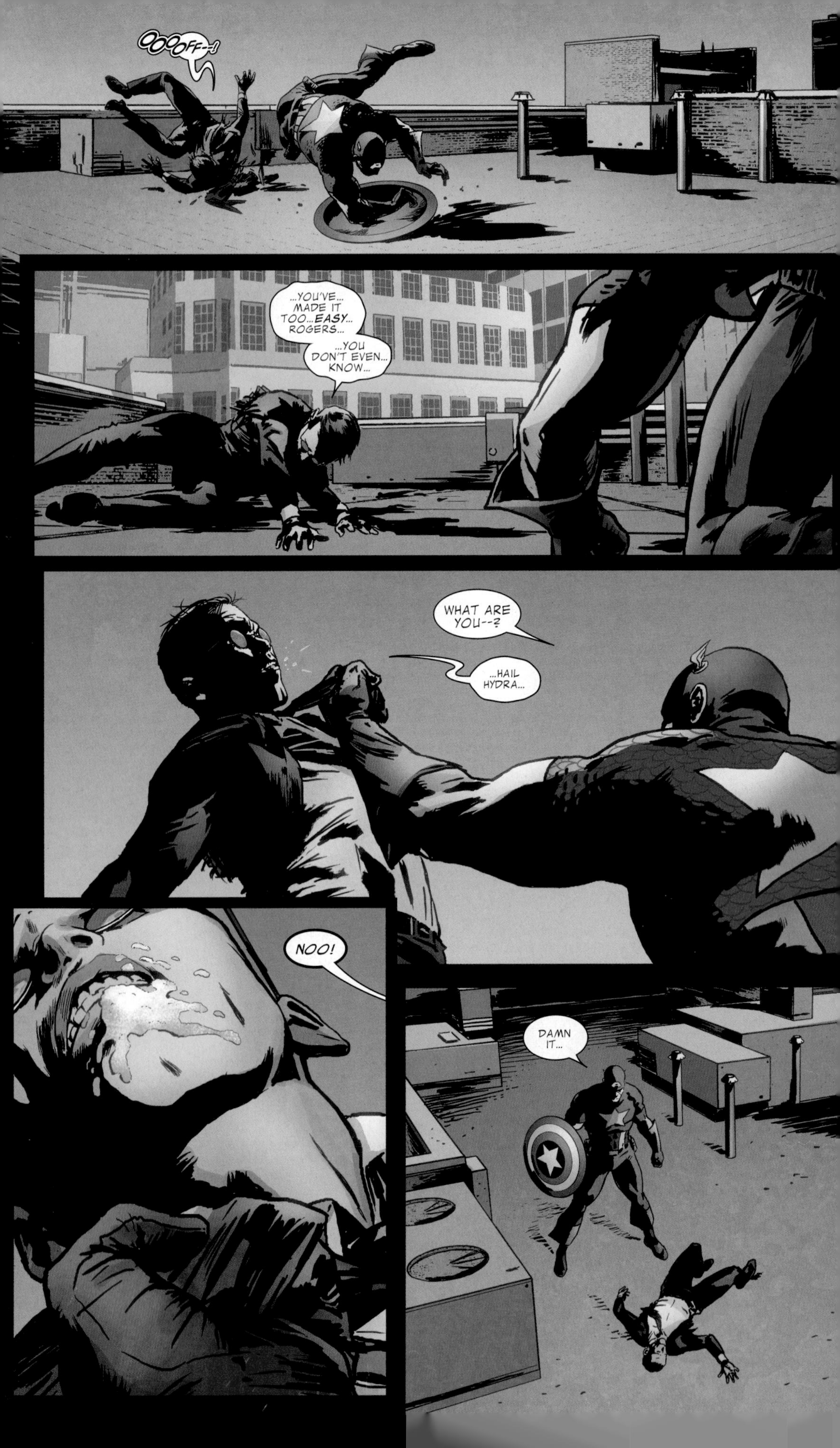
OOOOFF--!
...YOU'VE... MADE IT TOO...EASY... ROGERS...
...YOU DON'T EVEN... KNOW...
WHAT ARE YOU--?
...HAIL HYDRA...
NOO!
DAMN IT...

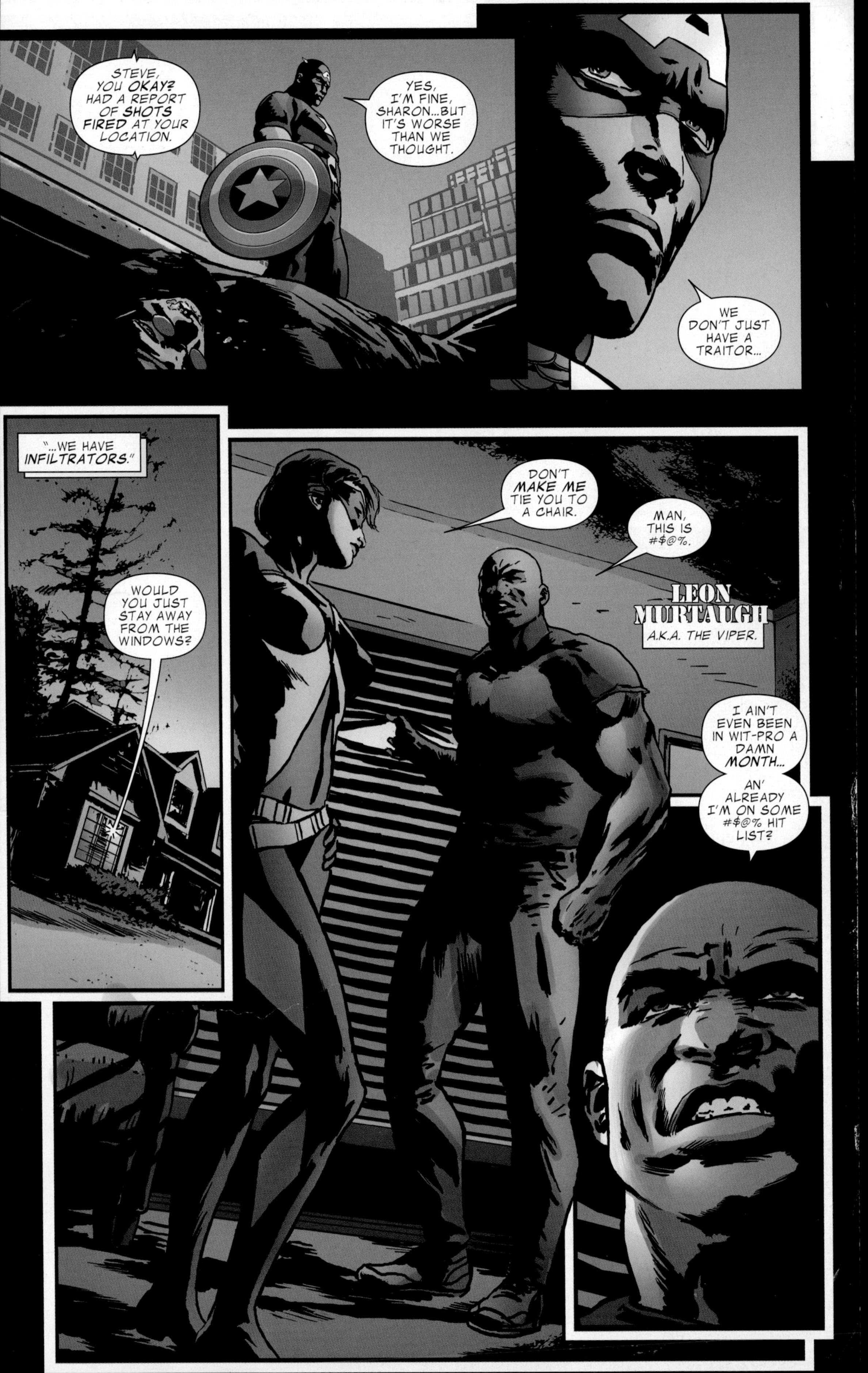
STEVE, YOU OKAY? HAD A REPORT OF SHOTS FIRED AT YOUR LOCATION.
YES, I'M FINE, SHARON...BUT IT'S WORSE THAN WE THOUGHT.
WE DON'T JUST HAVE A TRAITOR...
"...WE HAVE INFILTRATORS."
WOULD YOU JUST STAY AWAY FROM THE WINDOWS?
DON'T MAKE ME TIE YOU TO A CHAIR.
MAN, THIS IS #$@%.
LEON MURTAUGH
A.K.A. THE VIPER.
I AIN'T EVEN BEEN IN WIT-PRO A DAMN MONTH...
AN' ALREADY I'M ON SOME #$@% HIT LIST?

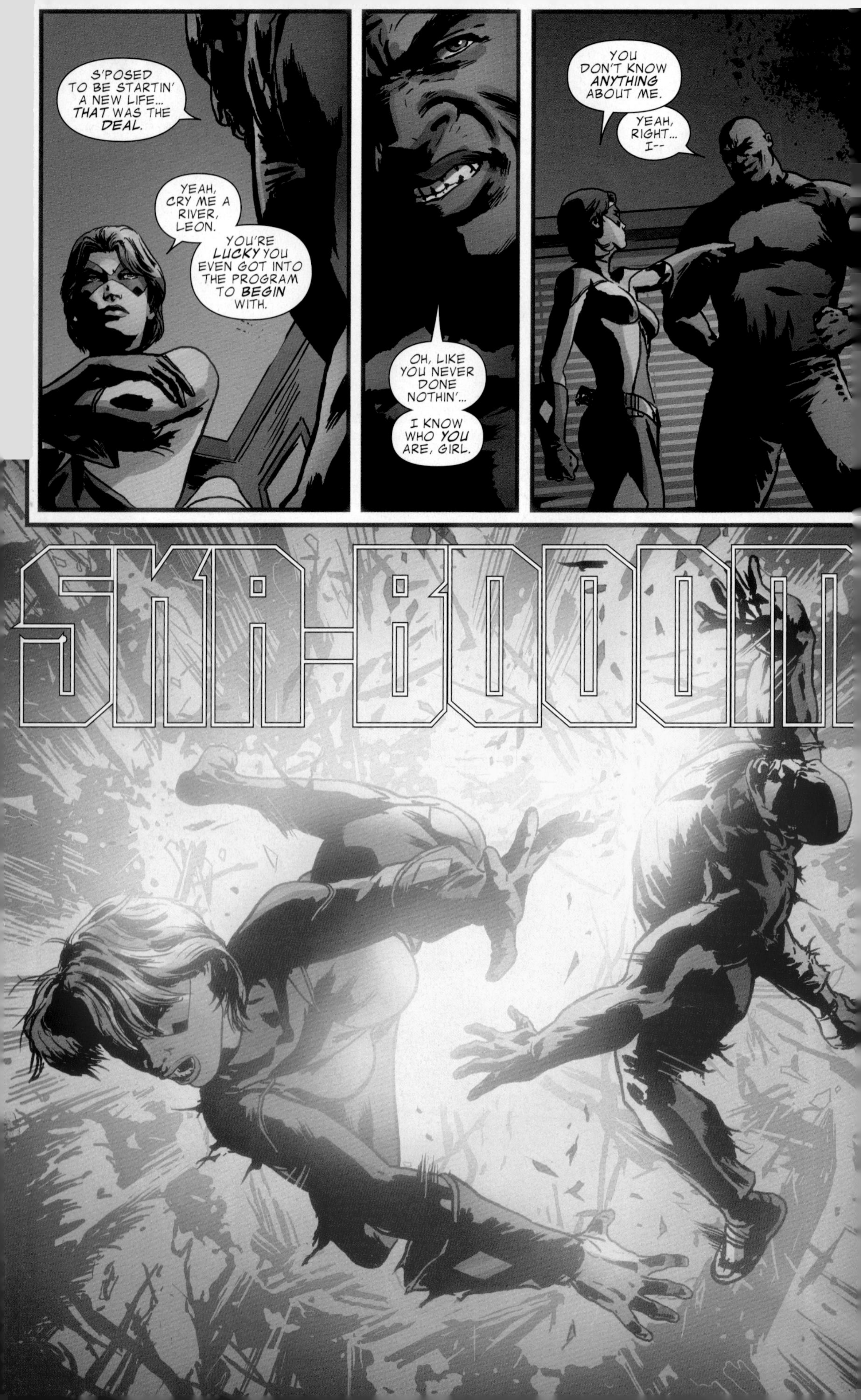
S'POSED TO BE STARTIN' A NEW LIFE... THAT WAS THE DEAL.
YEAH, CRY ME A RIVER, LEON.
YOU'RE LUCKY YOU EVEN GOT INTO THE PROGRAM TO BEGIN WITH.
OH, LIKE YOU NEVER DONE NOTHIN'...
I KNOW WHO YOU ARE, GIRL.
YOU DON'T KNOW ANYTHING ABOUT ME.
YEAH, RIGHT... I--
SKA-BOOOM

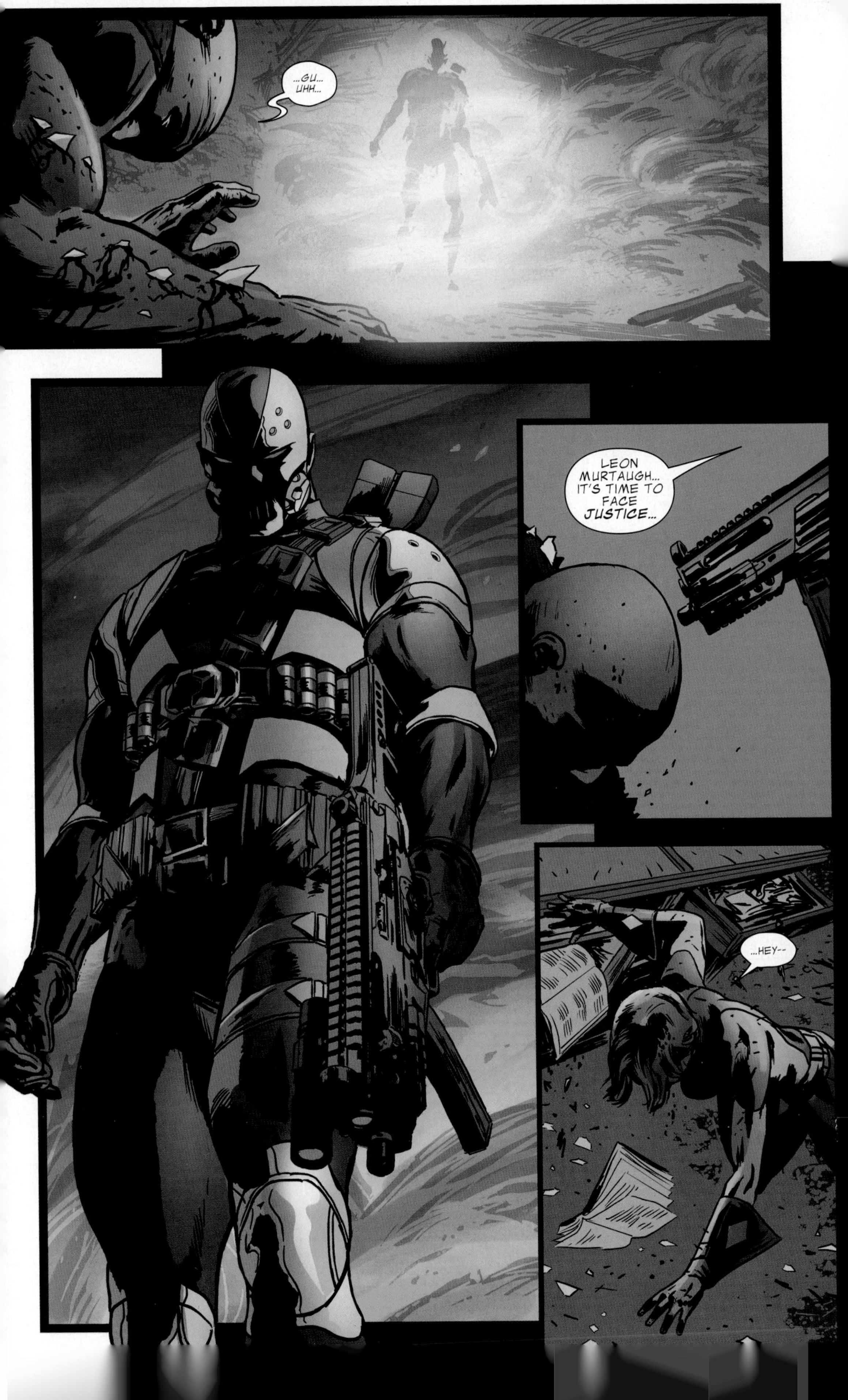
...GU... UHH...
LEON MURTAUGH... IT'S TIME TO FACE JUSTICE...
...HEY--

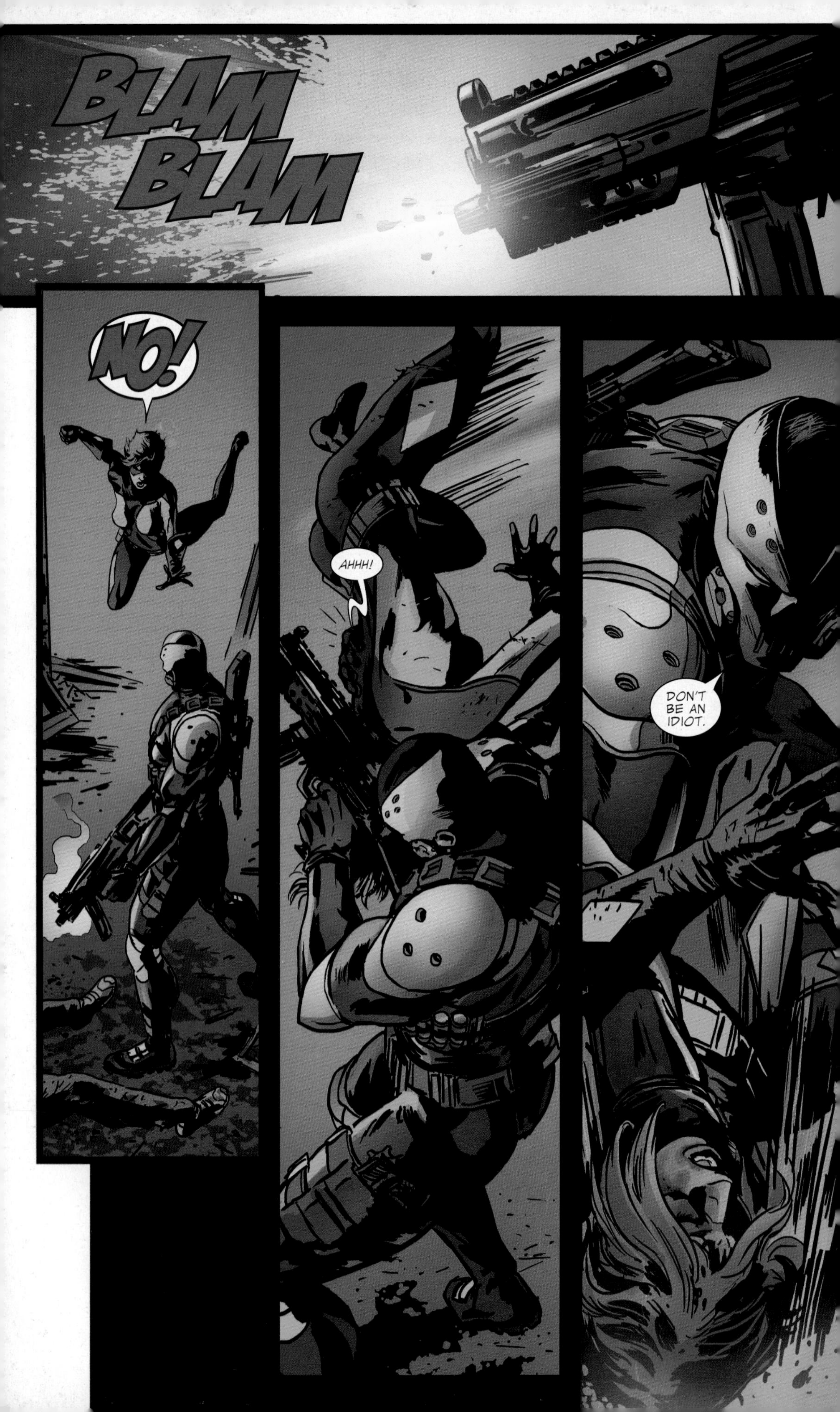
BLAM
BLAM
NO!
AHHH!
DON'T BE AN IDIOT.

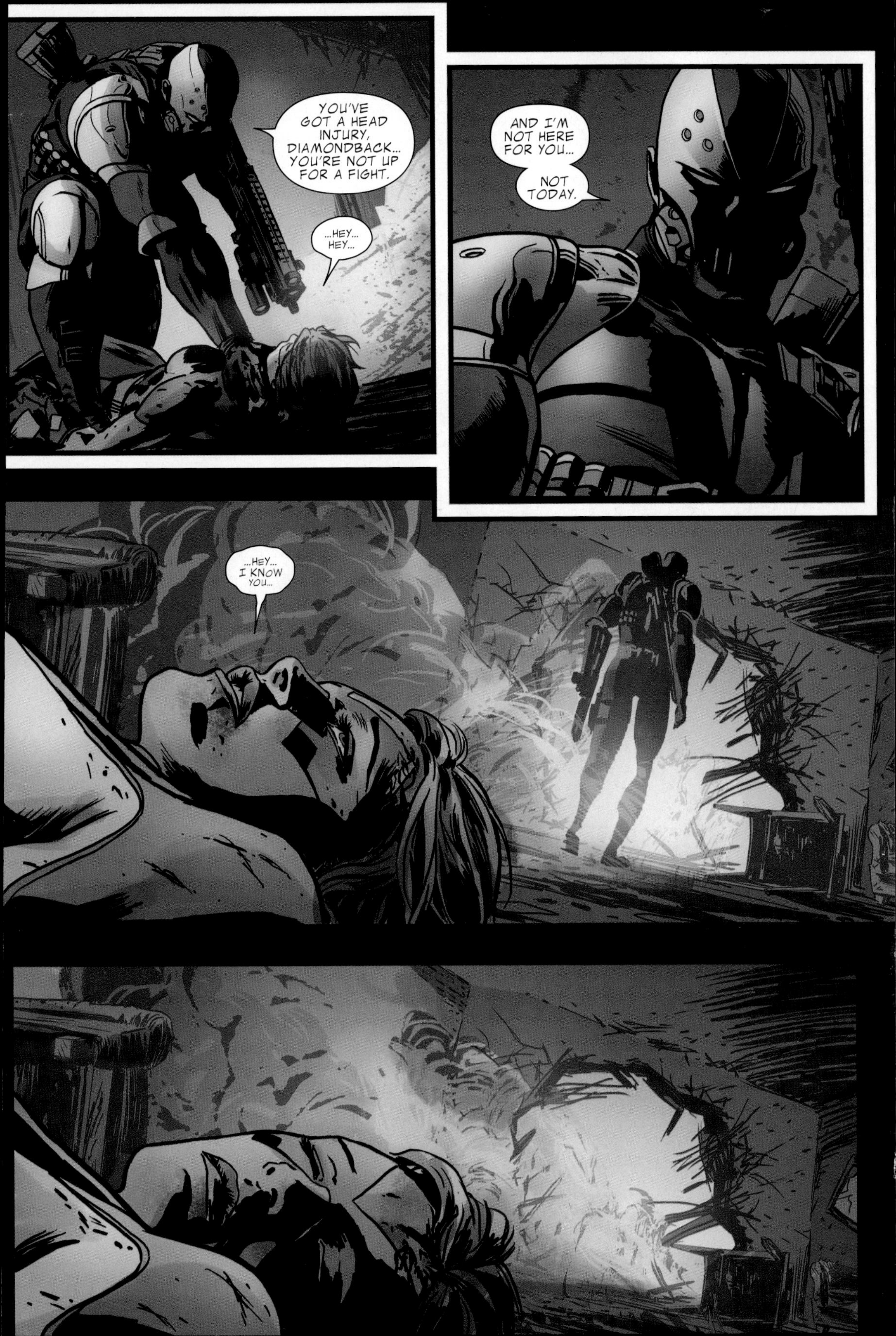
YOU'VE GOT A HEAD INJURY, DIAMONDBACK... YOU'RE NOT UP FOR A FIGHT.
...HEY... HEY...
AND I'M NOT HERE FOR YOU...
NOT TODAY.
...HEY... I KNOW YOU...

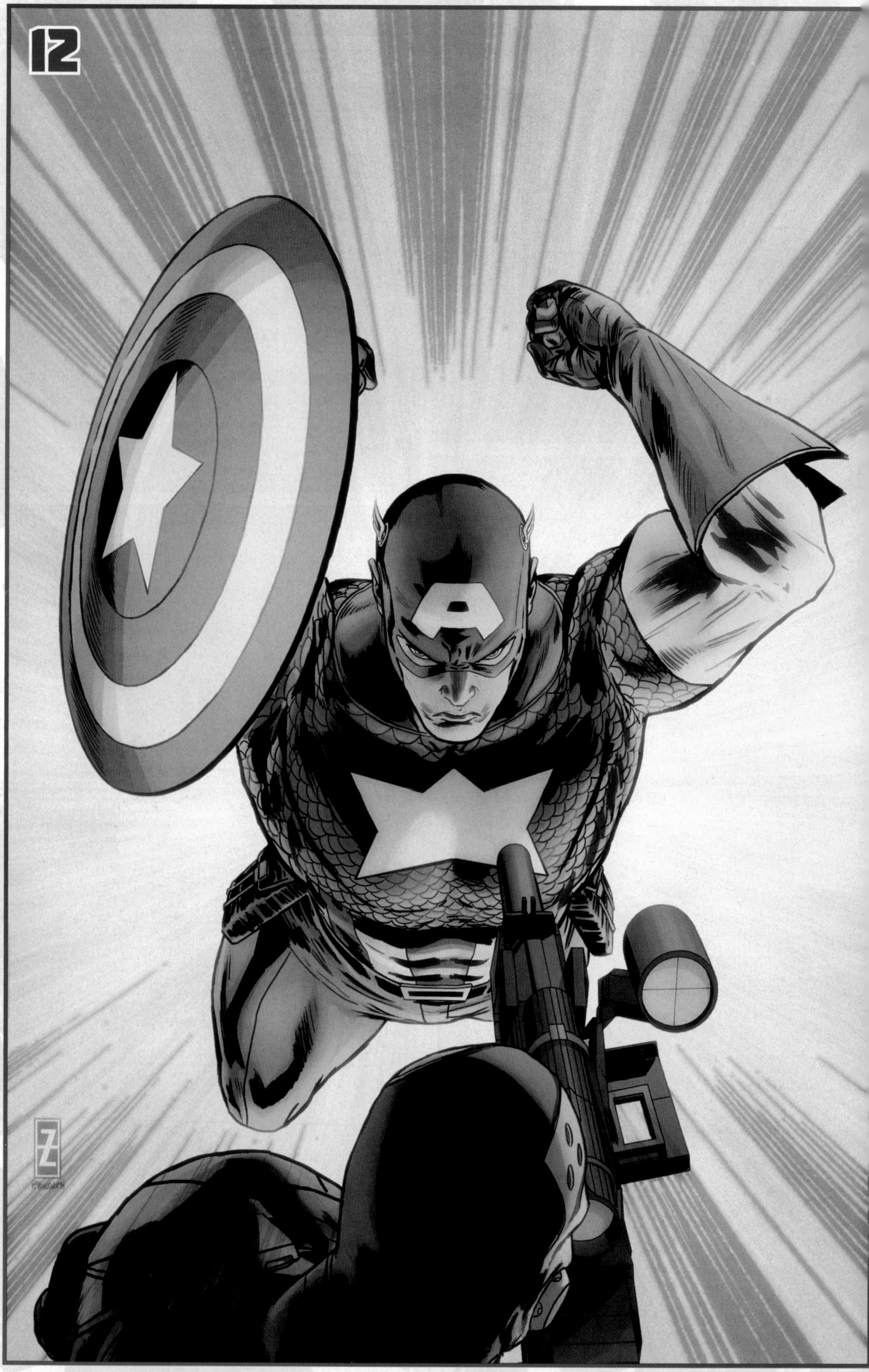
12

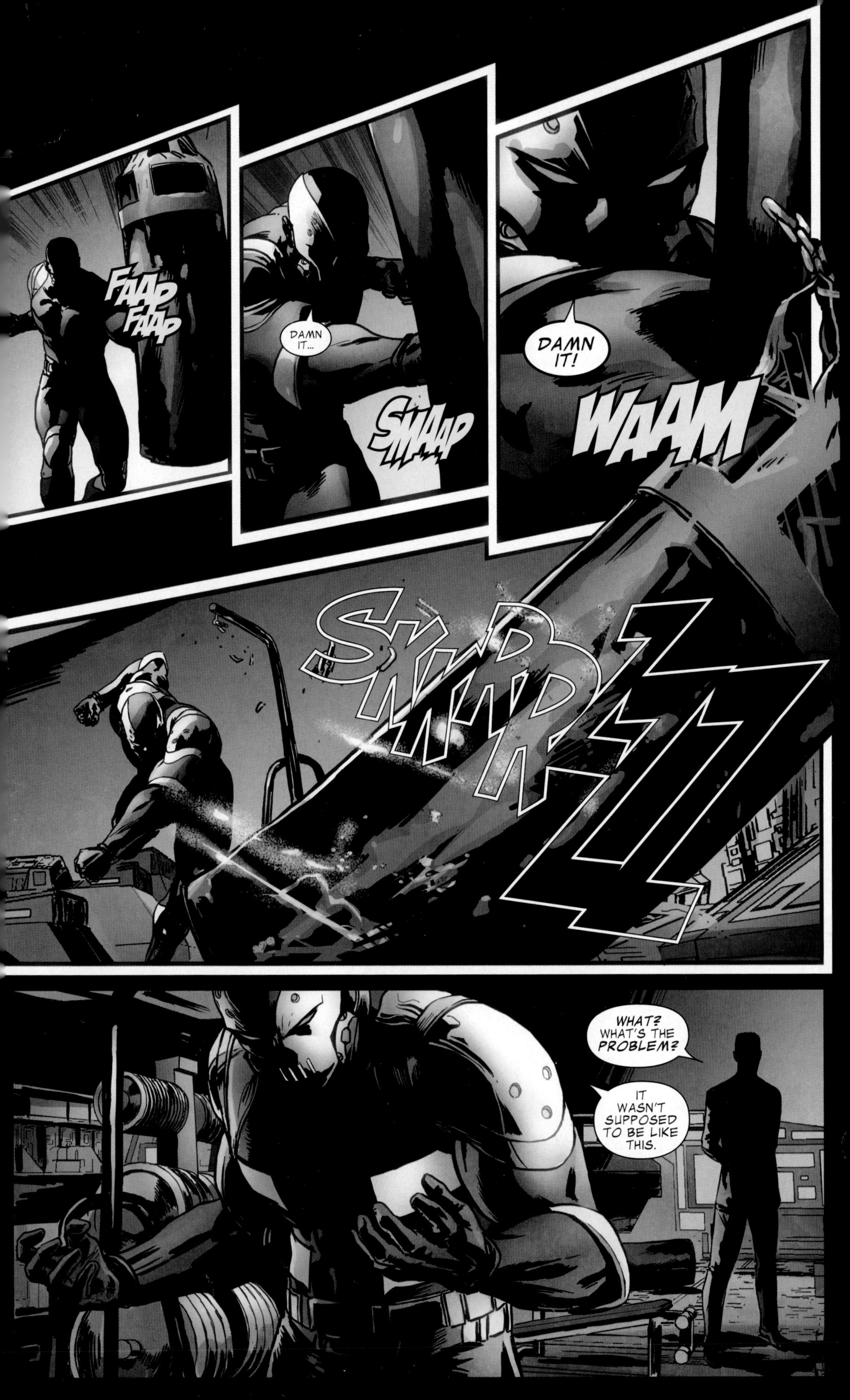
FAAP
FAAP
DAMN IT...
SMAAP
DAMN IT!
WAAM
SKRRRZ
WHAT? WHAT'S THE PROBLEM?
IT WASN'T SUPPOSED TO BE LIKE THIS.

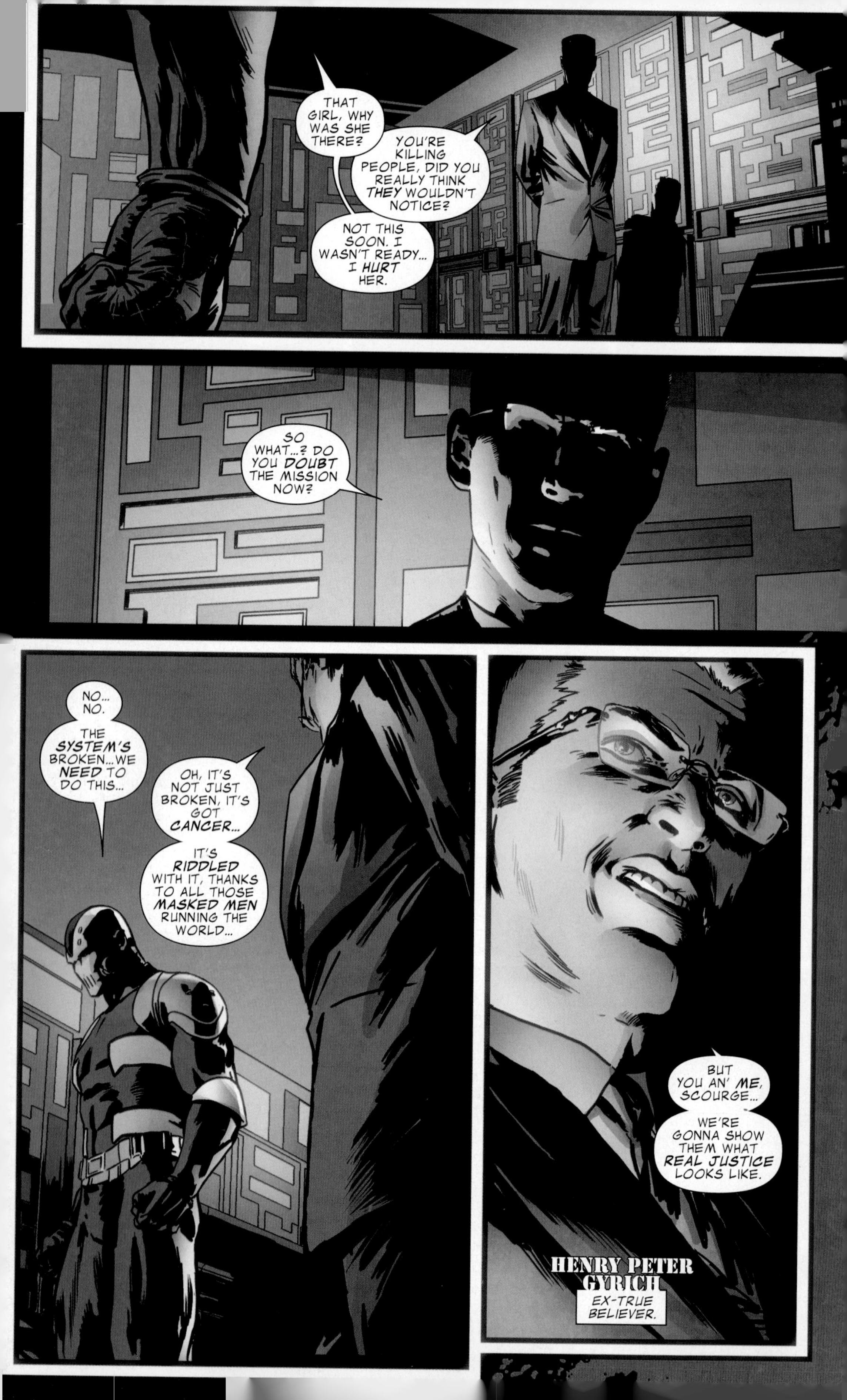

THAT GIRL, WHY WAS SHE THERE?
YOU'RE KILLING PEOPLE, DID YOU REALLY THINK THEY WOULDN'T NOTICE?
NOT THIS SOON. I WASN'T READY... I HURT HER.
SO WHAT...? DO YOU DOUBT THE MISSION NOW?
NO... NO.
THE SYSTEM'S BROKEN...WE NEED TO DO THIS...
OH, IT'S NOT JUST BROKEN, IT'S GOT CANCER...
IT'S RIDDLED WITH IT, THANKS TO ALL THOSE MASKED MEN RUNNING THE WORLD...
BUT YOU AN' ME, SCOURGE...
WE'RE GONNA SHOW THEM WHAT REAL JUSTICE LOOKS LIKE.
HENRY PETER GYRICH
EX-TRUE BELIEVER.

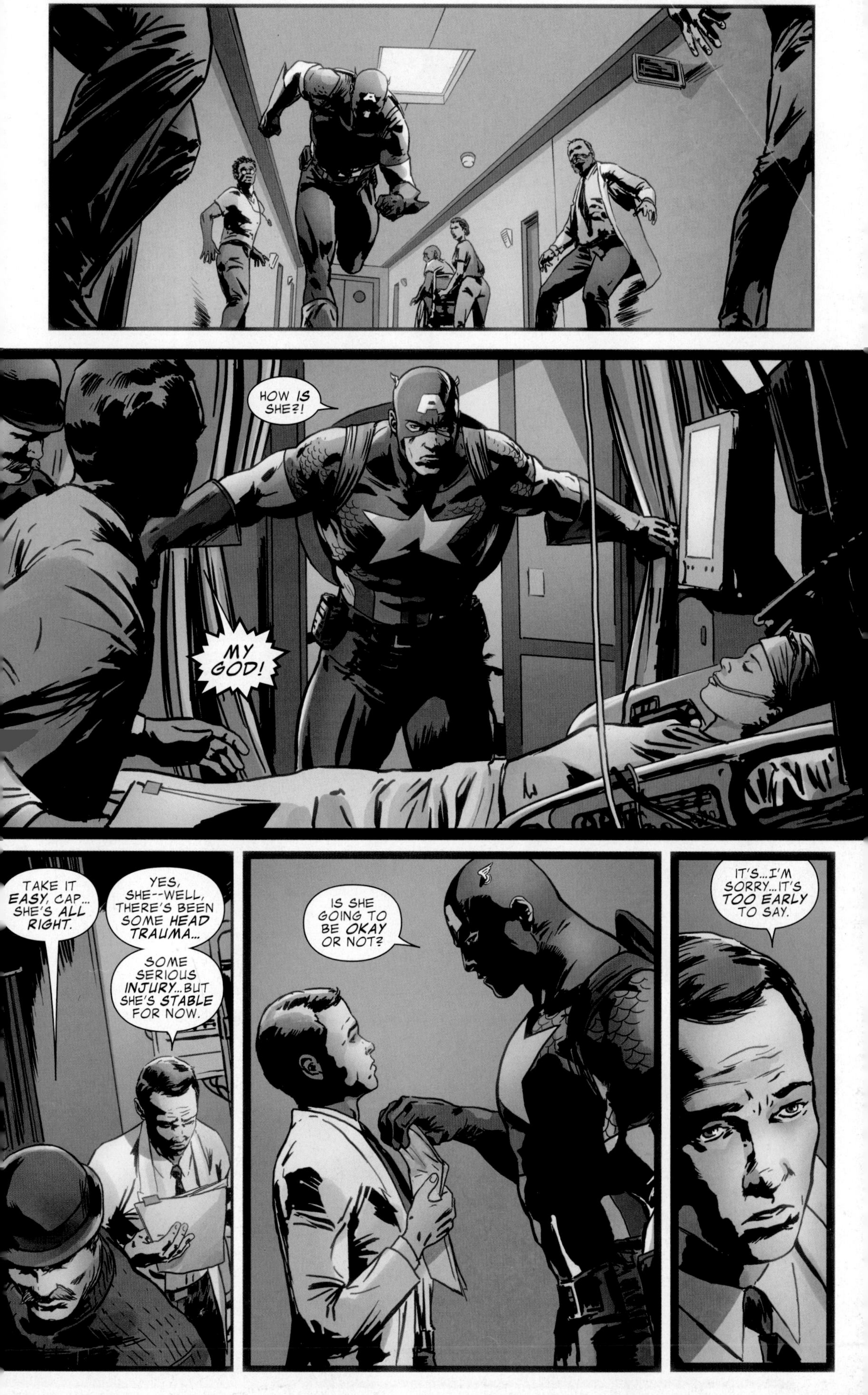
HOW IS SHE?!
MY GOD!
TAKE IT EASY, CAP... SHE'S ALL RIGHT.
YES, SHE--WELL, THERE'S BEEN SOME HEAD TRAUMA...
SOME SERIOUS INJURY...BUT SHE'S STABLE FOR NOW.
IS SHE GOING TO BE OKAY OR NOT?
IT'S...I'M SORRY...IT'S TOO EARLY TO SAY.

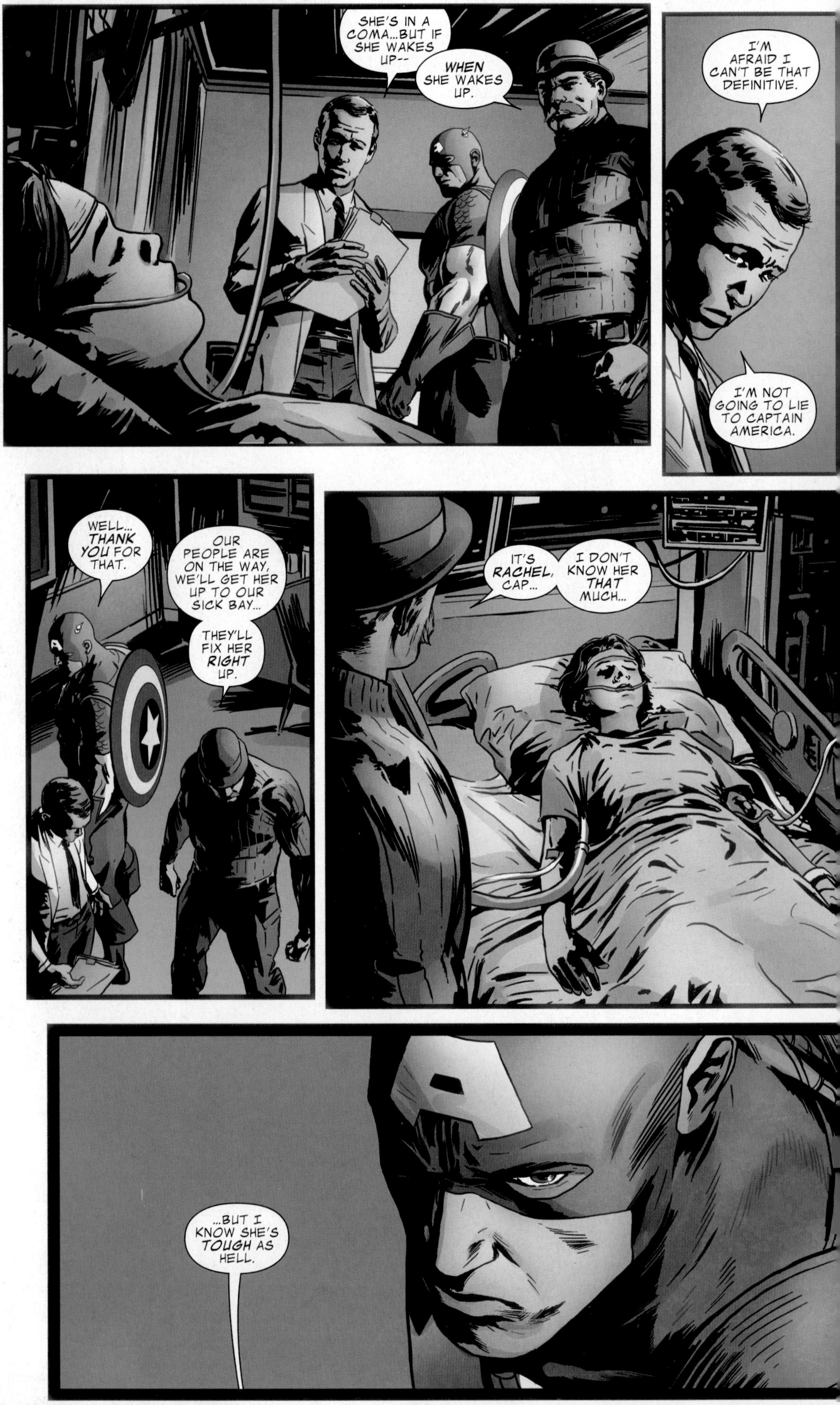
SHE'S IN A COMA...BUT IF SHE WAKES UP--
WHEN SHE WAKES UP.
I'M AFRAID I CAN'T BE THAT DEFINITIVE.
I'M NOT GOING TO LIE TO CAPTAIN AMERICA.
WELL... THANK YOU FOR THAT.
OUR PEOPLE ARE ON THE WAY, WE'LL GET HER UP TO OUR SICK BAY...
THEY'LL FIX HER RIGHT UP.
IT'S RACHEL, CAP...
I DON'T KNOW HER THAT MUCH...
...BUT I KNOW SHE'S TOUGH AS HELL.

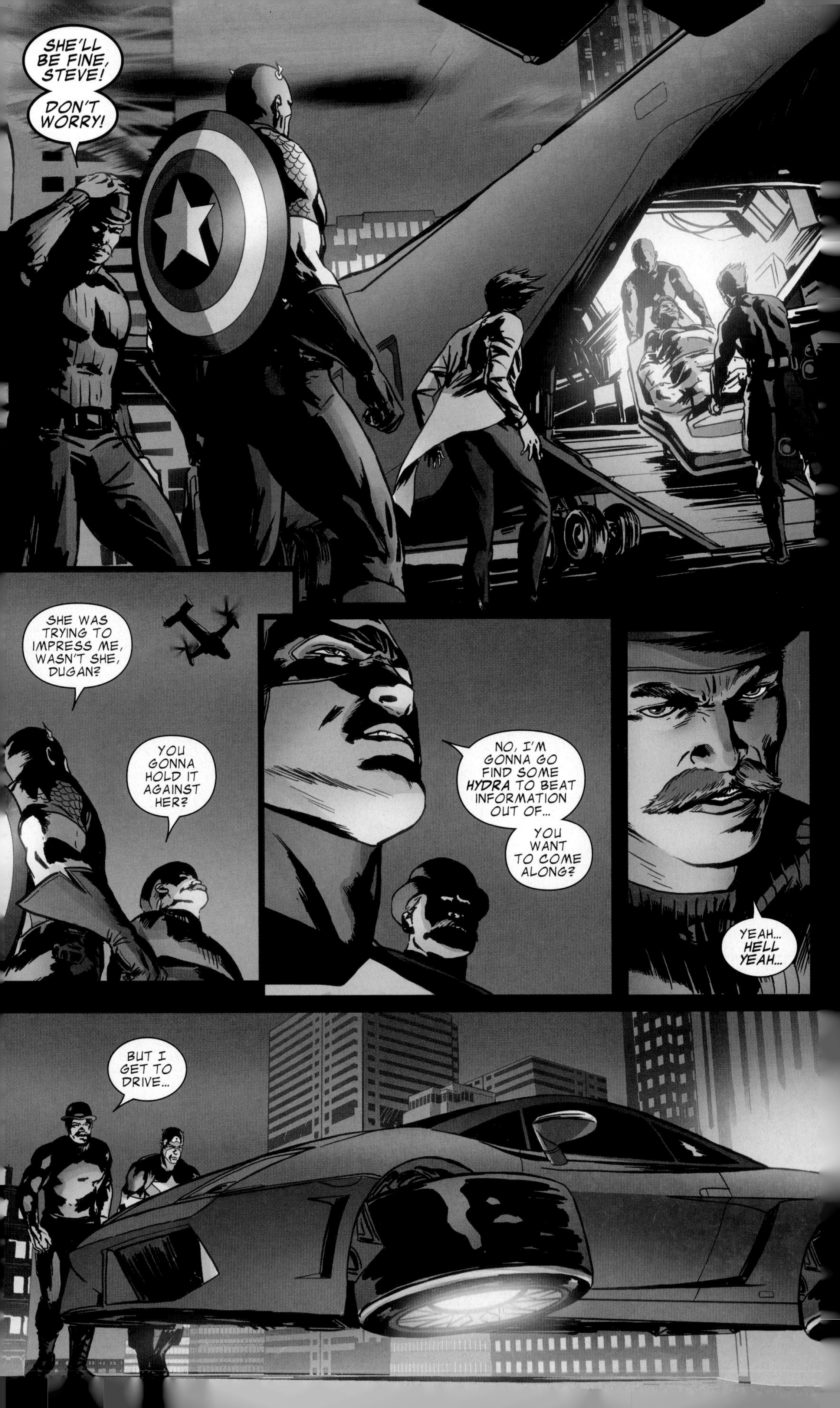

SHE'LL BE FINE, STEVE!
DON'T WORRY!
SHE WAS TRYING TO IMPRESS ME, WASN'T SHE, DUGAN?
YOU GONNA HOLD IT AGAINST HER?
NO, I'M GONNA GO FIND SOME HYDRA TO BEAT INFORMATION OUT OF...
YOU WANT TO COME ALONG?
YEAH... HELL YEAH...
BUT I GET TO DRIVE...

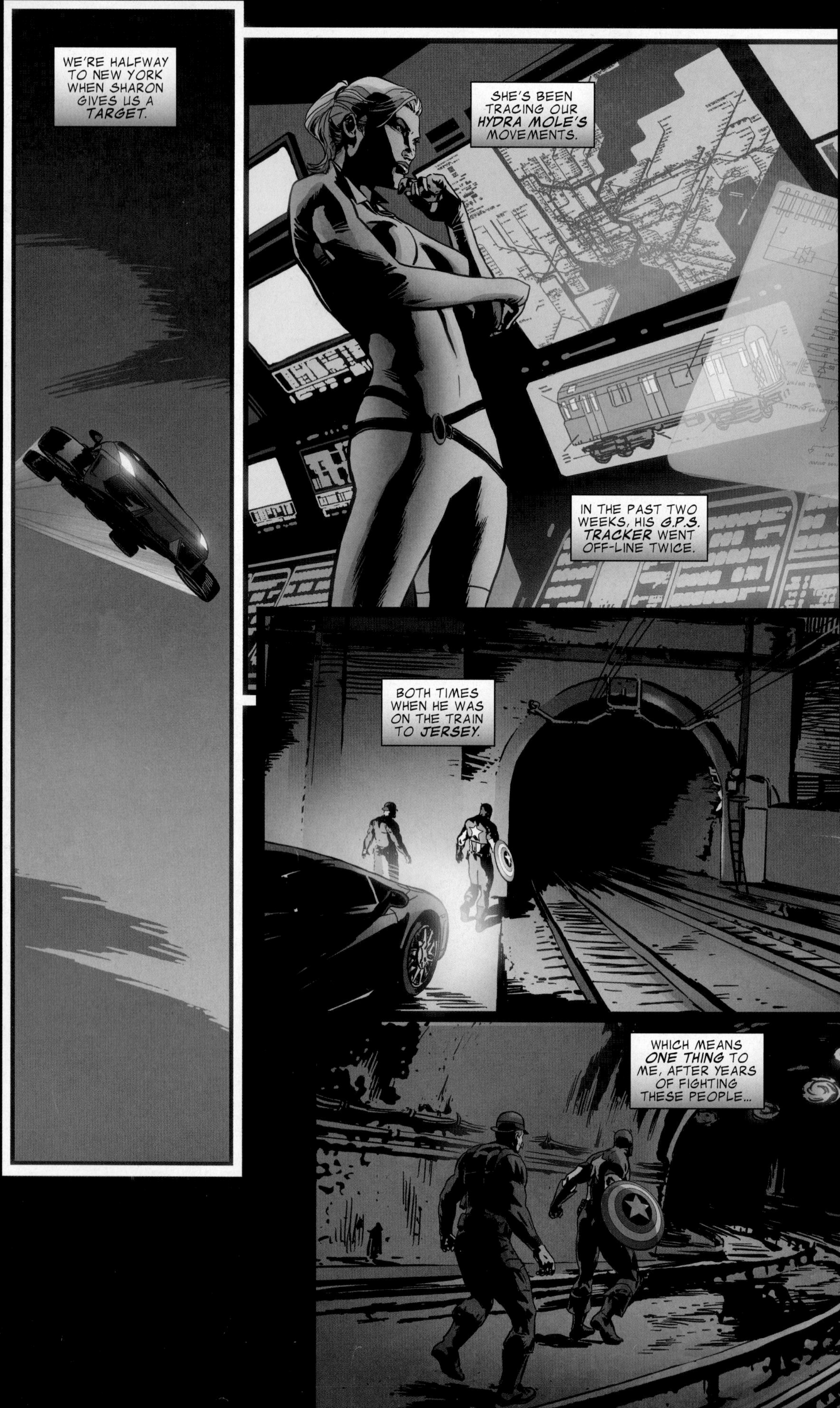
WE'RE HALFWAY TO NEW YORK WHEN SHARON GIVES US A TARGET.
SHE'S BEEN TRACING OUR HYDRA MOLE'S MOVEMENTS.
IN THE PAST TWO WEEKS, HIS G.P.S. TRACKER WENT OFF-LINE TWICE.
BOTH TIMES WHEN HE WAS ON THE TRAIN TO JERSEY.
WHICH MEANS ONE THING TO ME, AFTER YEARS OF FIGHTING THESE PEOPLE...

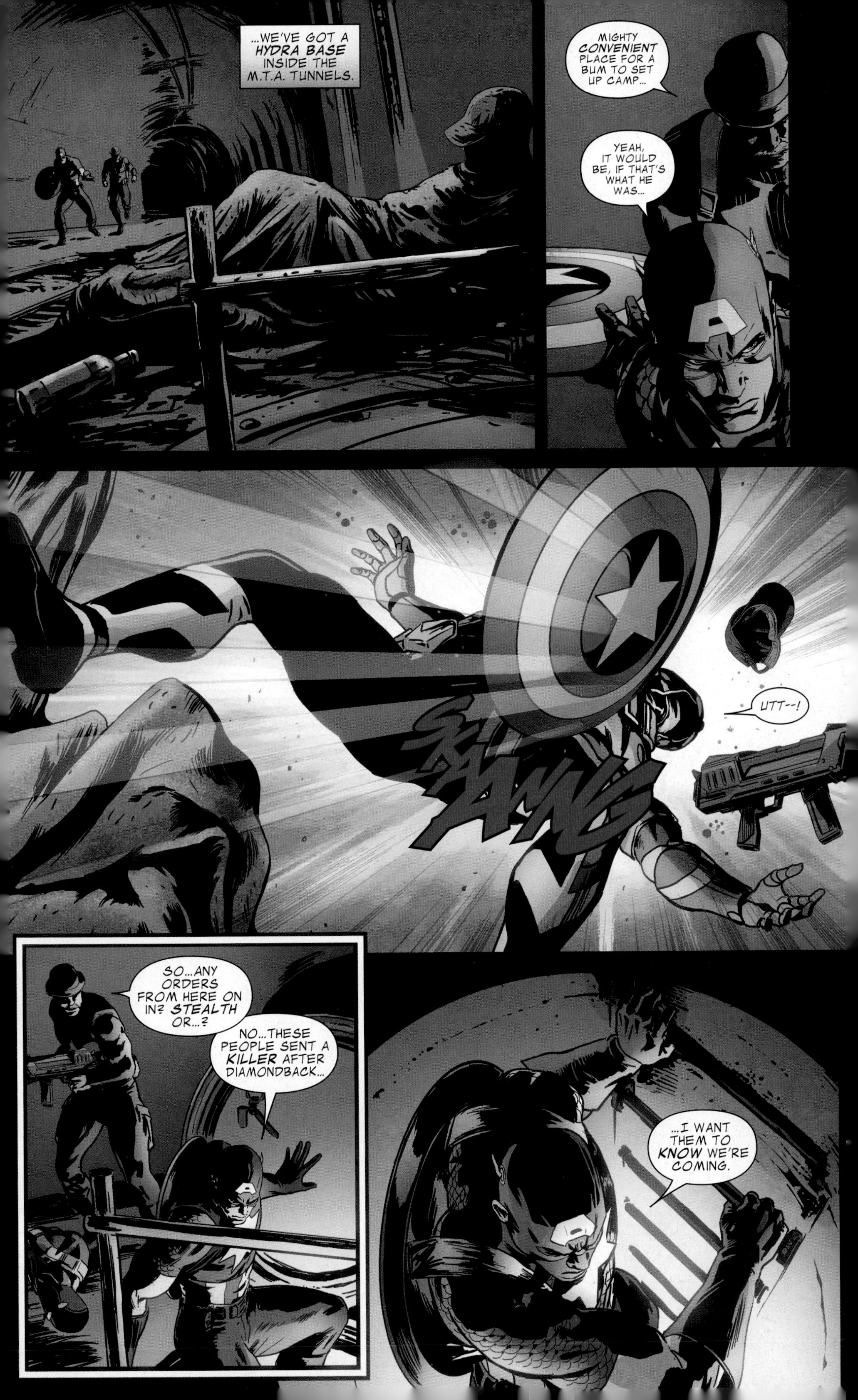
...WE'VE GOT A HYDRA BASE INSIDE THE M.T.A. TUNNELS.
MIGHTY CONVENIENT PLACE FOR A BUM TO SET UP CAMP...
YEAH, IT WOULD BE, IF THAT'S WHAT HE WAS...
UTT--!
SO...ANY ORDERS FROM HERE ON IN? STEALTH OR...?
NO...THESE PEOPLE SENT A KILLER AFTER DIAMONDBACK...
...I WANT THEM TO KNOW WE'RE COMING.

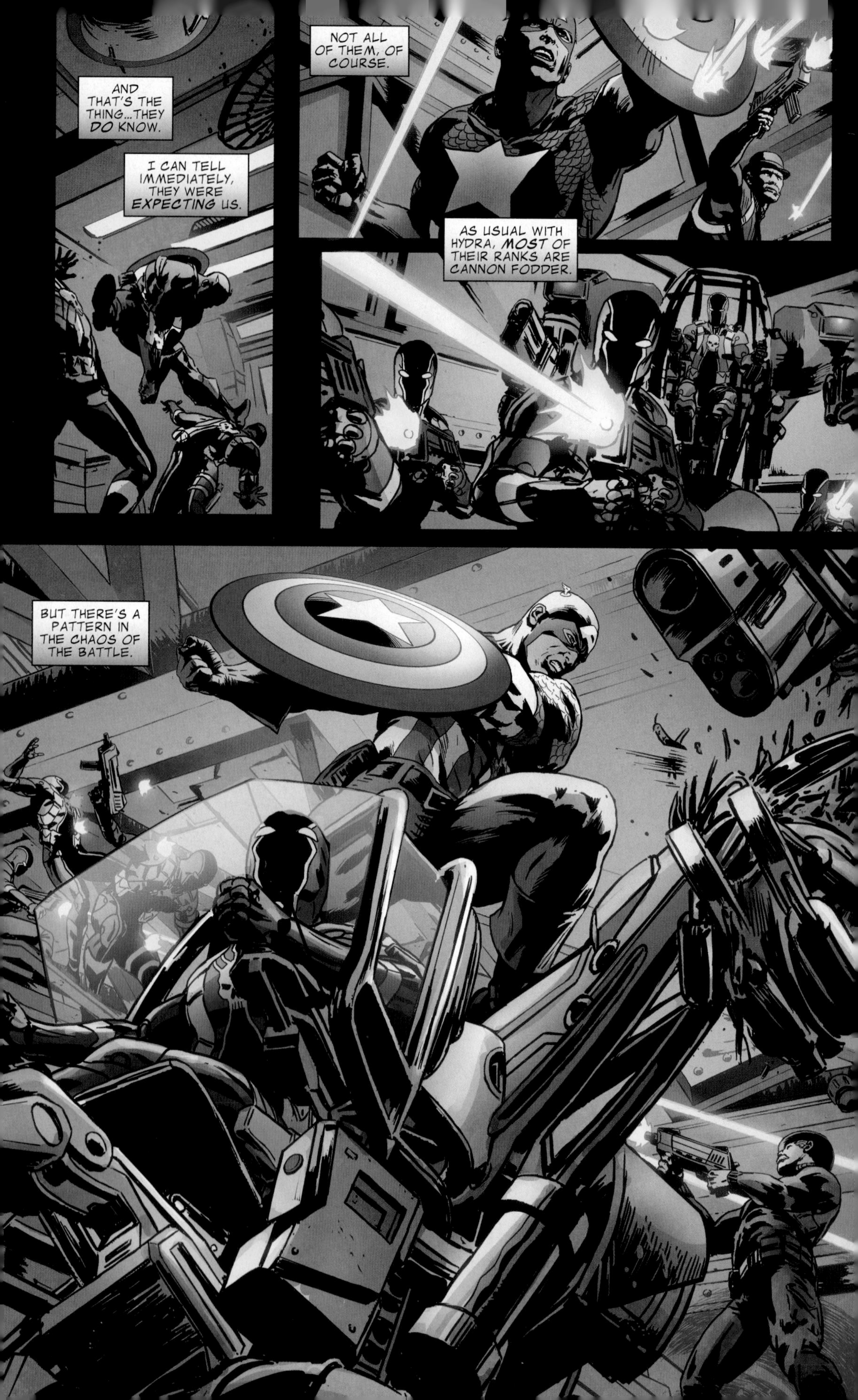
AND THAT'S THE THING...THEY DO KNOW.
I CAN TELL IMMEDIATELY, THEY WERE EXPECTING US.
NOT ALL OF THEM, OF COURSE.
AS USUAL WITH HYDRA, MOST OF THEIR RANKS ARE CANNON FODDER.
BUT THERE'S A PATTERN IN THE CHAOS OF THE BATTLE.

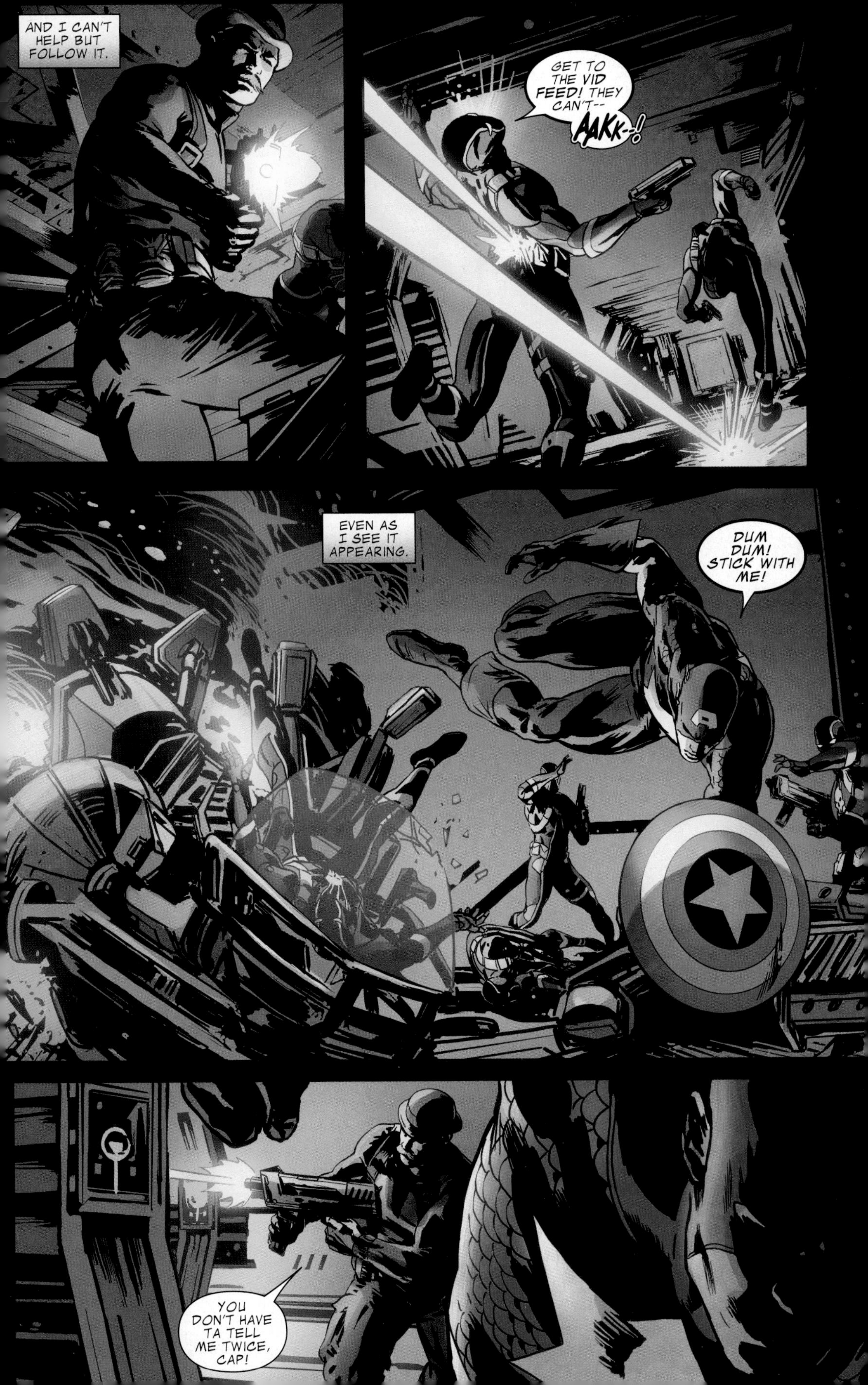
AND I CAN'T HELP BUT FOLLOW IT.
GET TO THE VID FEED! THEY CAN'T--
AAKK--!
EVEN AS I SEE IT APPEARING.
DUM DUM! STICK WITH ME!
YOU DON'T HAVE TA TELL ME TWICE, CAP!

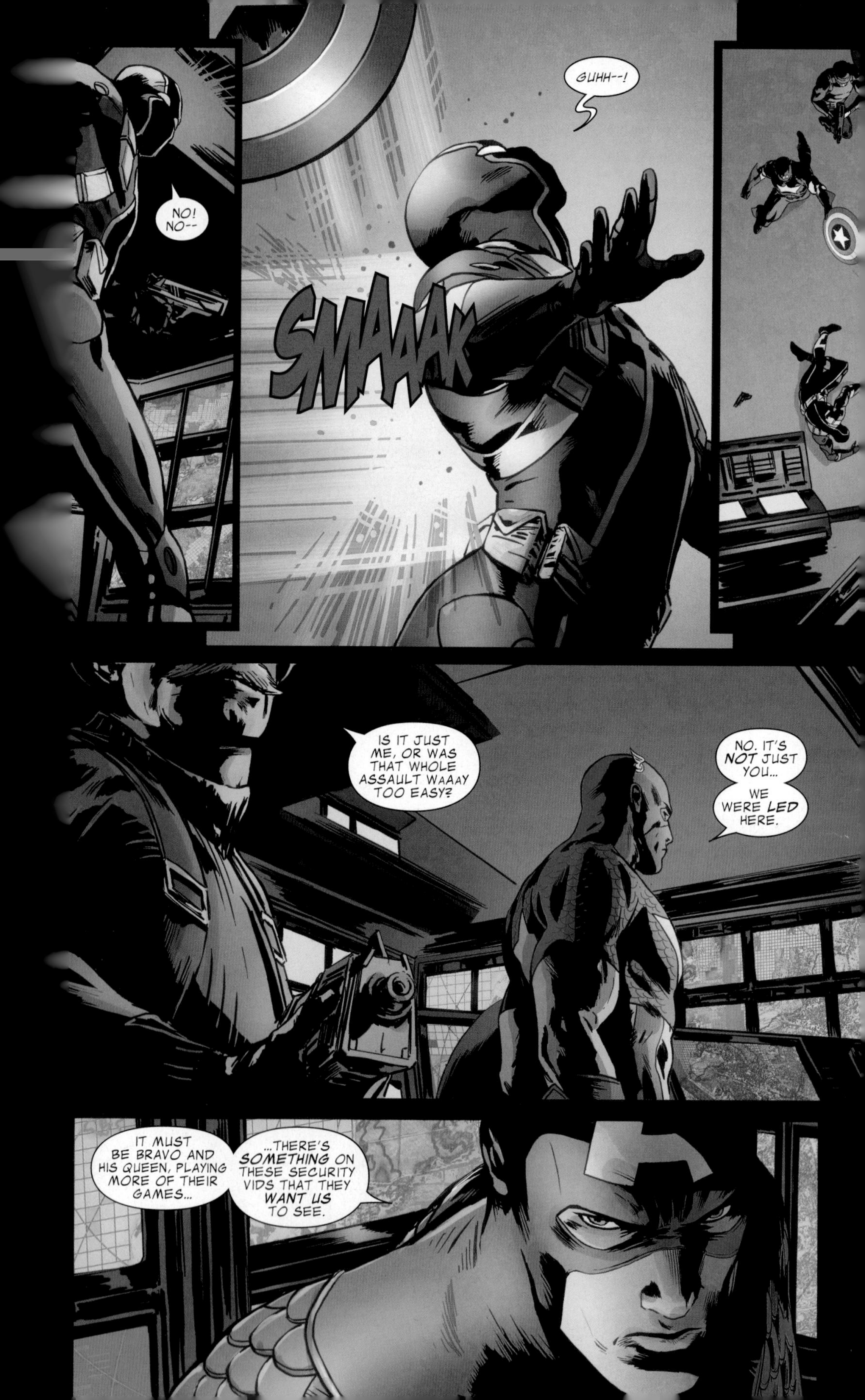
GUHH--!
NO! NO--
SMAAAK
IS IT JUST ME, OR WAS THAT WHOLE ASSAULT WAAAY TOO EASY?
NO. IT'S NOT JUST YOU...
WE WERE LED HERE.
IT MUST BE BRAVO AND HIS QUEEN, PLAYING MORE OF THEIR GAMES...
...THERE'S SOMETHING ON THESE SECURITY VIDS THAT THEY WANT US TO SEE.

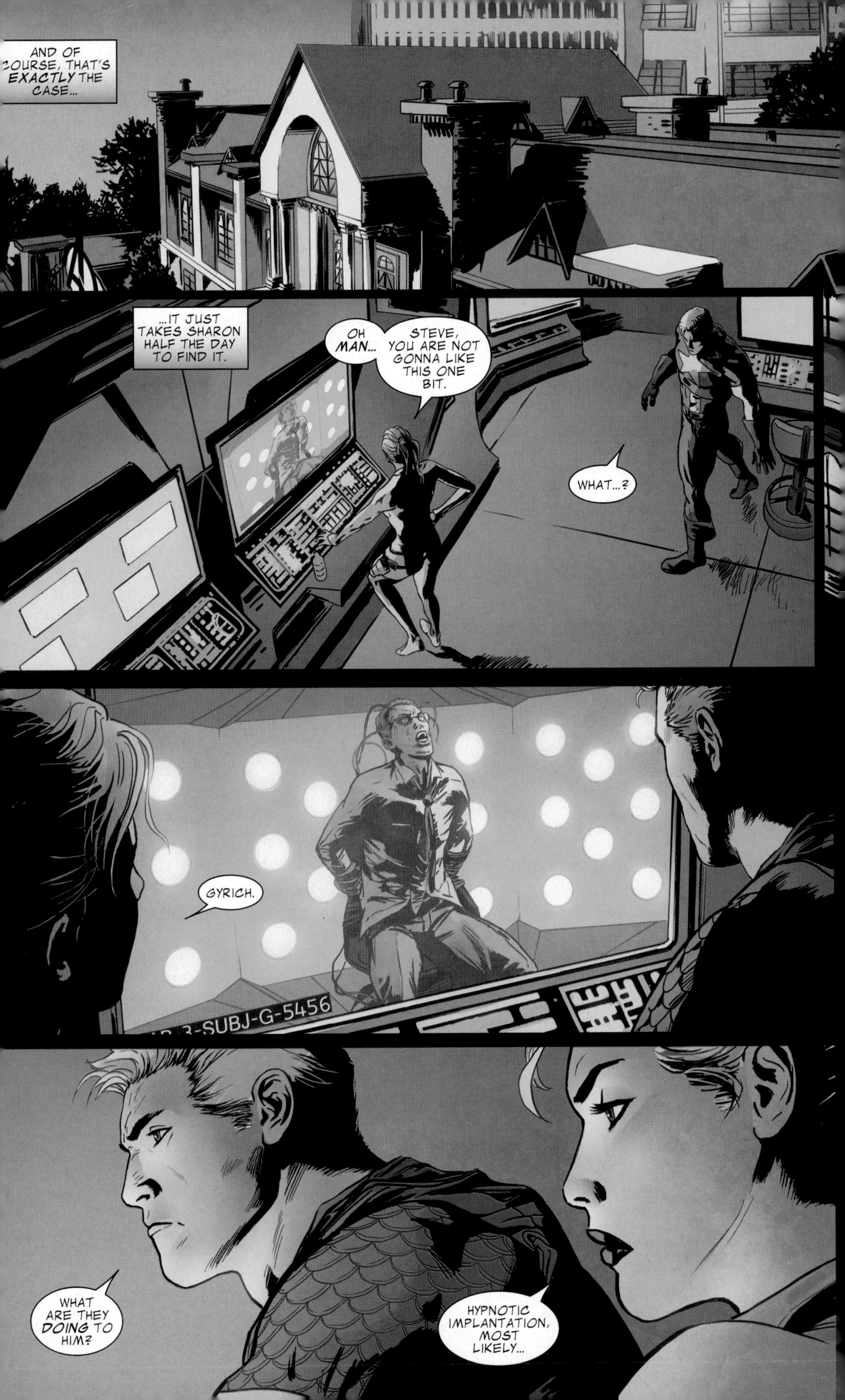
AND OF COURSE, THAT'S EXACTLY THE CASE...
...IT JUST TAKES SHARON HALF THE DAY TO FIND IT.
OH MAN...
STEVE, YOU ARE NOT GONNA LIKE THIS ONE BIT.
WHAT...?
GYRICH.
-SUBJ-G-5456
WHAT ARE THEY DOING TO HIM?
HYPNOTIC IMPLANTATION, MOST LIKELY...

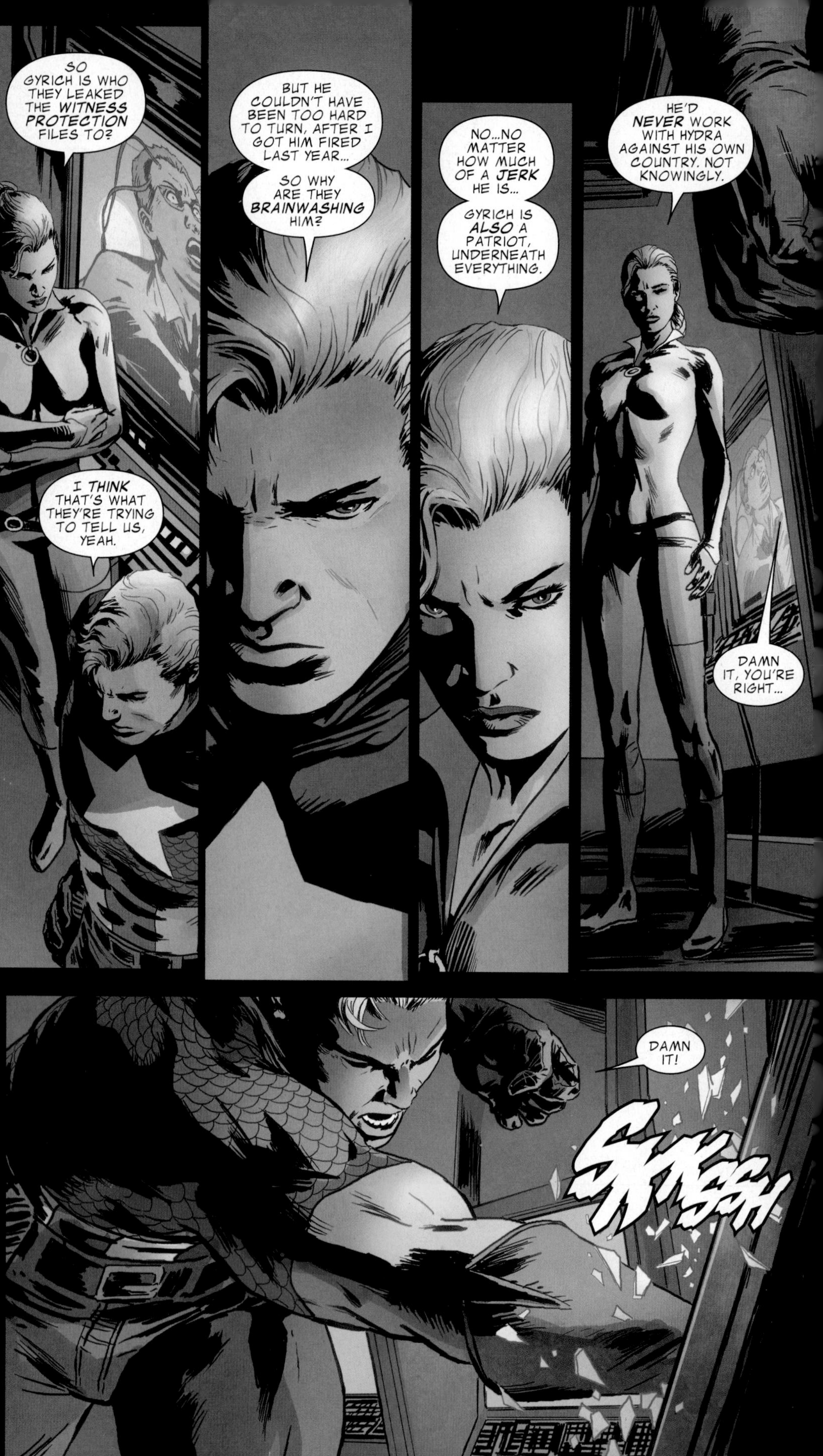

SO GYRICH IS WHO THEY LEAKED THE WITNESS PROTECTION FILES TO?
I THINK THAT'S WHAT THEY'RE TRYING TO TELL US, YEAH.
BUT HE COULDN'T HAVE BEEN TOO HARD TO TURN, AFTER I GOT HIM FIRED LAST YEAR...
SO WHY ARE THEY BRAINWASHING HIM?
NO...NO MATTER HOW MUCH OF A JERK HE IS...
GYRICH IS ALSO A PATRIOT, UNDERNEATH EVERYTHING.
HE'D NEVER WORK WITH HYDRA AGAINST HIS OWN COUNTRY. NOT KNOWINGLY.
DAMN IT, YOU'RE RIGHT...
DAMN IT!
SKKSSH

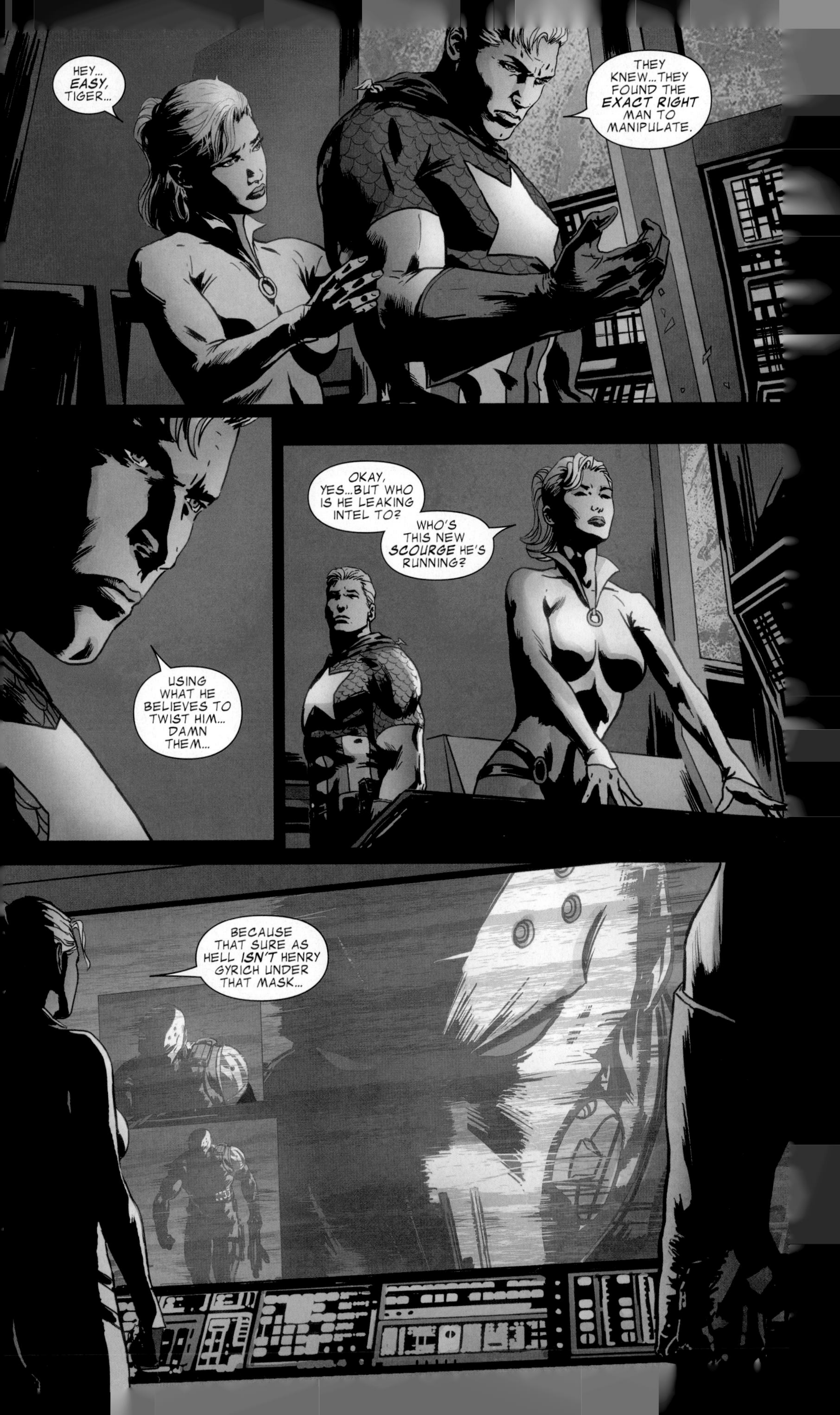
HEY... EASY, TIGER...
THEY KNEW...THEY FOUND THE EXACT RIGHT MAN TO MANIPULATE.
USING WHAT HE BELIEVES TO TWIST HIM... DAMN THEM...
OKAY, YES...BUT WHO IS HE LEAKING INTEL TO?
WHO'S THIS NEW SCOURGE HE'S RUNNING?
BECAUSE THAT SURE AS HELL ISN'T HENRY GYRICH UNDER THAT MASK...

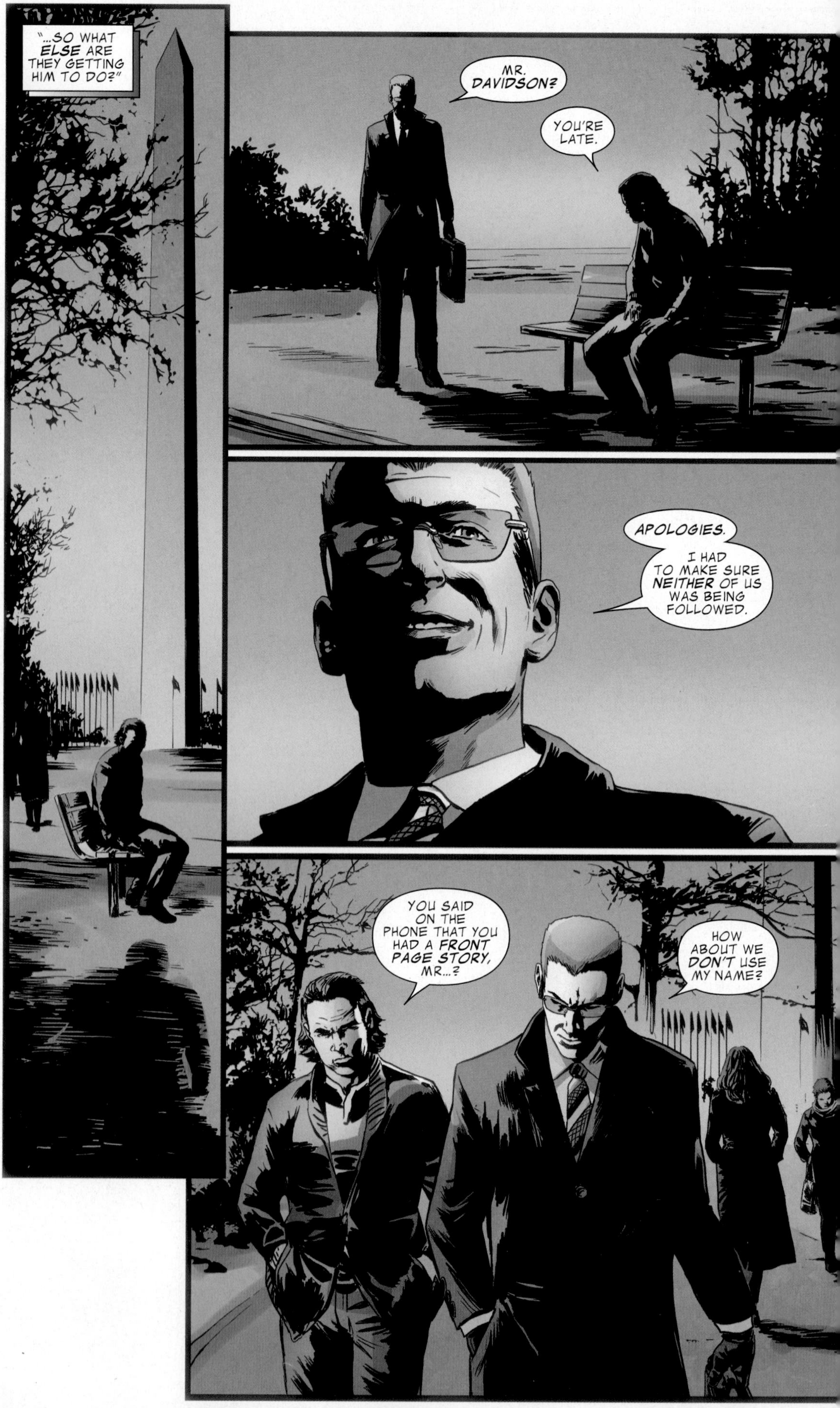
"...SO WHAT ELSE ARE THEY GETTING HIM TO DO?"
MR. DAVIDSON?
YOU'RE LATE.
APOLOGIES.
I HAD TO MAKE SURE NEITHER OF US WAS BEING FOLLOWED.
YOU SAID ON THE PHONE THAT YOU HAD A FRONT PAGE STORY, MR...?
HOW ABOUT WE DON'T USE MY NAME?

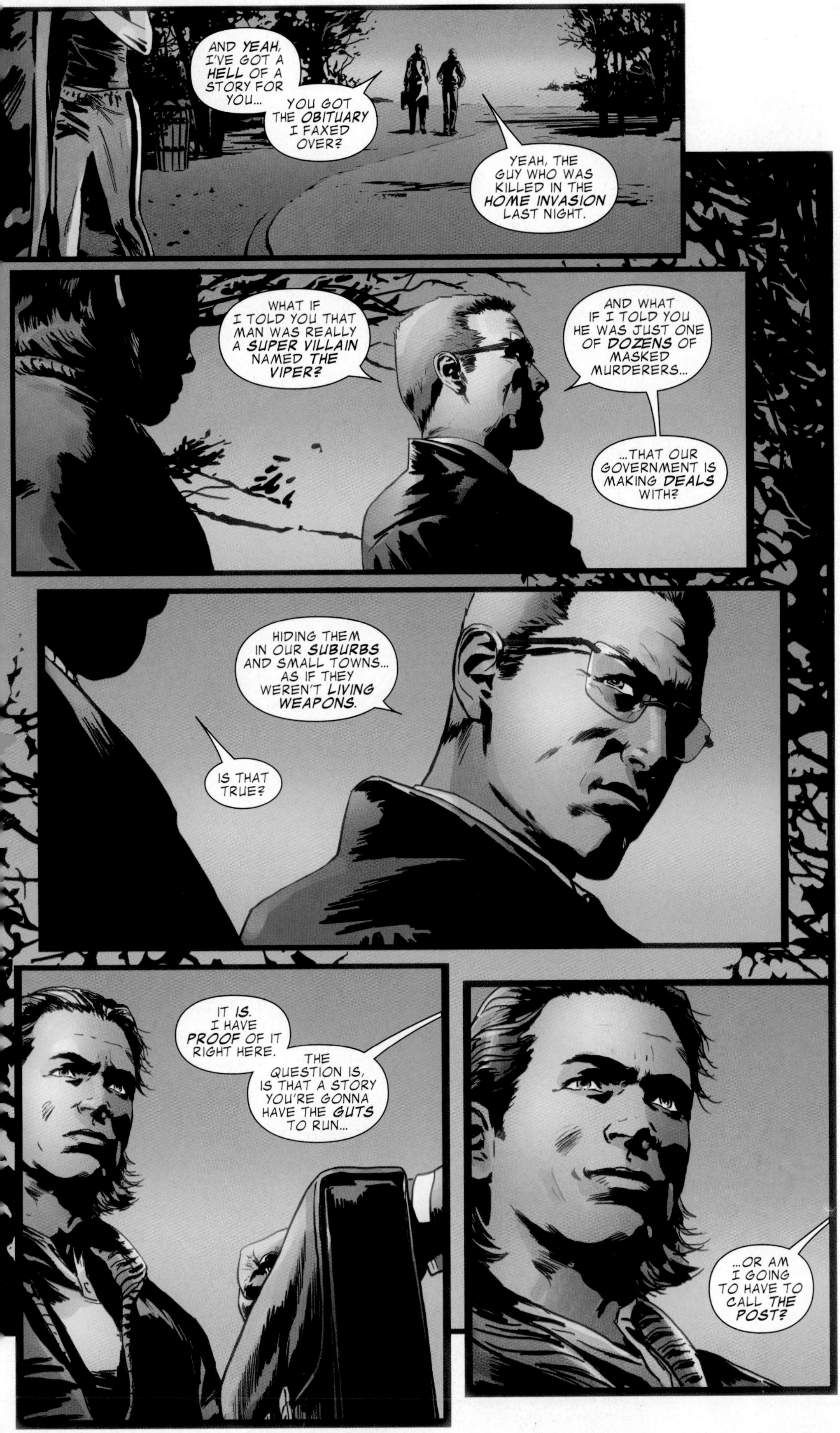
AND YEAH, I'VE GOT A HELL OF A STORY FOR YOU...
YOU GOT THE OBITUARY I FAXED OVER?
YEAH, THE GUY WHO WAS KILLED IN THE HOME INVASION LAST NIGHT.
WHAT IF I TOLD YOU THAT MAN WAS REALLY A SUPER VILLAIN NAMED THE VIPER?
AND WHAT IF I TOLD YOU HE WAS JUST ONE OF DOZENS OF MASKED MURDERERS...
...THAT OUR GOVERNMENT IS MAKING DEALS WITH?
HIDING THEM IN OUR SUBURBS AND SMALL TOWNS... AS IF THEY WEREN'T LIVING WEAPONS.
IS THAT TRUE?
IT IS. I HAVE PROOF OF IT RIGHT HERE.
THE QUESTION IS, IS THAT A STORY YOU'RE GONNA HAVE THE GUTS TO RUN...
...OR AM I GOING TO HAVE TO CALL THE POST?

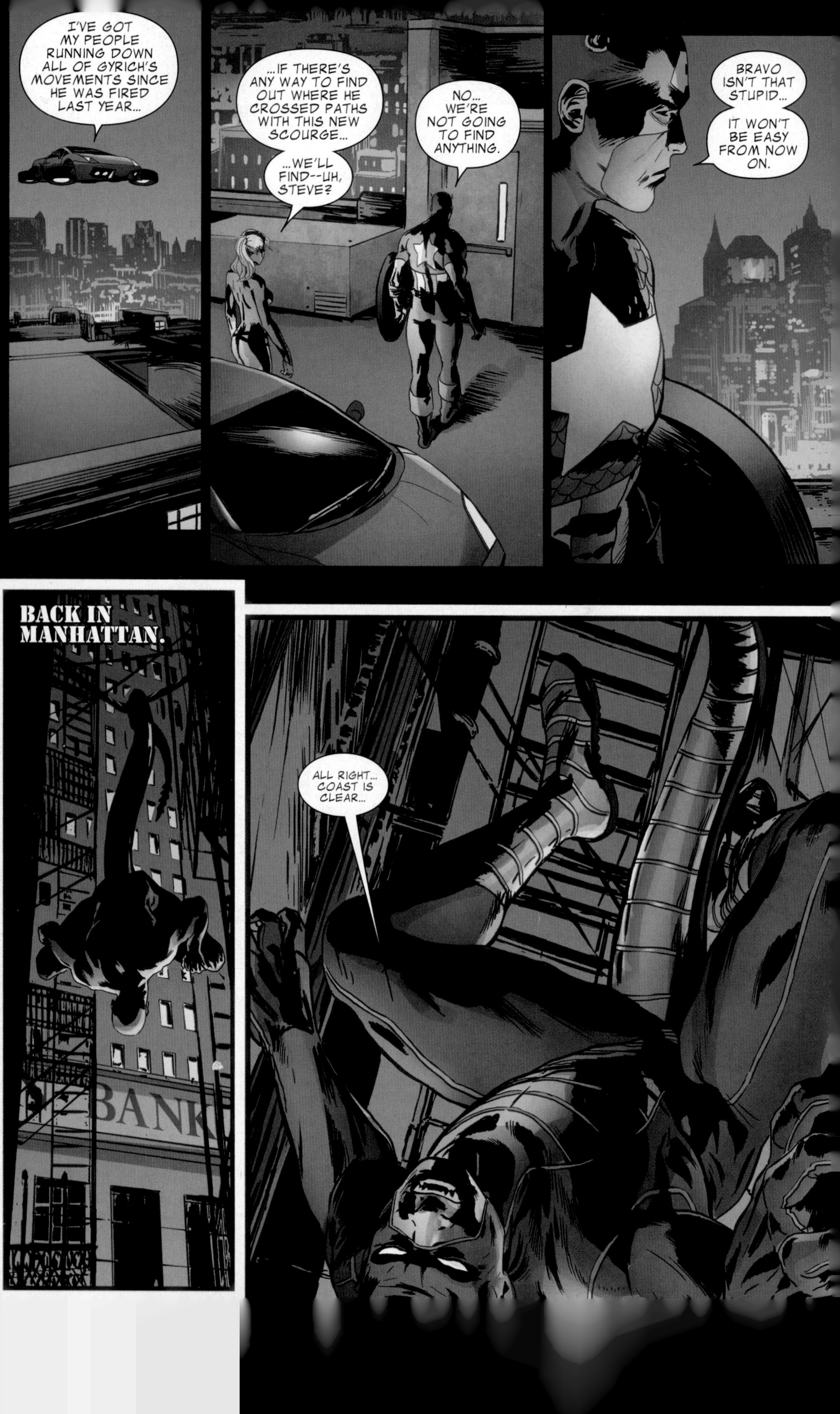
I'VE GOT MY PEOPLE RUNNING DOWN ALL OF GYRICH'S MOVEMENTS SINCE HE WAS FIRED LAST YEAR...
...IF THERE'S ANY WAY TO FIND OUT WHERE HE CROSSED PATHS WITH THIS NEW SCOURGE...
...WE'LL FIND--UH, STEVE?
NO... WE'RE NOT GOING TO FIND ANYTHING.
BRAVO ISN'T THAT STUPID...
IT WON'T BE EASY FROM NOW ON.
BACK IN MANHATTAN.
BANK
ALL RIGHT... COAST IS CLEAR...

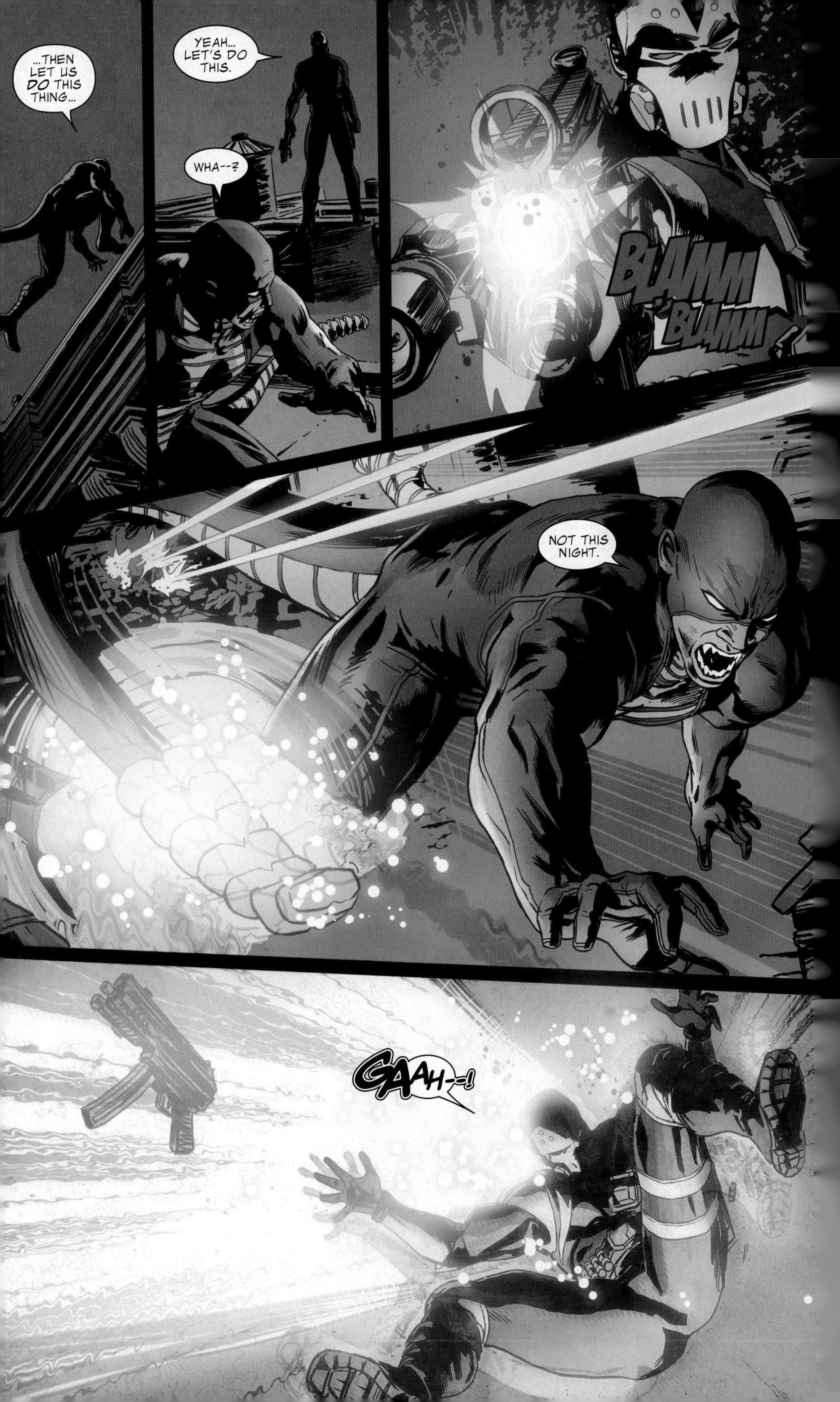
...THEN LET US DO THIS THING...
YEAH... LET'S DO THIS.
WHA--?
BLAMM BLAMM
NOT THIS NIGHT.
GAAH--!

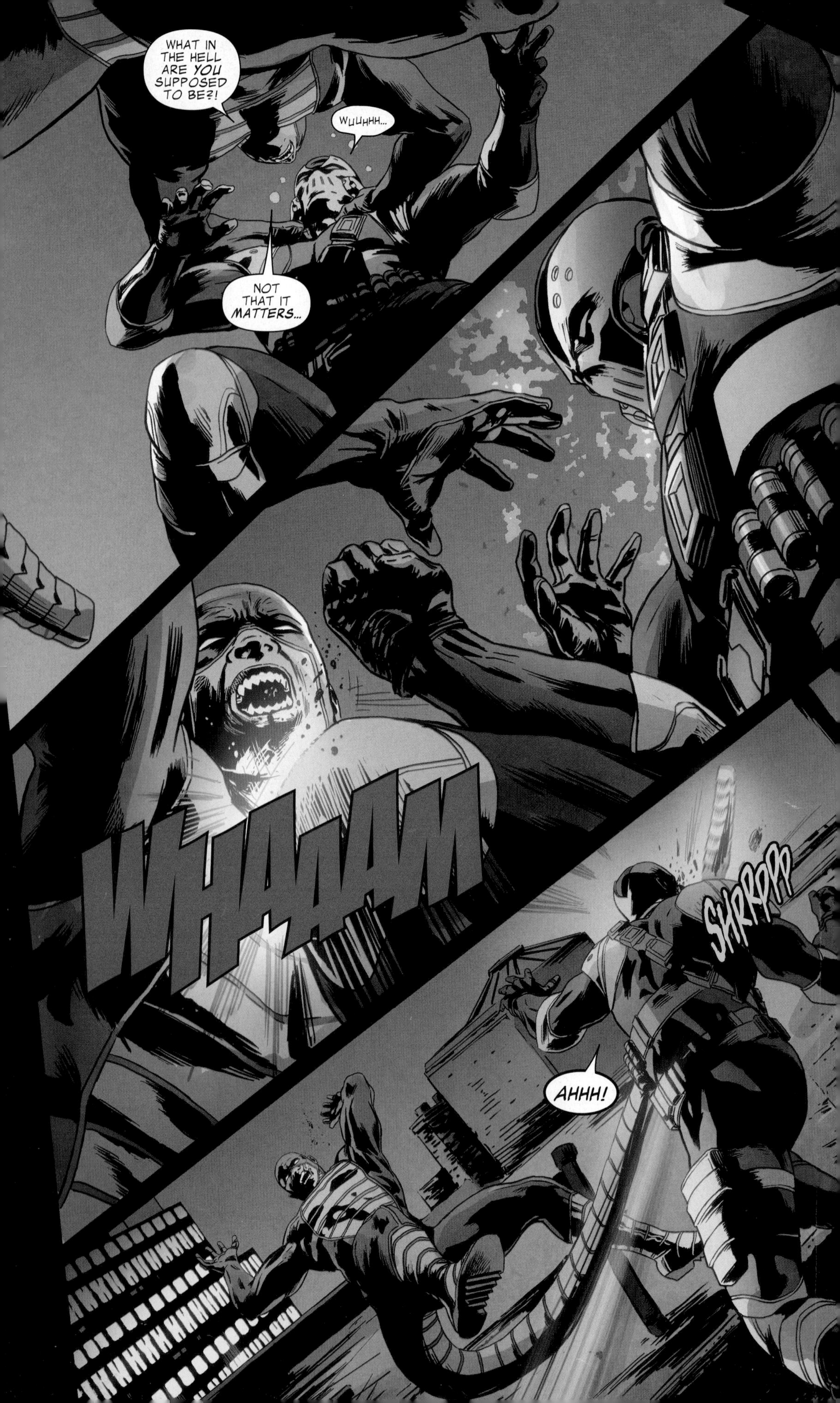

WHAT IN THE HELL ARE YOU SUPPOSED TO BE?!
WUUHHH...
NOT THAT IT MATTERS...
WHAAAM
SHRPPP
AHHH!

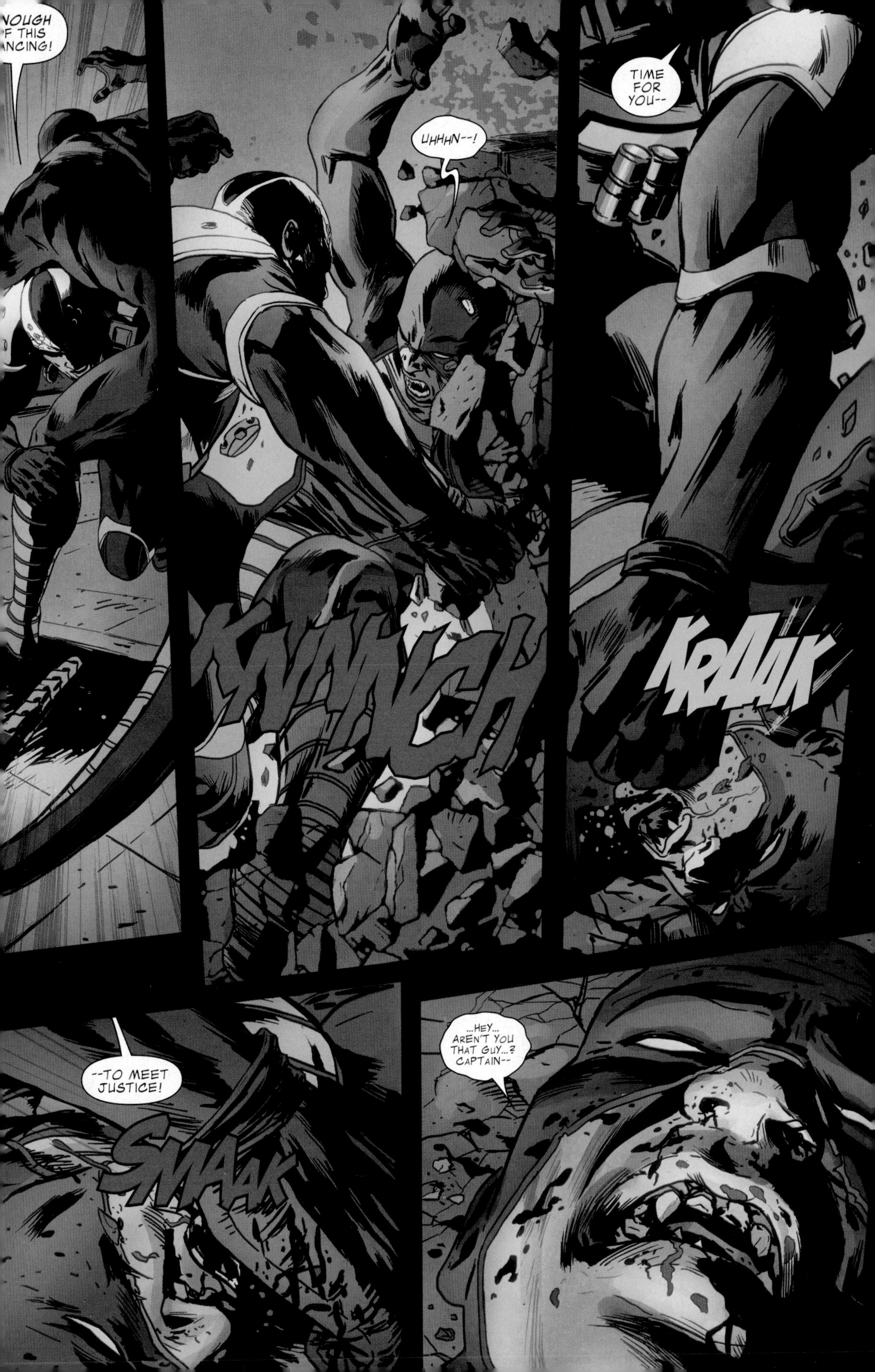
NOUGH
F THIS
ANCING!
UHHHN--!
KWWNCH
TIME FOR YOU--
KRAAK
--TO MEET JUSTICE!
SMAAK
...HEY... AREN'T YOU THAT GUY...? CAPTAIN--

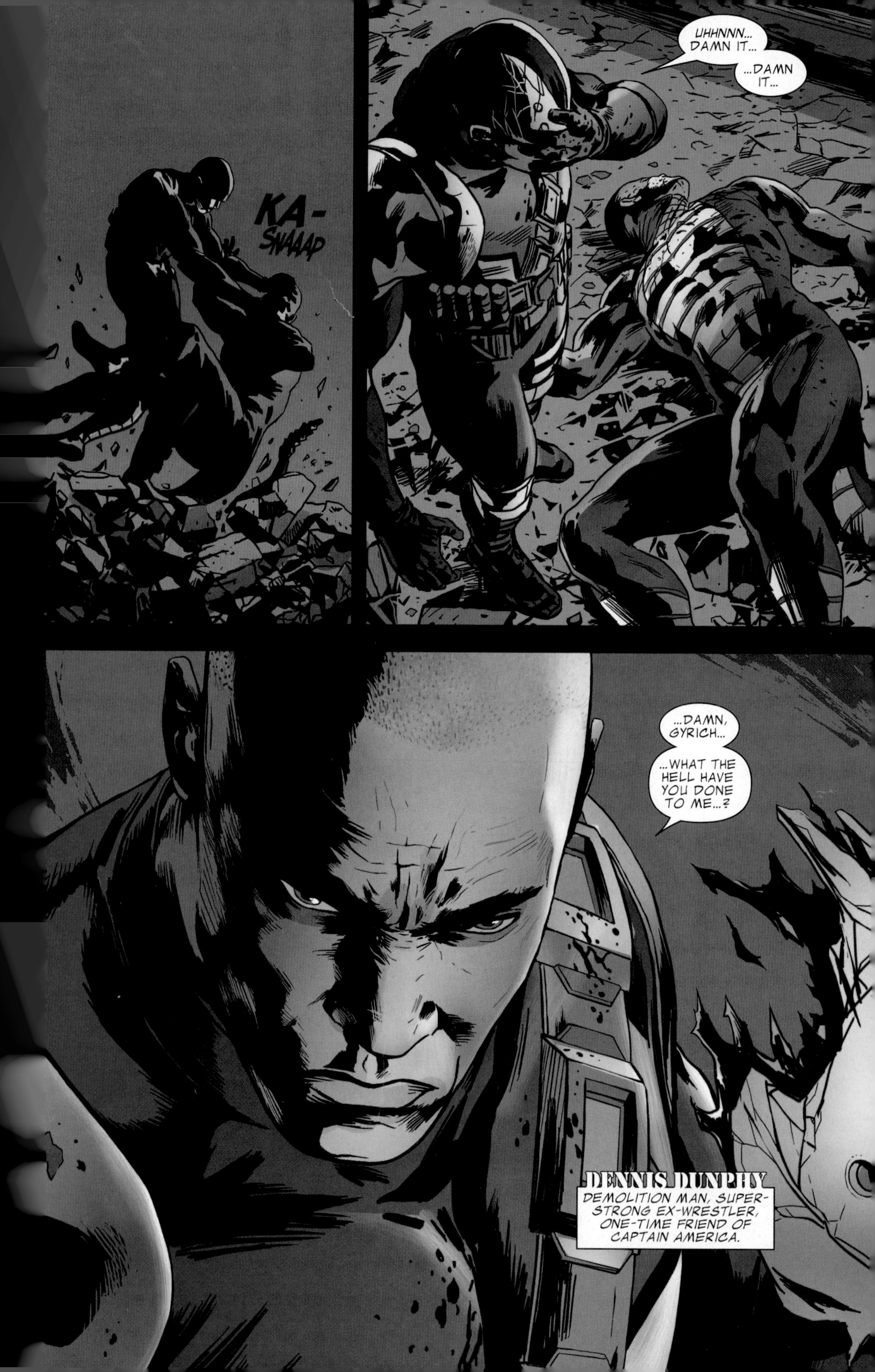
KA-SNAAAP
UHHNNN... DAMN IT...
...DAMN IT...
...DAMN, GYRICH...
...WHAT THE HELL HAVE YOU DONE TO ME...?
DENNIS DUNPHY
DEMOLITION MAN, SUPER-STRONG EX-WRESTLER, ONE-TIME FRIEND OF CAPTAIN AMERICA.

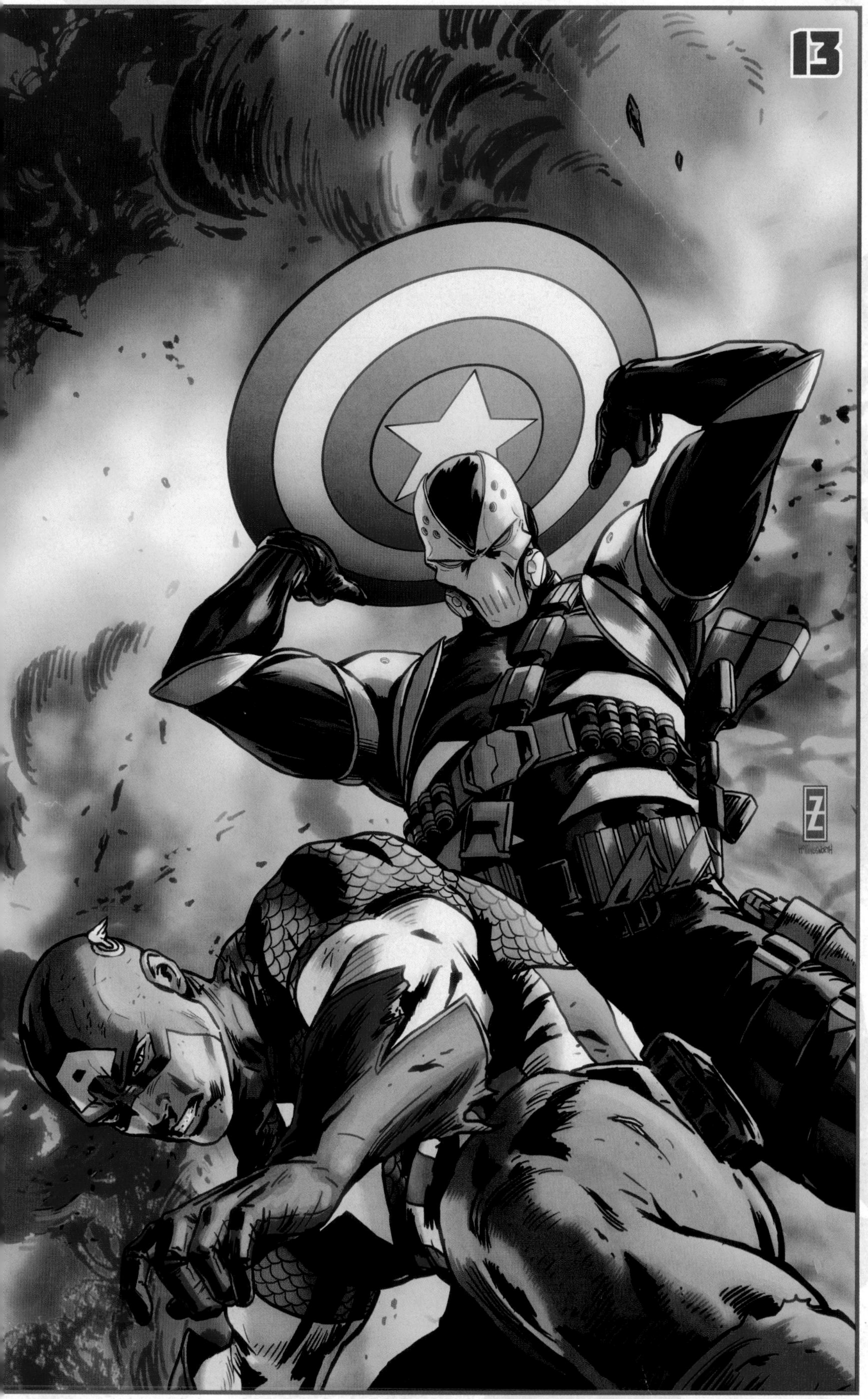
13

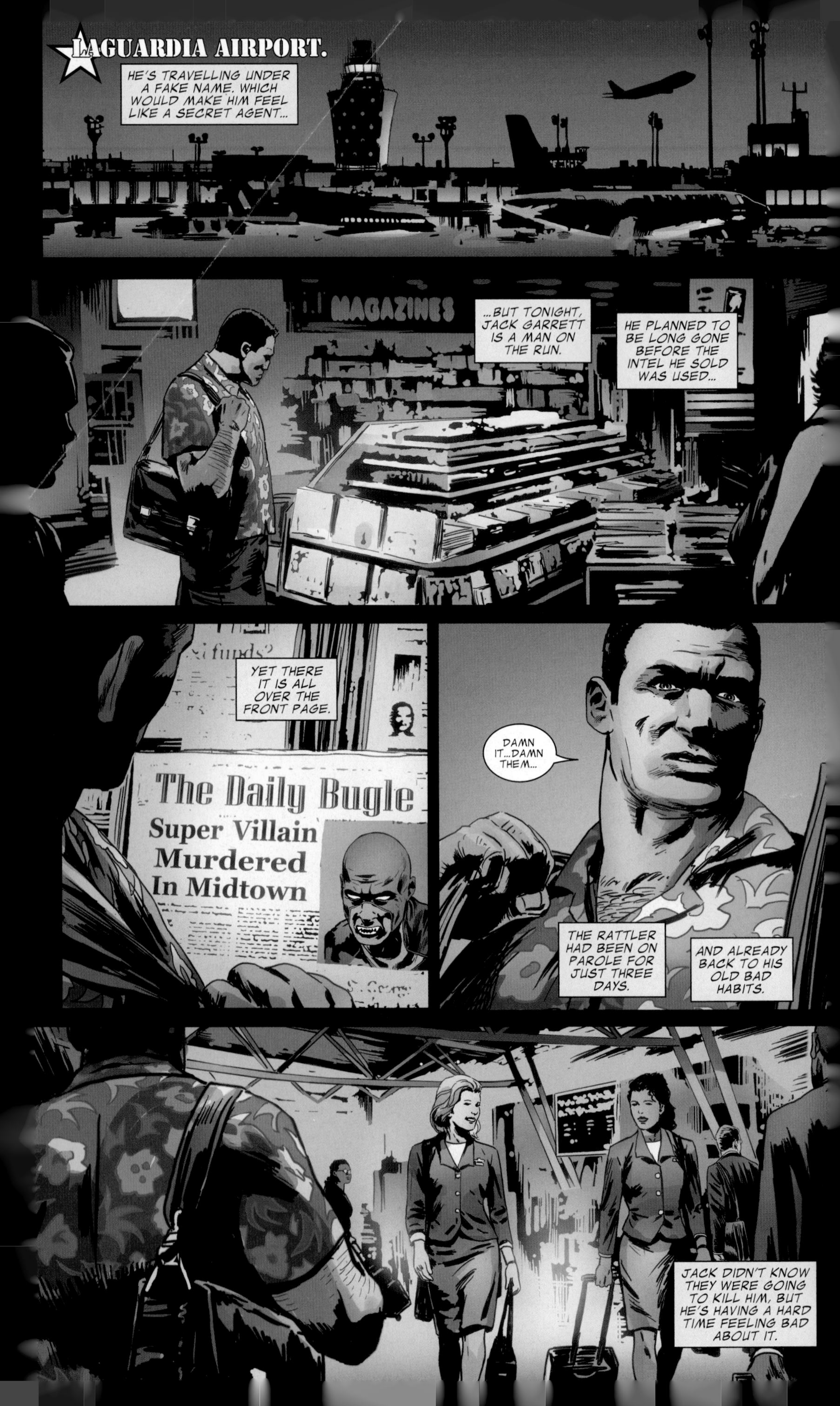
LAGUARDIA AIRPORT.
HE'S TRAVELLING UNDER A FAKE NAME. WHICH WOULD MAKE HIM FEEL LIKE A SECRET AGENT...
MAGAZINES
...BUT TONIGHT, JACK GARRETT IS A MAN ON THE RUN.
HE PLANNED TO BE LONG GONE BEFORE THE INTEL HE SOLD WAS USED...
YET THERE IT IS ALL OVER THE FRONT PAGE.
The Daily Bugle
Super Villain Murdered In Midtown
DAMN IT...DAMN THEM...
THE RATTLER HAD BEEN ON PAROLE FOR JUST THREE DAYS.
AND ALREADY BACK TO HIS OLD BAD HABITS.
JACK DIDN'T KNOW THEY WERE GOING TO KILL HIM, BUT HE'S HAVING A HARD TIME FEELING BAD ABOUT IT.

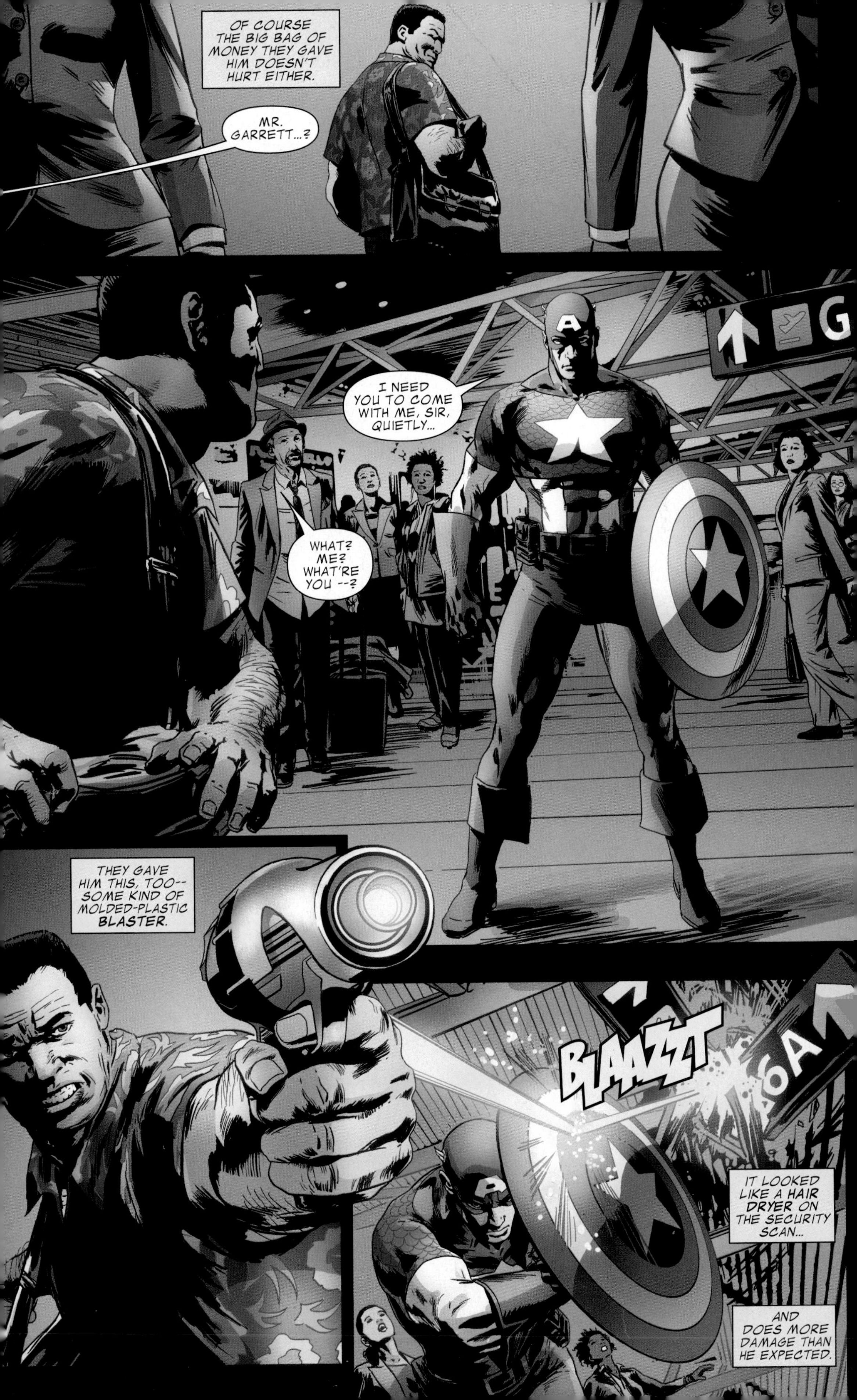
OF COURSE THE BIG BAG OF MONEY THEY GAVE HIM DOESN'T HURT EITHER.
MR. GARRETT...?
I NEED YOU TO COME WITH ME, SIR, QUIETLY...
WHAT? ME? WHAT'RE YOU --?
THEY GAVE HIM THIS, TOO-- SOME KIND OF MOLDED-PLASTIC BLASTER.
BLAAZZT
IT LOOKED LIKE A HAIR DRYER ON THE SECURITY SCAN...
AND DOES MORE DAMAGE THAN HE EXPECTED.

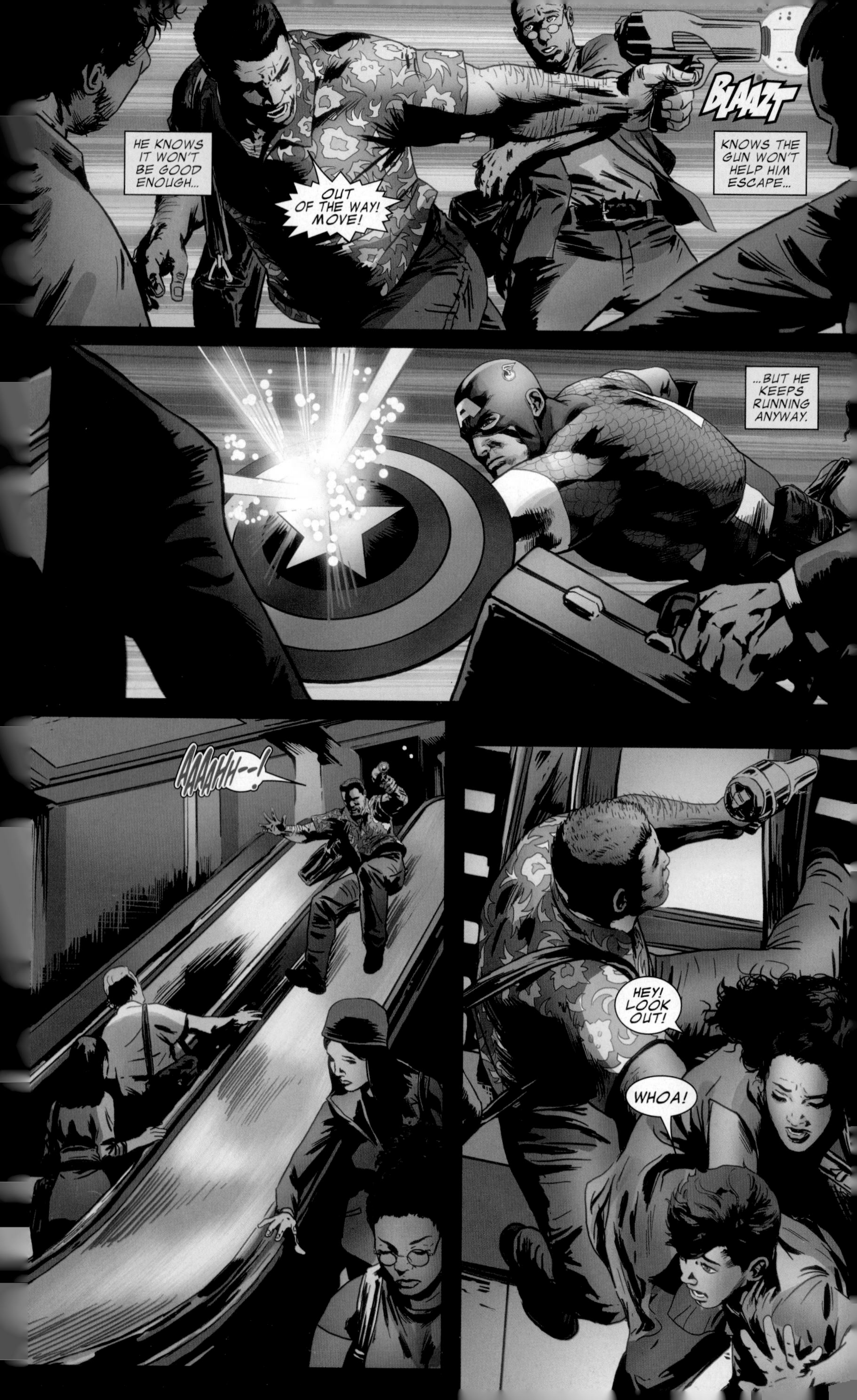
HE KNOWS IT WON'T BE GOOD ENOUGH...
OUT OF THE WAY! MOVE!
BLAAZT
KNOWS THE GUN WON'T HELP HIM ESCAPE...
...BUT HE KEEPS RUNNING ANYWAY.
AAAAHH--!
HEY! LOOK OUT!
WHOA!

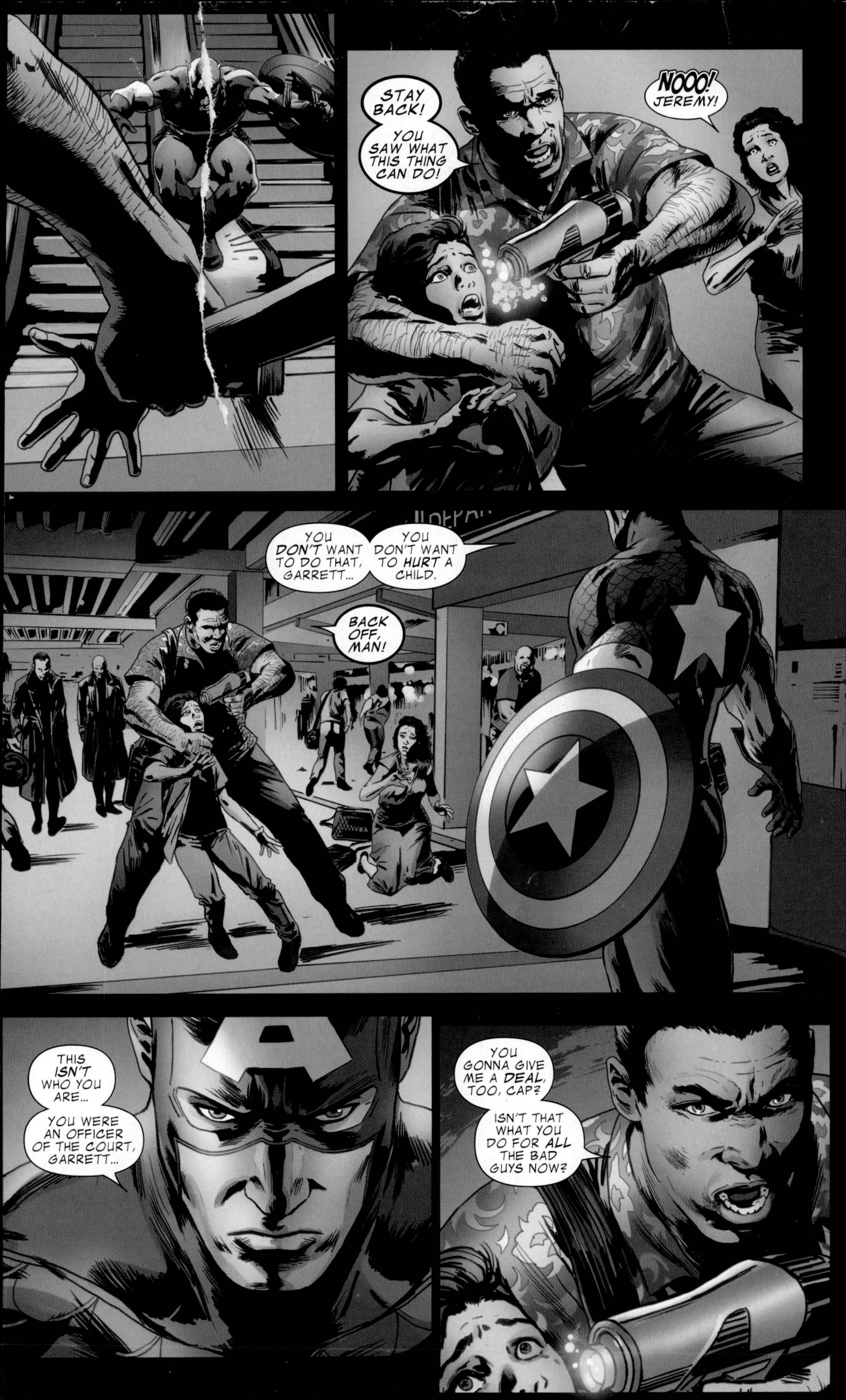
STAY BACK!
YOU SAW WHAT THIS THING CAN DO!
NOOO! JEREMY!
YOU DON'T WANT TO DO THAT, GARRETT...
YOU DON'T WANT TO HURT A CHILD.
BACK OFF, MAN!
THIS ISN'T WHO YOU ARE...
YOU WERE AN OFFICER OF THE COURT, GARRETT...
YOU GONNA GIVE ME A DEAL, TOO, CAP?
ISN'T THAT WHAT YOU DO FOR ALL THE BAD GUYS NOW?

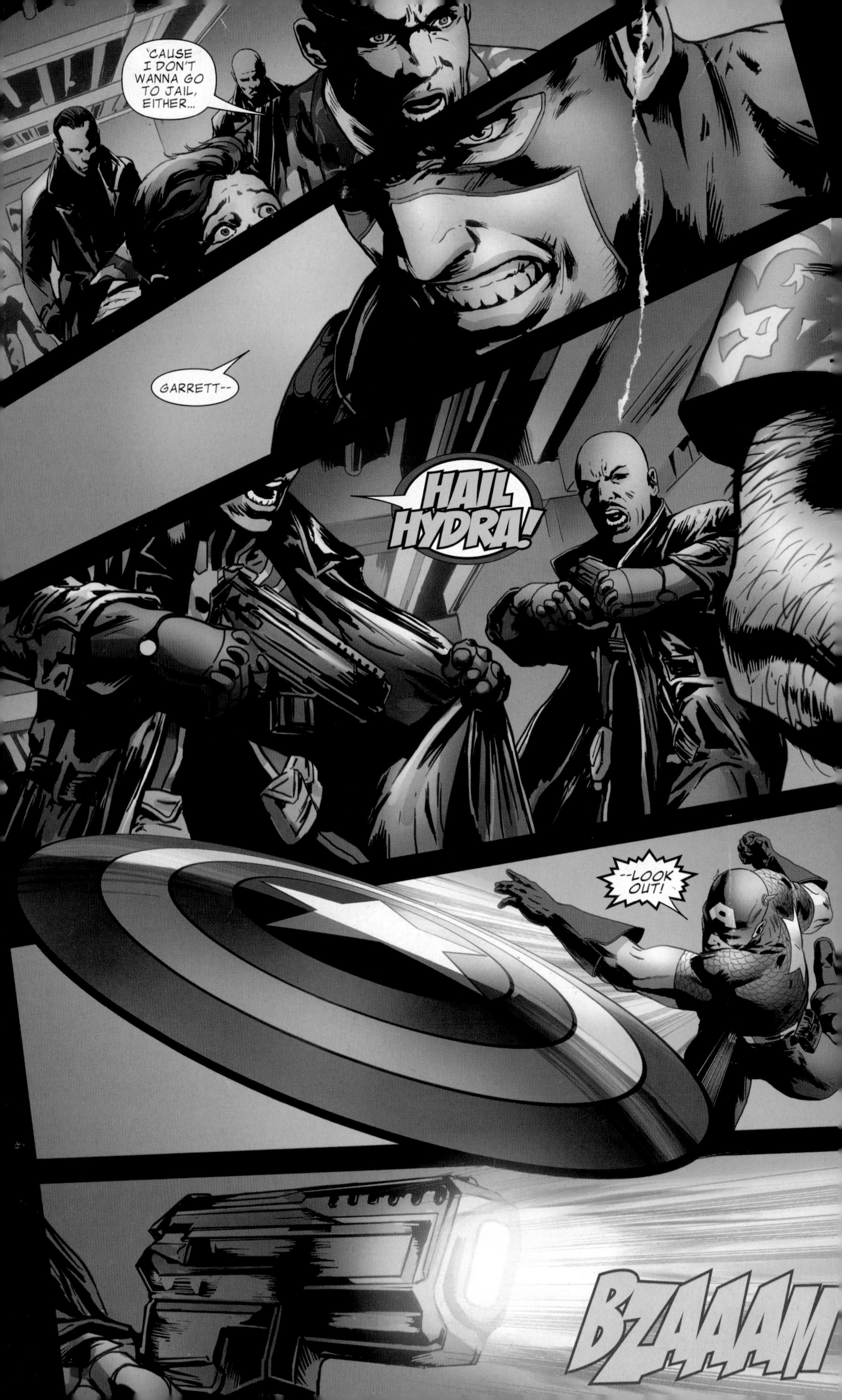
'CAUSE I DON'T WANNA GO TO JAIL, EITHER...
GARRETT--
HAIL HYDRA!
--LOOK OUT!
BZAAAM

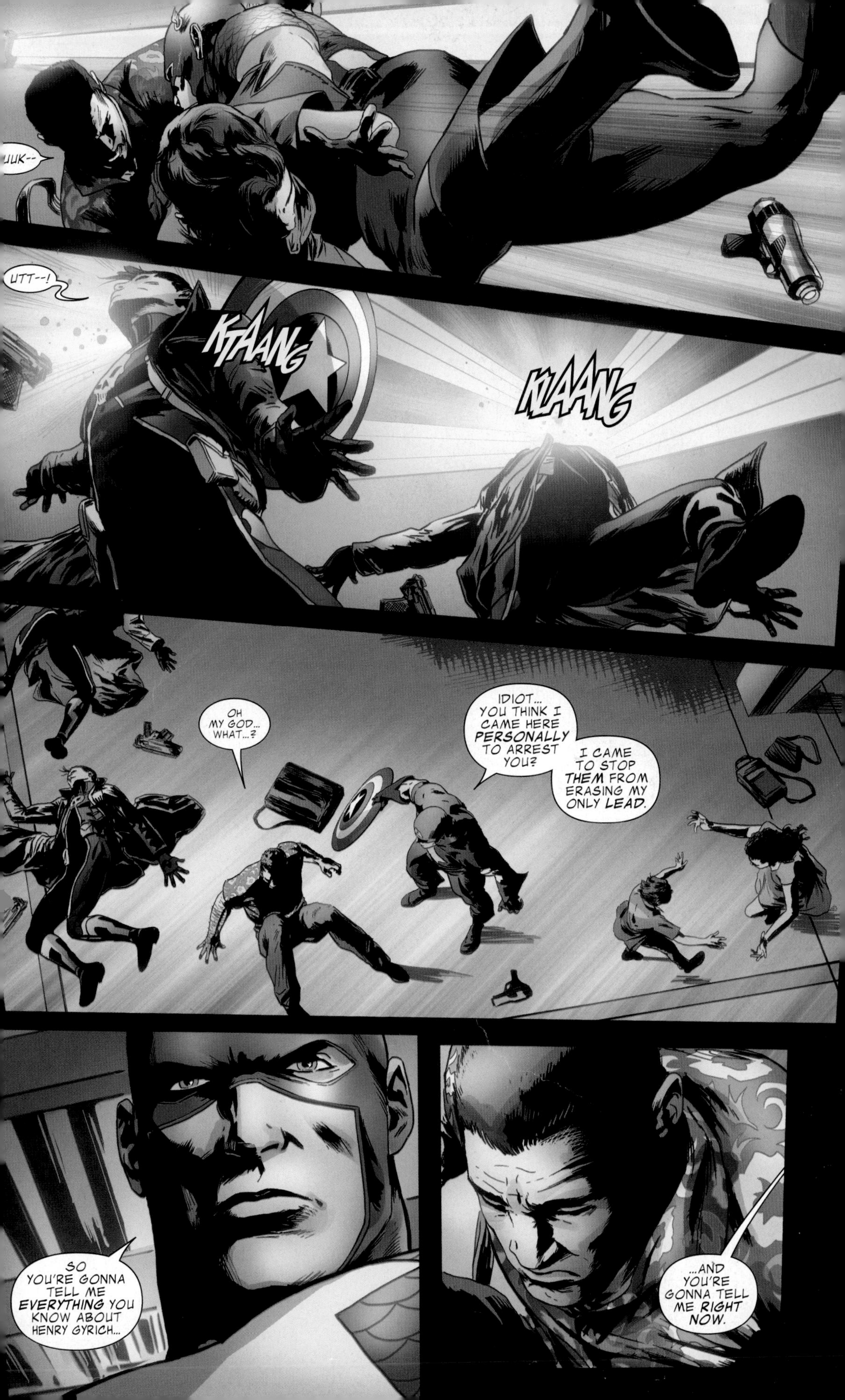
UUK--
UTT--!
KTAANG
KLAANG
OH MY GOD... WHAT...?
IDIOT... YOU THINK I CAME HERE PERSONALLY TO ARREST YOU?
I CAME TO STOP THEM FROM ERASING MY ONLY LEAD.
SO YOU'RE GONNA TELL ME EVERYTHING YOU KNOW ABOUT HENRY GYRICH...
...AND YOU'RE GONNA TELL ME RIGHT NOW.

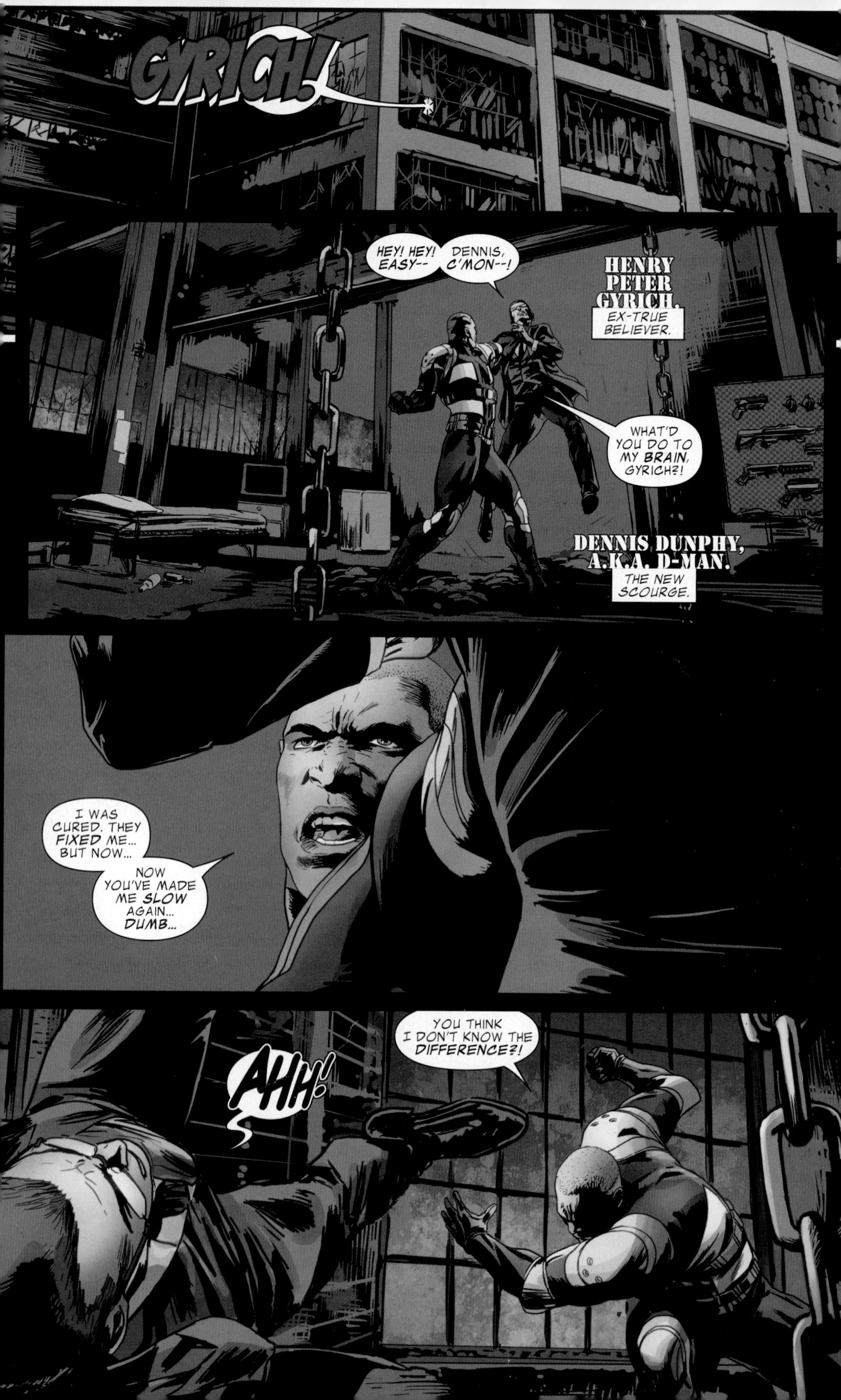
GYRICH!
HEY! HEY! EASY--
DENNIS, C'MON--!
HENRY PETER GYRICH.
EX-TRUE BELIEVER.
WHAT'D YOU DO TO MY BRAIN, GYRICH?!
DENNIS DUNPHY, A.K.A. D-MAN.
THE NEW SCOURGE.
I WAS CURED. THEY FIXED ME... BUT NOW...
NOW YOU'VE MADE ME SLOW AGAIN... DUMB...
YOU THINK I DON'T KNOW THE DIFFERENCE?!
AHH!

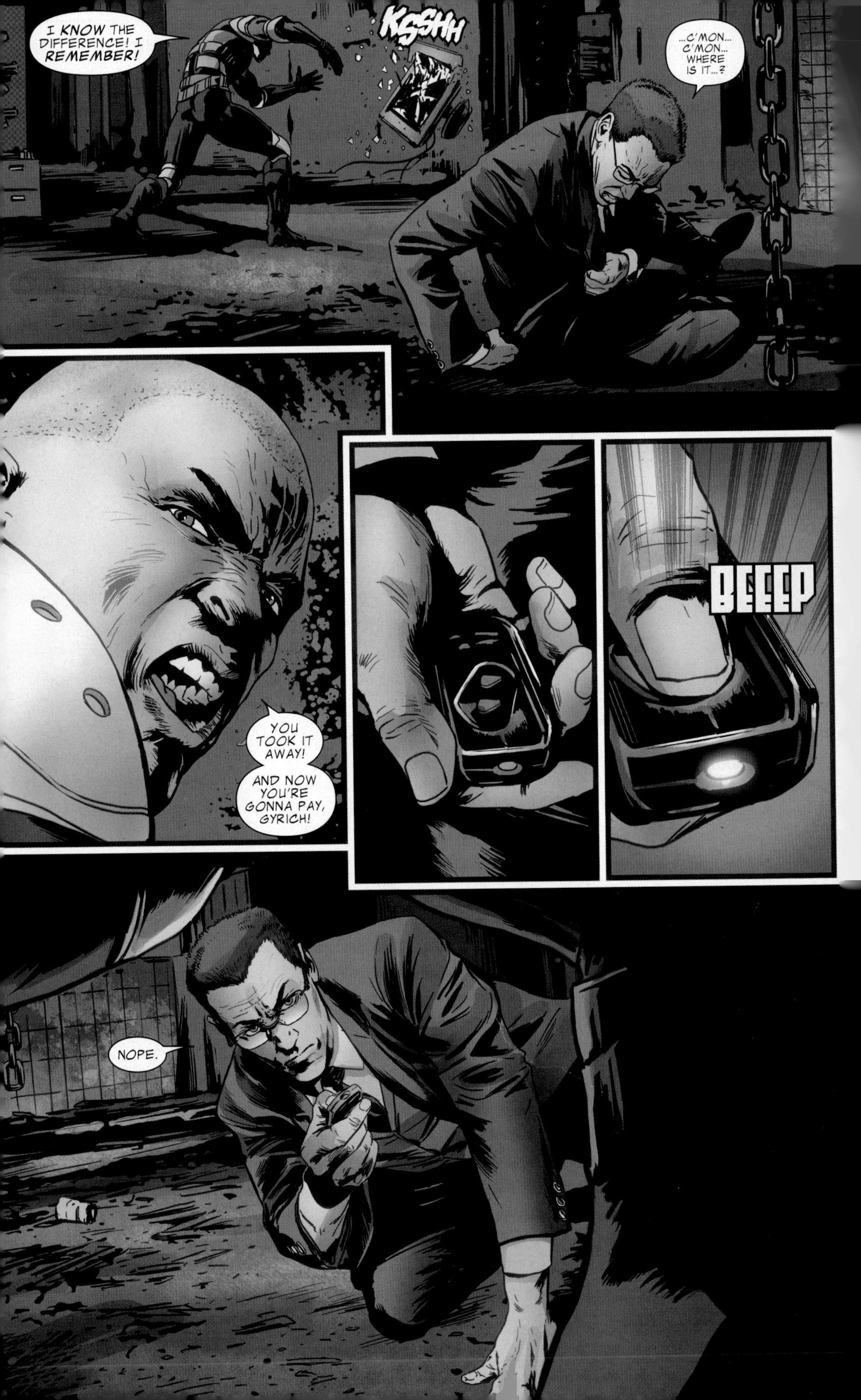
I KNOW THE DIFFERENCE! I REMEMBER!
KSSHH
...C'MON... C'MON... WHERE IS IT...?
YOU TOOK IT AWAY!
AND NOW YOU'RE GONNA PAY, GYRICH!
BEEEP
NOPE.

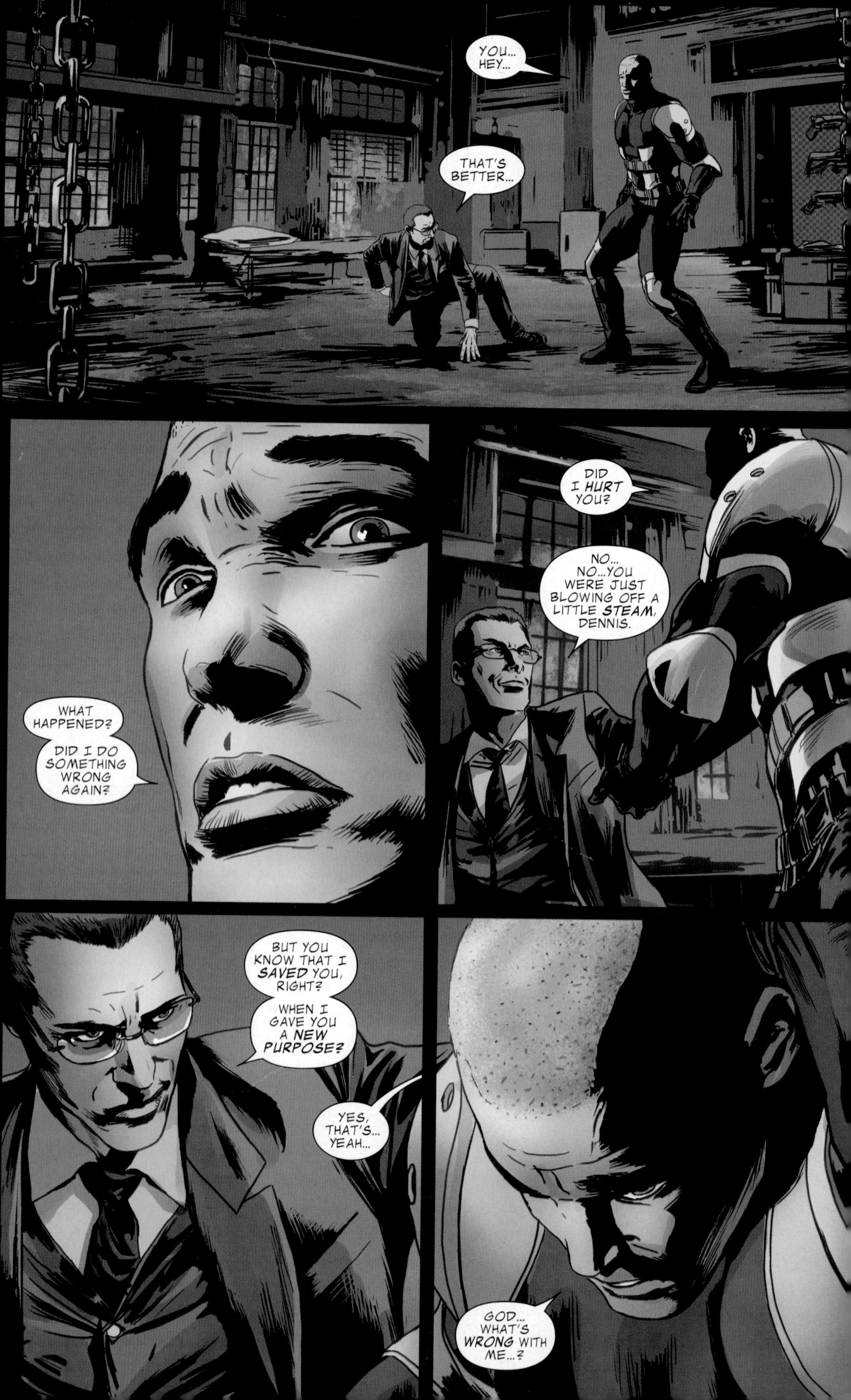
YOU... HEY...
THAT'S BETTER...
WHAT HAPPENED?
DID I DO SOMETHING WRONG AGAIN?
DID I HURT YOU?
NO... NO...YOU WERE JUST BLOWING OFF A LITTLE STEAM, DENNIS.
BUT YOU KNOW THAT I SAVED YOU, RIGHT?
WHEN I GAVE YOU A NEW PURPOSE?
YES, THAT'S... YEAH...
GOD... WHAT'S WRONG WITH ME...?

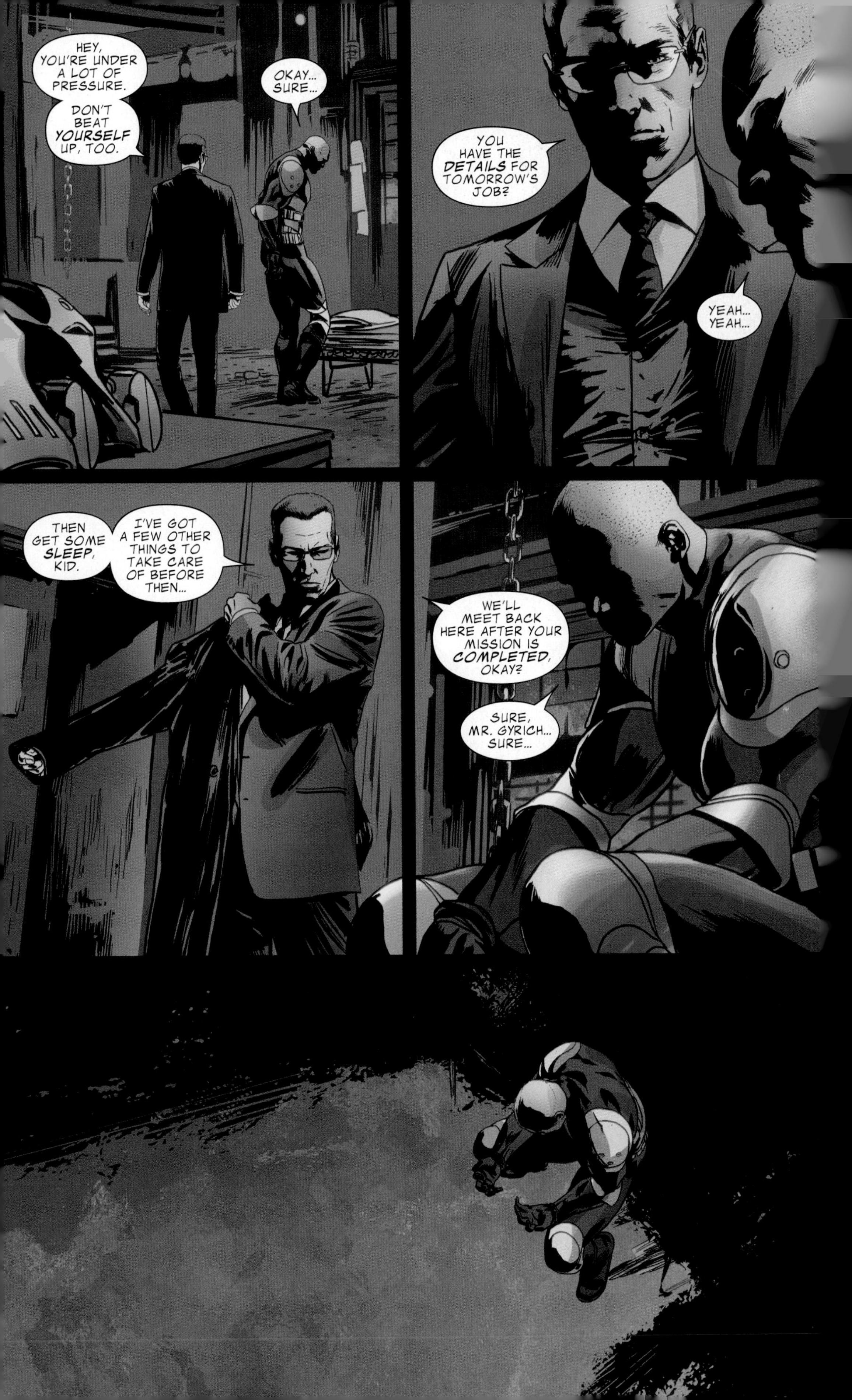
HEY, YOU'RE UNDER A LOT OF PRESSURE.
DON'T BEAT YOURSELF UP, TOO.
OKAY... SURE...
YOU HAVE THE DETAILS FOR TOMORROW'S JOB?
YEAH... YEAH...
THEN GET SOME SLEEP, KID.
I'VE GOT A FEW OTHER THINGS TO TAKE CARE OF BEFORE THEN...
WE'LL MEET BACK HERE AFTER YOUR MISSION IS COMPLETED, OKAY?
SURE, MR. GYRICH... SURE...

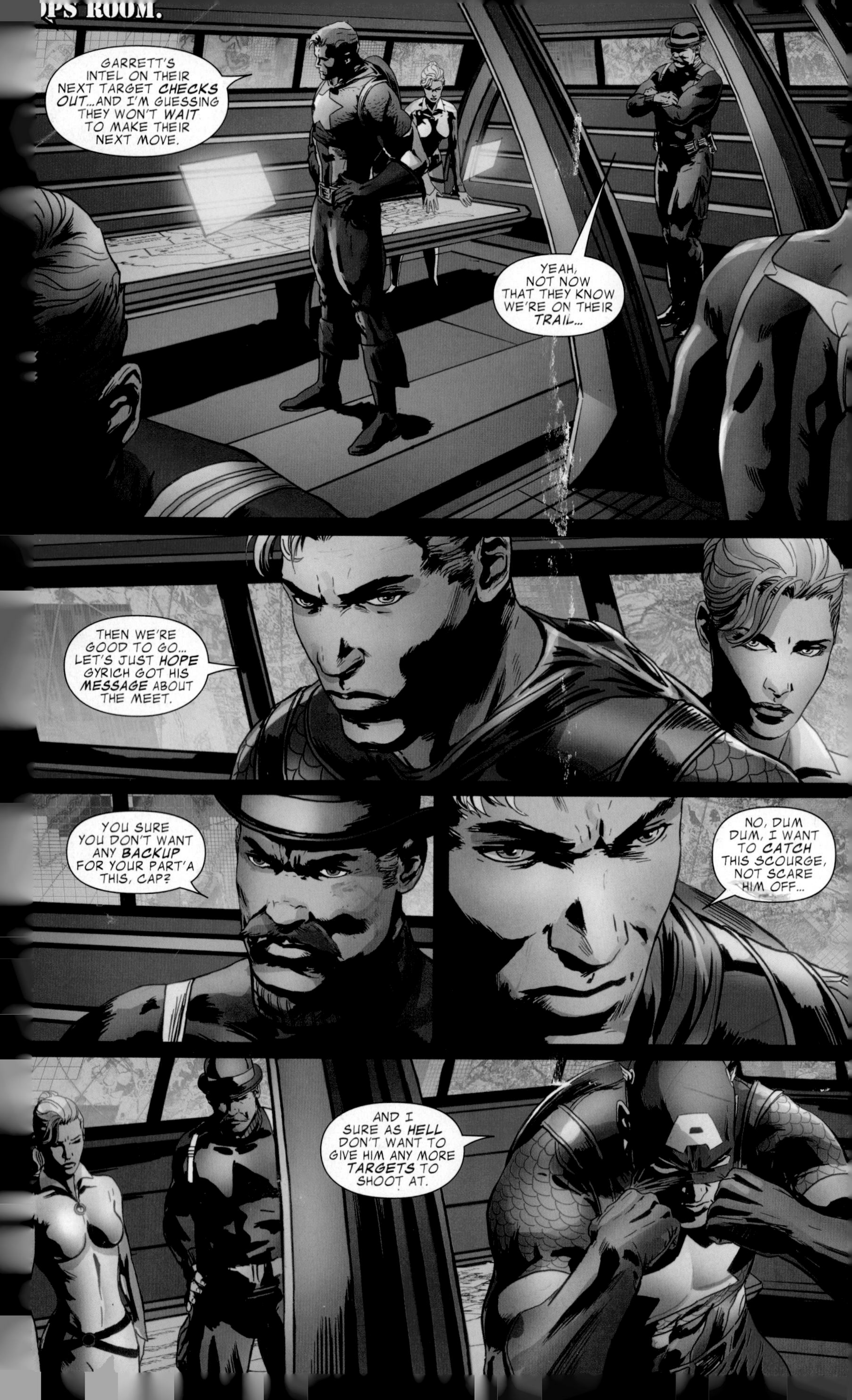

...OPS ROOM.
GARRETT'S INTEL ON THEIR NEXT TARGET CHECKS OUT...AND I'M GUESSING THEY WON'T WAIT TO MAKE THEIR NEXT MOVE.
YEAH, NOT NOW THAT THEY KNOW WE'RE ON THEIR TRAIL...
THEN WE'RE GOOD TO GO... LET'S JUST HOPE GYRICH GOT HIS MESSAGE ABOUT THE MEET.
YOU SURE YOU DON'T WANT ANY BACKUP FOR YOUR PART'A THIS, CAP?
NO, DUM DUM, I WANT TO CATCH THIS SCOURGE, NOT SCARE HIM OFF...
AND I SURE AS HELL DON'T WANT TO GIVE HIM ANY MORE TARGETS TO SHOOT AT.

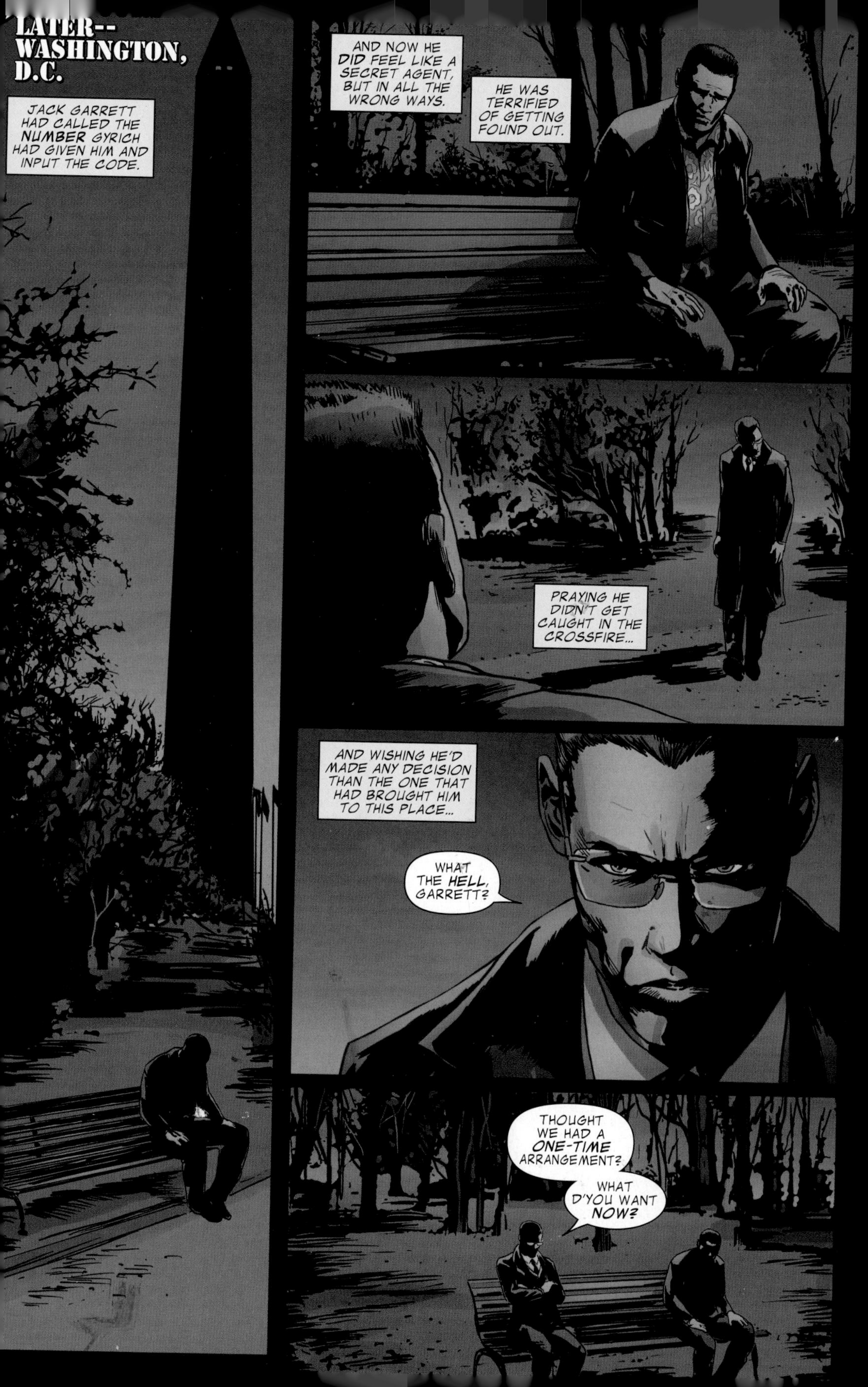
LATER-- WASHINGTON, D.C.
JACK GARRETT HAD CALLED THE NUMBER GYRICH HAD GIVEN HIM AND INPUT THE CODE.
AND NOW HE DID FEEL LIKE A SECRET AGENT, BUT IN ALL THE WRONG WAYS.
HE WAS TERRIFIED OF GETTING FOUND OUT.
PRAYING HE DIDN'T GET CAUGHT IN THE CROSSFIRE...
AND WISHING HE'D MADE ANY DECISION THAN THE ONE THAT HAD BROUGHT HIM TO THIS PLACE...
WHAT THE HELL, GARRETT?
THOUGHT WE HAD A ONE-TIME ARRANGEMENT?
WHAT D'YOU WANT NOW?

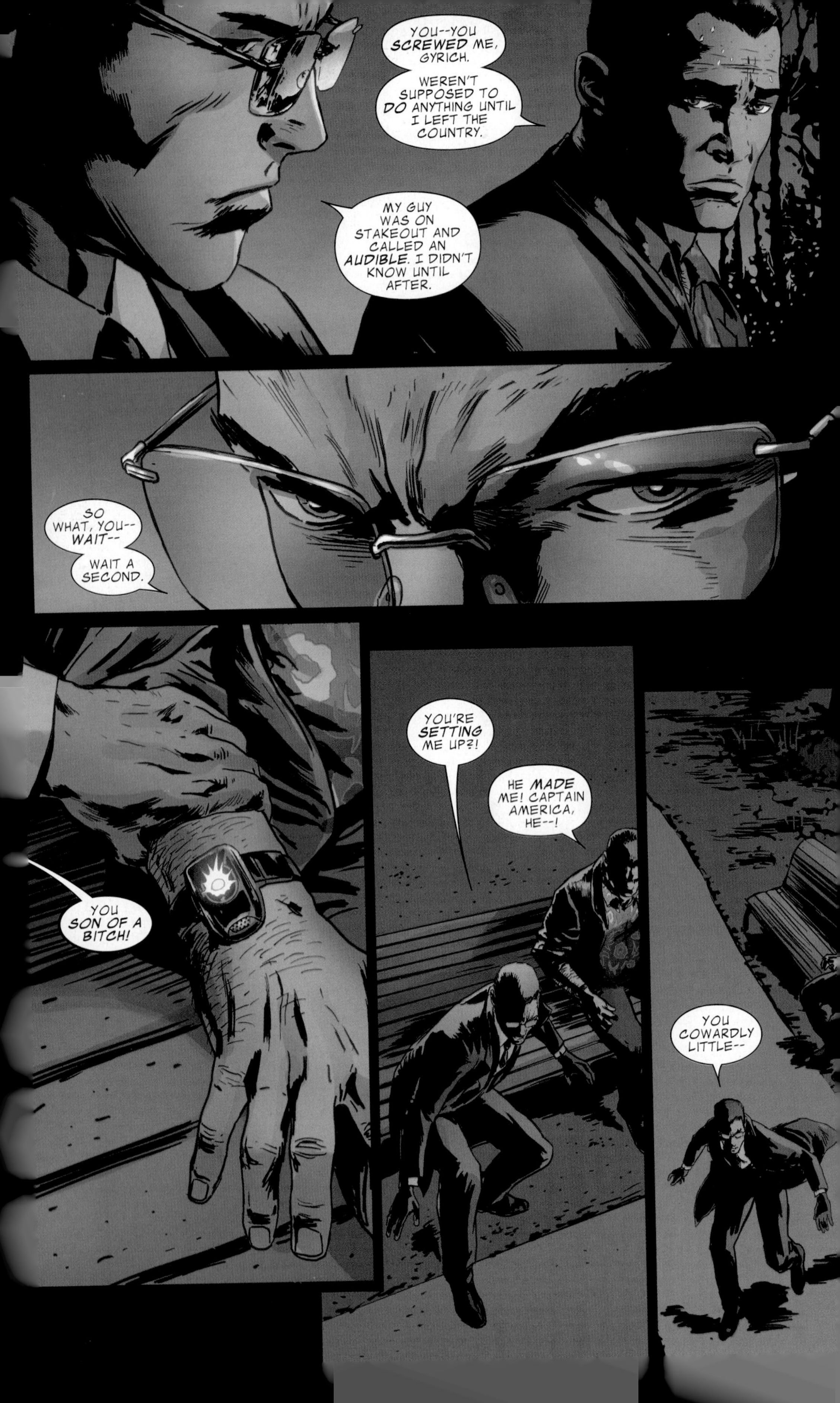
YOU--YOU **SCREWED** ME, GYRICH.
WEREN'T SUPPOSED TO **DO** ANYTHING UNTIL I LEFT THE COUNTRY.
MY GUY WAS ON STAKEOUT AND CALLED AN **AUDIBLE**. I DIDN'T KNOW UNTIL AFTER.
SO WHAT, YOU-- **WAIT**--
WAIT A SECOND.
YOU **SON OF A BITCH**!
YOU'RE **SETTING** ME UP?!
HE **MADE** ME! CAPTAIN AMERICA, HE--!
YOU COWARDLY LITTLE--

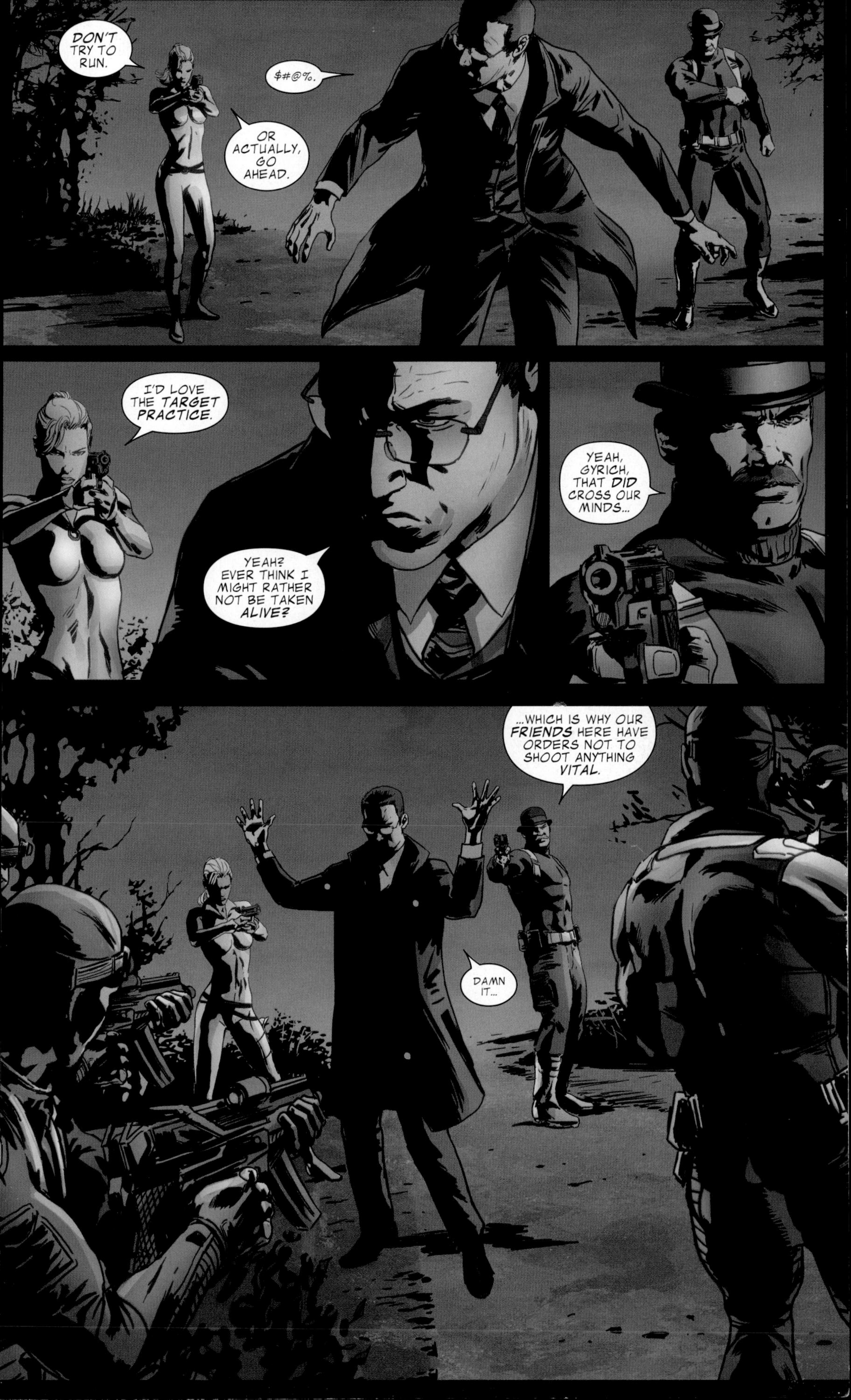
DON'T TRY TO RUN.
$#@%.
OR ACTUALLY, GO AHEAD.
I'D LOVE THE TARGET PRACTICE.
YEAH? EVER THINK I MIGHT RATHER NOT BE TAKEN ALIVE?
YEAH, GYRICH, THAT DID CROSS OUR MINDS...
...WHICH IS WHY OUR FRIENDS HERE HAVE ORDERS NOT TO SHOOT ANYTHING VITAL.
DAMN IT...

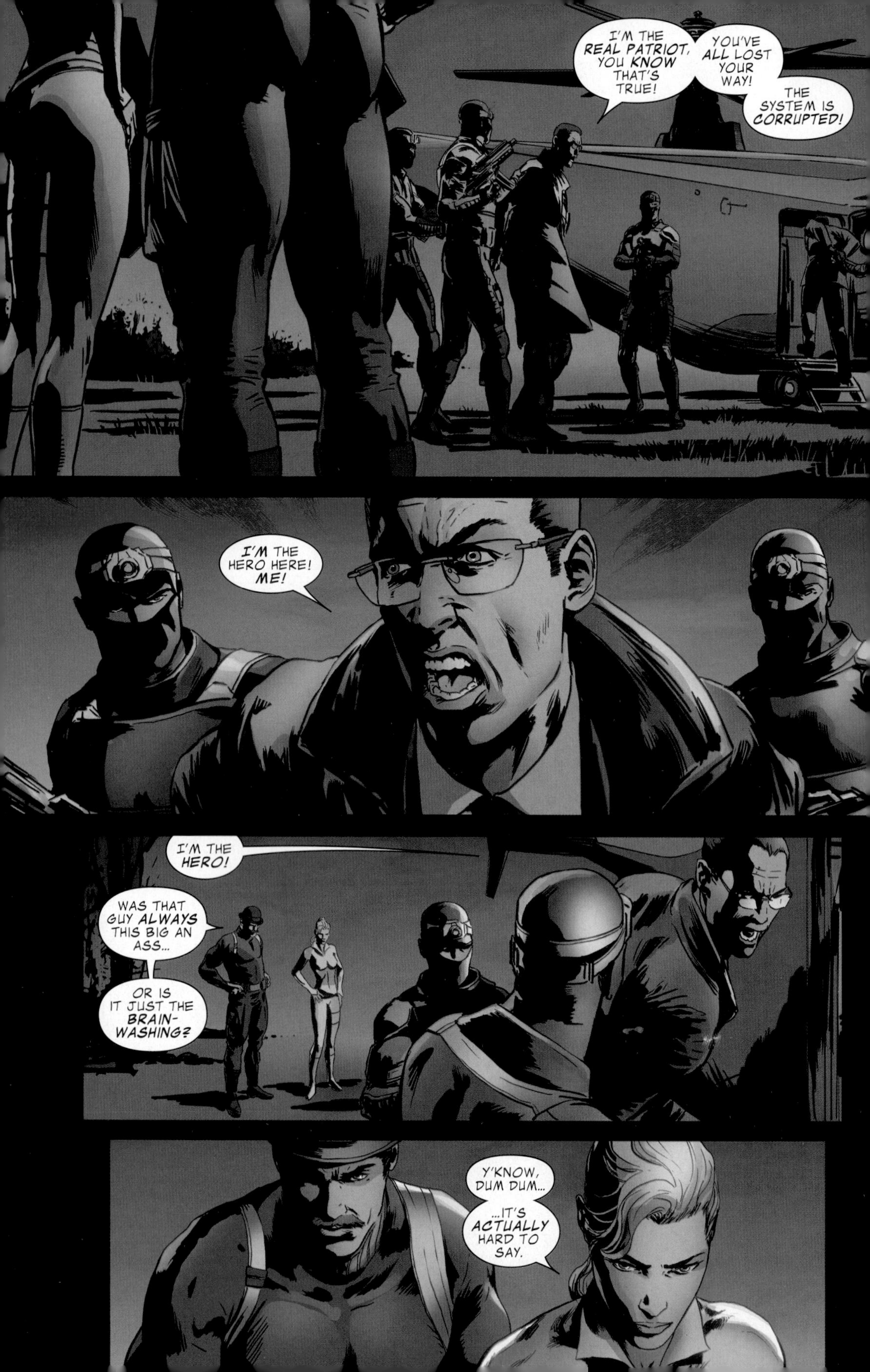
I'M THE REAL PATRIOT, YOU KNOW THAT'S TRUE!
YOU'VE ALL LOST YOUR WAY!
THE SYSTEM IS CORRUPTED!
I'M THE HERO HERE! ME!
I'M THE HERO!
WAS THAT GUY ALWAYS THIS BIG AN ASS...
OR IS IT JUST THE BRAIN-WASHING?
Y'KNOW, DUM DUM...
...IT'S ACTUALLY HARD TO SAY.

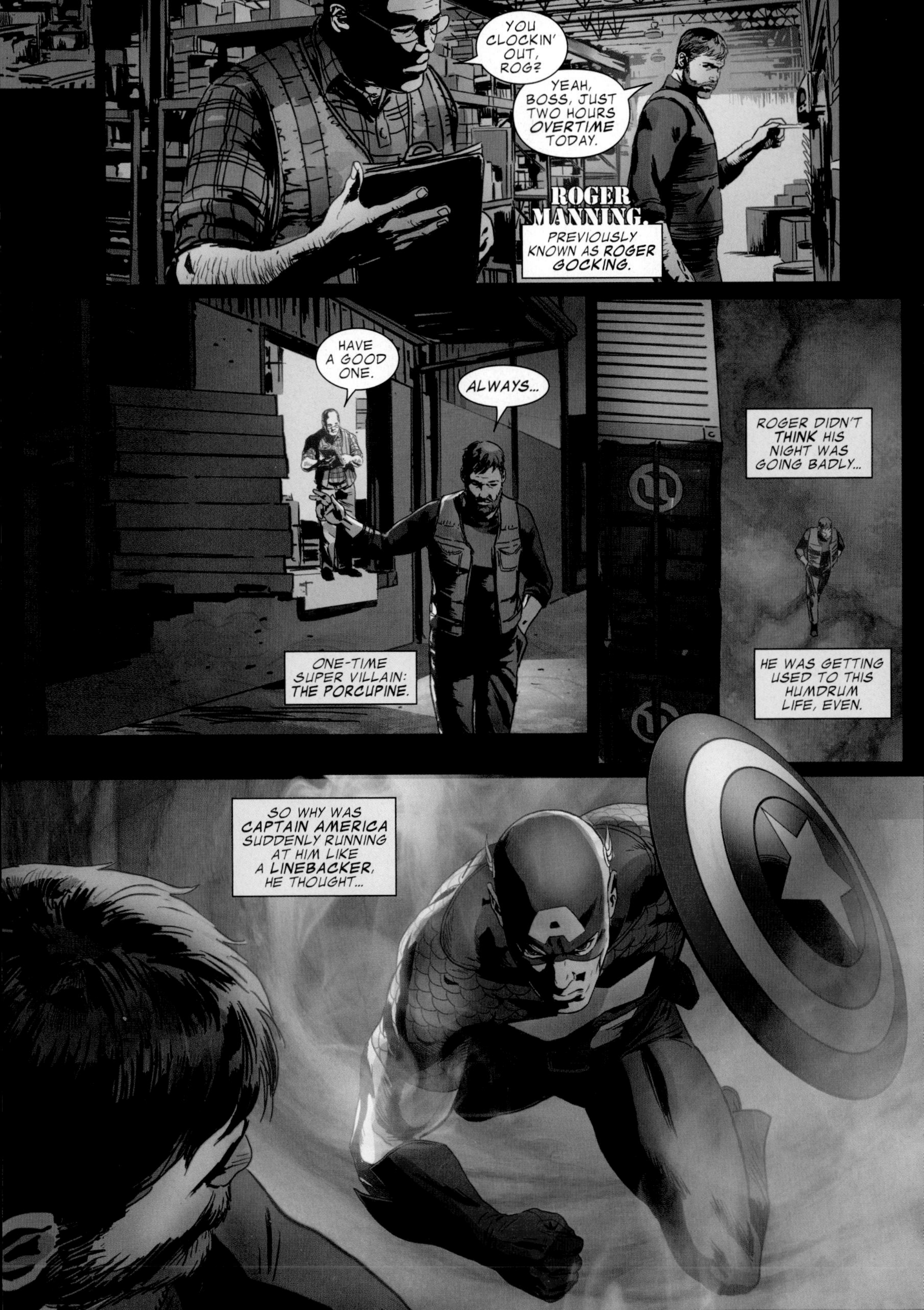

YOU CLOCKIN' OUT, ROG?
YEAH, BOSS, JUST TWO HOURS OVERTIME TODAY.
ROGER MANNING.
PREVIOUSLY KNOWN AS ROGER GOCKING.
HAVE A GOOD ONE.
ALWAYS...
ONE-TIME SUPER VILLAIN: THE PORCUPINE.
ROGER DIDN'T THINK HIS NIGHT WAS GOING BADLY...
HE WAS GETTING USED TO THIS HUMDRUM LIFE, EVEN.
SO WHY WAS CAPTAIN AMERICA SUDDENLY RUNNING AT HIM LIKE A LINEBACKER, HE THOUGHT...

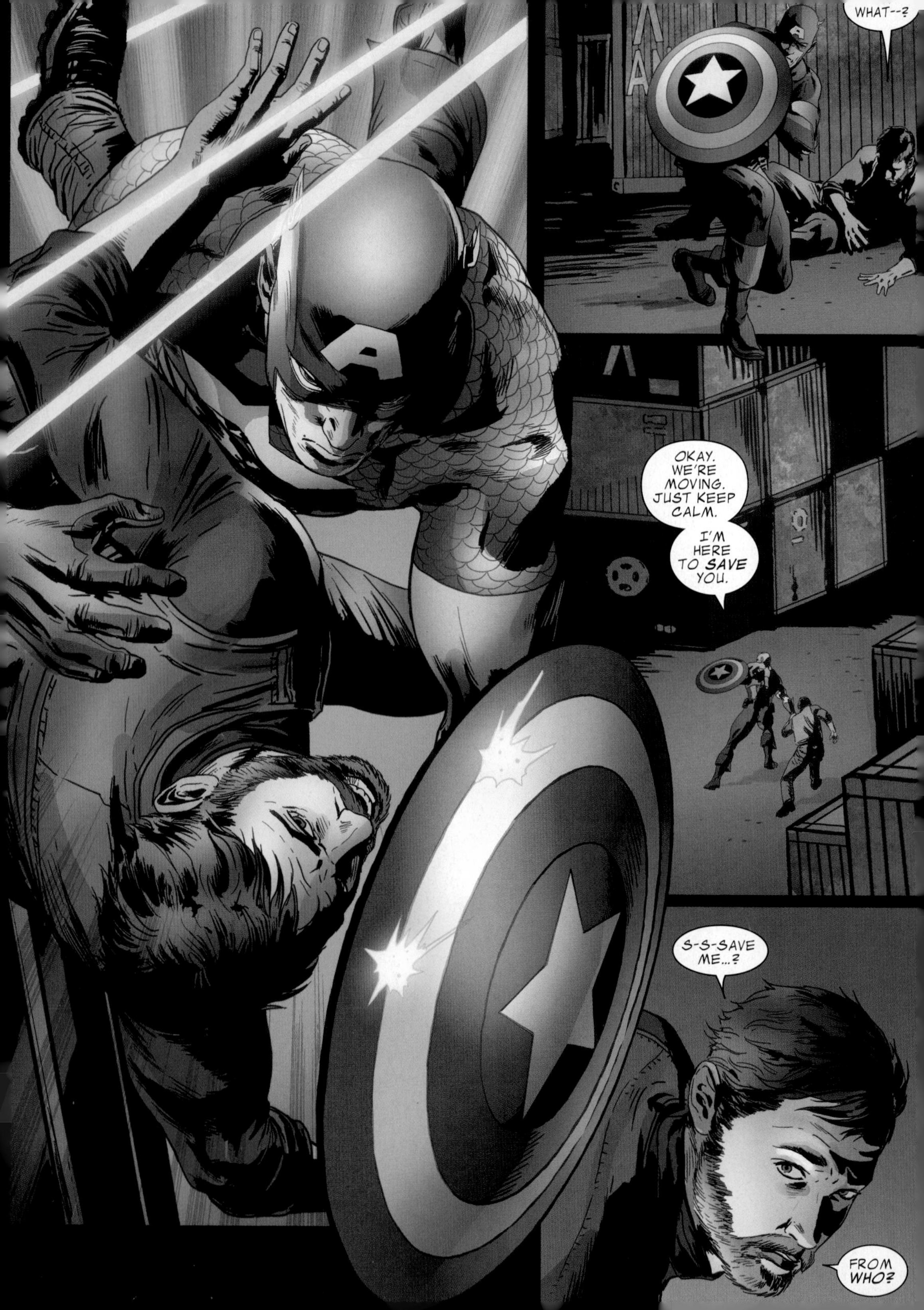
WHAT--?
OKAY. WE'RE MOVING. JUST KEEP CALM.
I'M HERE TO SAVE YOU.
S-S-SAVE ME...?
FROM WHO?

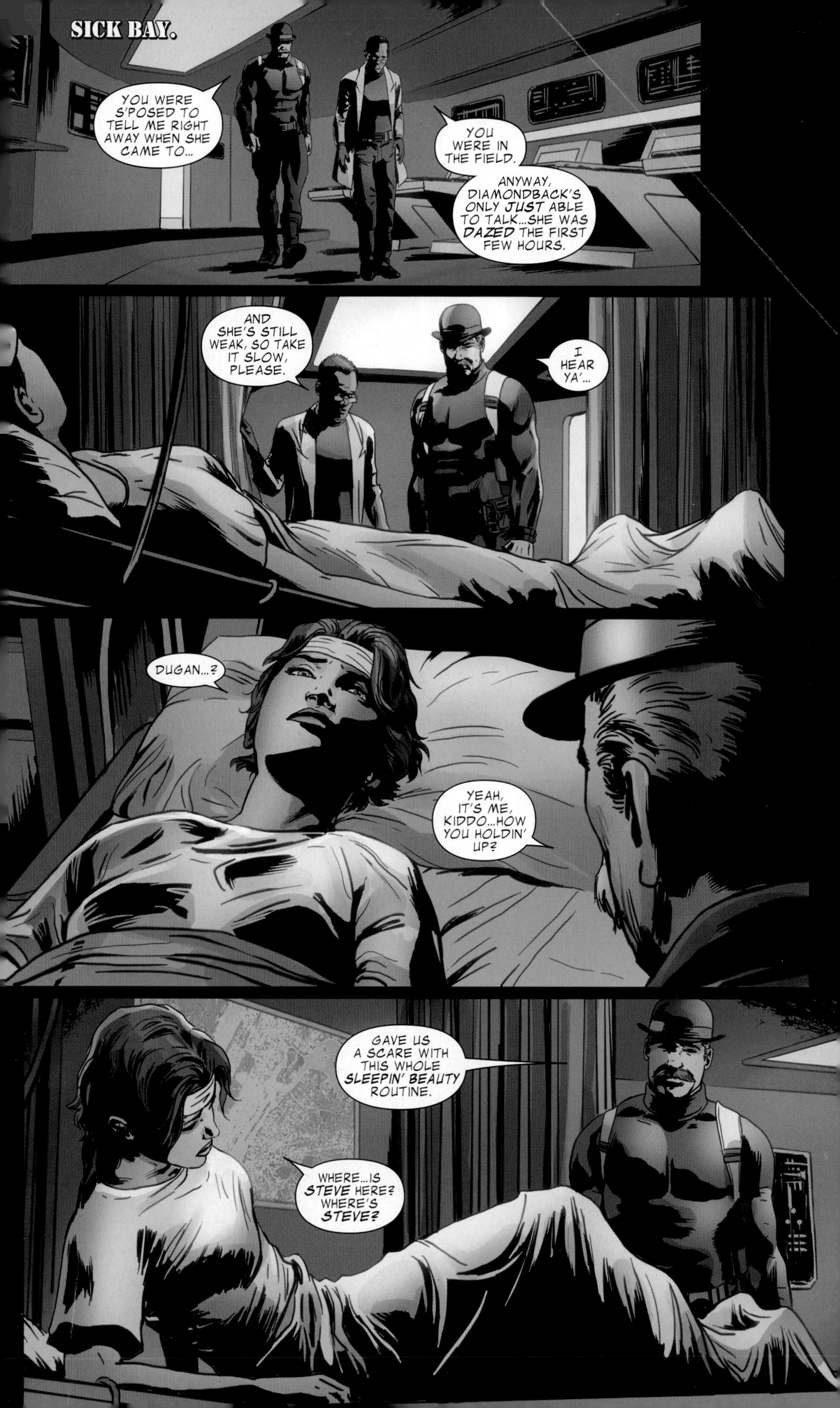
SICK BAY.
YOU WERE S'POSED TO TELL ME RIGHT AWAY WHEN SHE CAME TO...
YOU WERE IN THE FIELD.
ANYWAY, DIAMONDBACK'S ONLY JUST ABLE TO TALK...SHE WAS DAZED THE FIRST FEW HOURS.
AND SHE'S STILL WEAK, SO TAKE IT SLOW, PLEASE.
I HEAR YA'...
DUGAN...?
YEAH, IT'S ME, KIDDO...HOW YOU HOLDIN' UP?
GAVE US A SCARE WITH THIS WHOLE SLEEPIN' BEAUTY ROUTINE.
WHERE...IS STEVE HERE? WHERE'S STEVE?

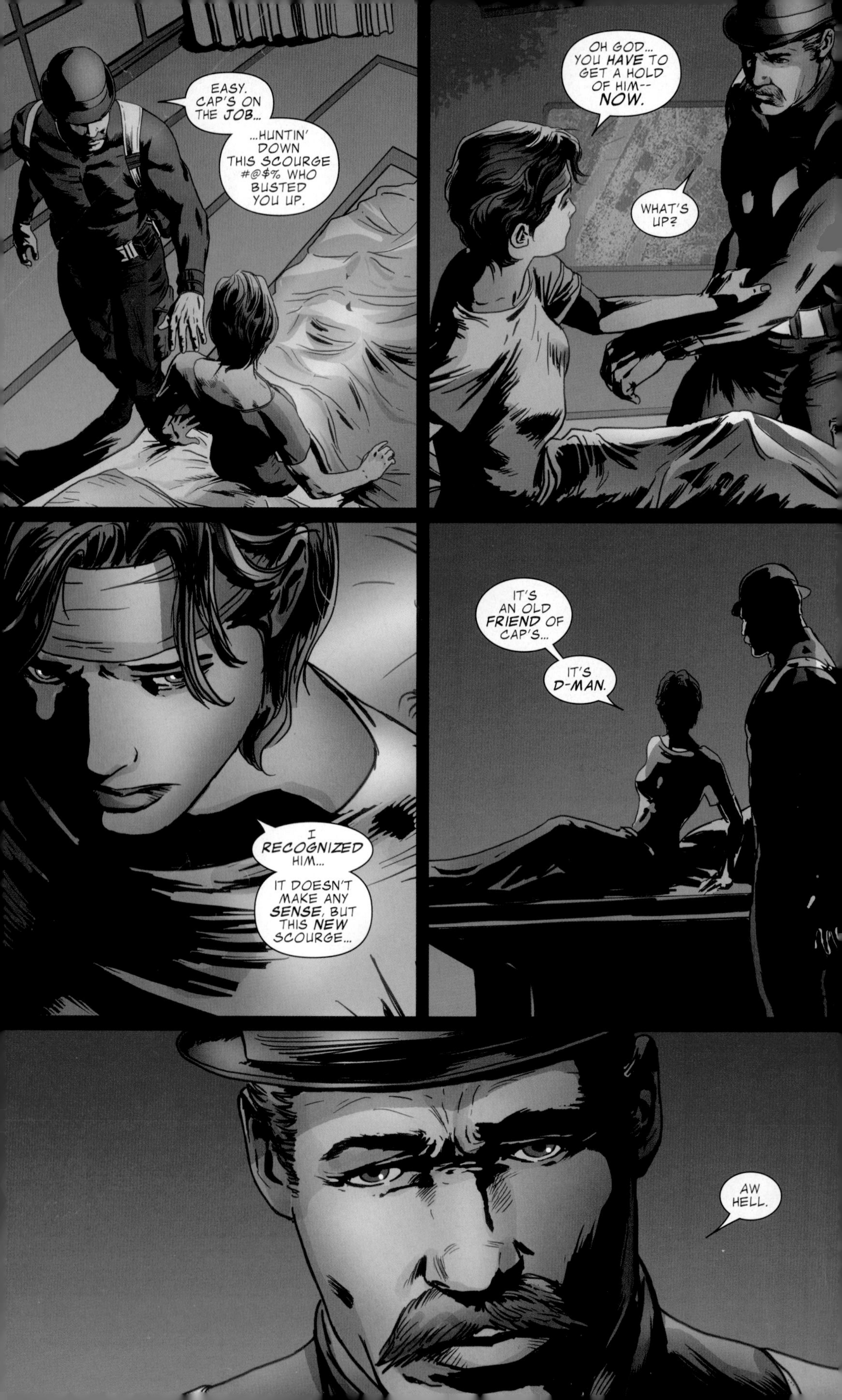
EASY. CAP'S ON THE JOB...
...HUNTIN' DOWN THIS SCOURGE #@$% WHO BUSTED YOU UP.
OH GOD... YOU HAVE TO GET A HOLD OF HIM-- NOW.
WHAT'S UP?
I RECOGNIZED HIM...
IT DOESN'T MAKE ANY SENSE, BUT THIS NEW SCOURGE...
IT'S AN OLD FRIEND OF CAP'S...
IT'S D-MAN.
AW HELL.

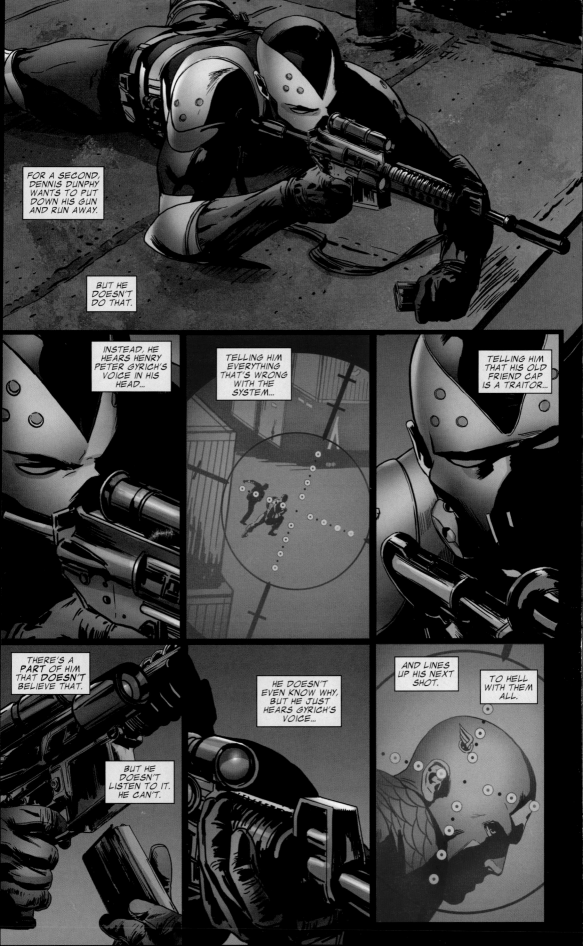

FOR A SECOND, DENNIS DUNPHY WANTS TO PUT DOWN HIS GUN AND RUN AWAY.

BUT HE DOESN'T DO THAT.

INSTEAD, HE HEARS HENRY PETER GYRICH'S VOICE IN HIS HEAD...

TELLING HIM EVERYTHING THAT'S WRONG WITH THE SYSTEM...

TELLING HIM THAT HIS OLD FRIEND CAP IS A TRAITOR...

THERE'S A PART OF HIM THAT DOESN'T BELIEVE THAT.

BUT HE DOESN'T LISTEN TO IT. HE CAN'T.

HE DOESN'T EVEN KNOW WHY, BUT HE JUST HEARS GYRICH'S VOICE...

AND LINES UP HIS NEXT SHOT.

TO HELL WITH THEM ALL.

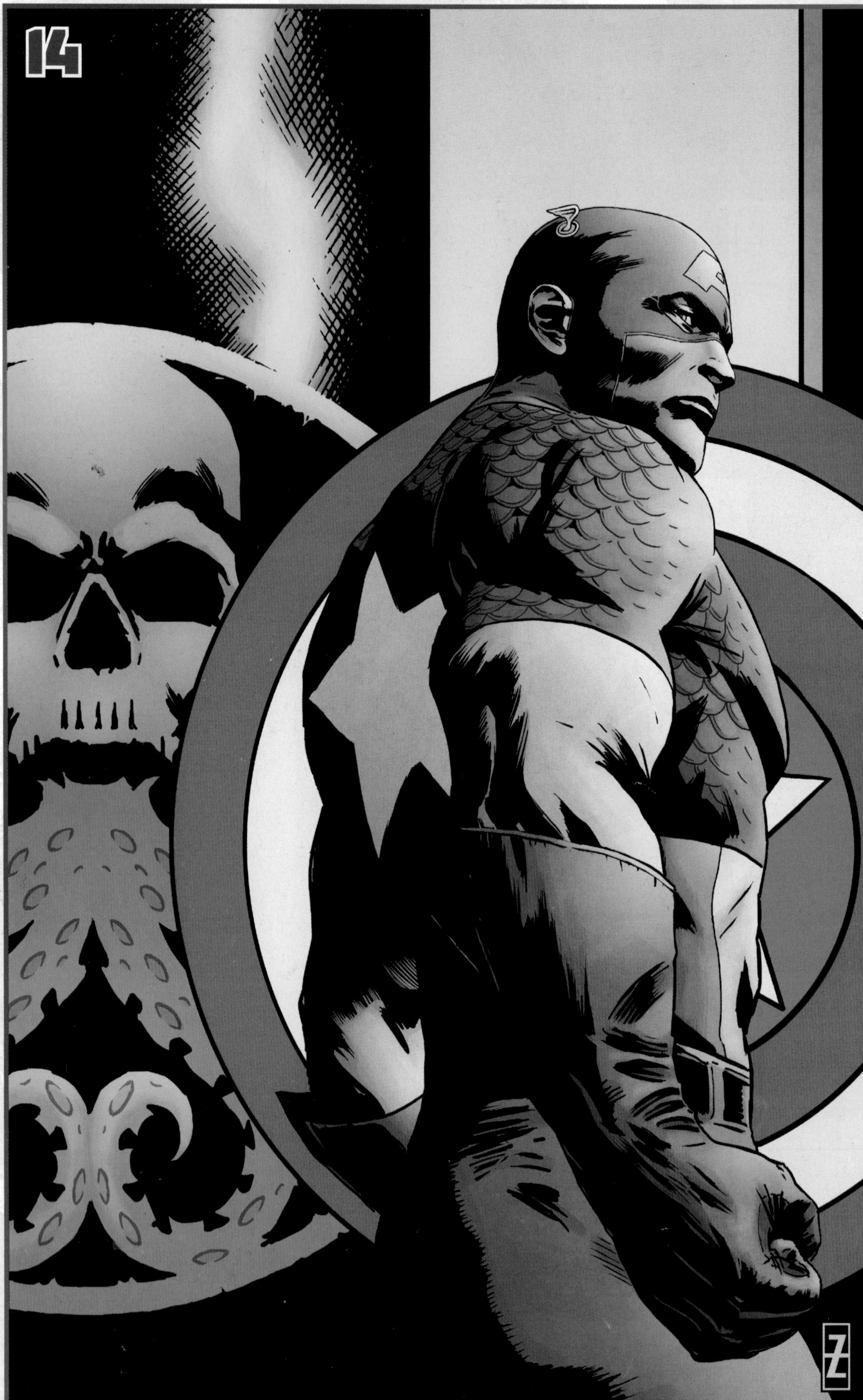
14

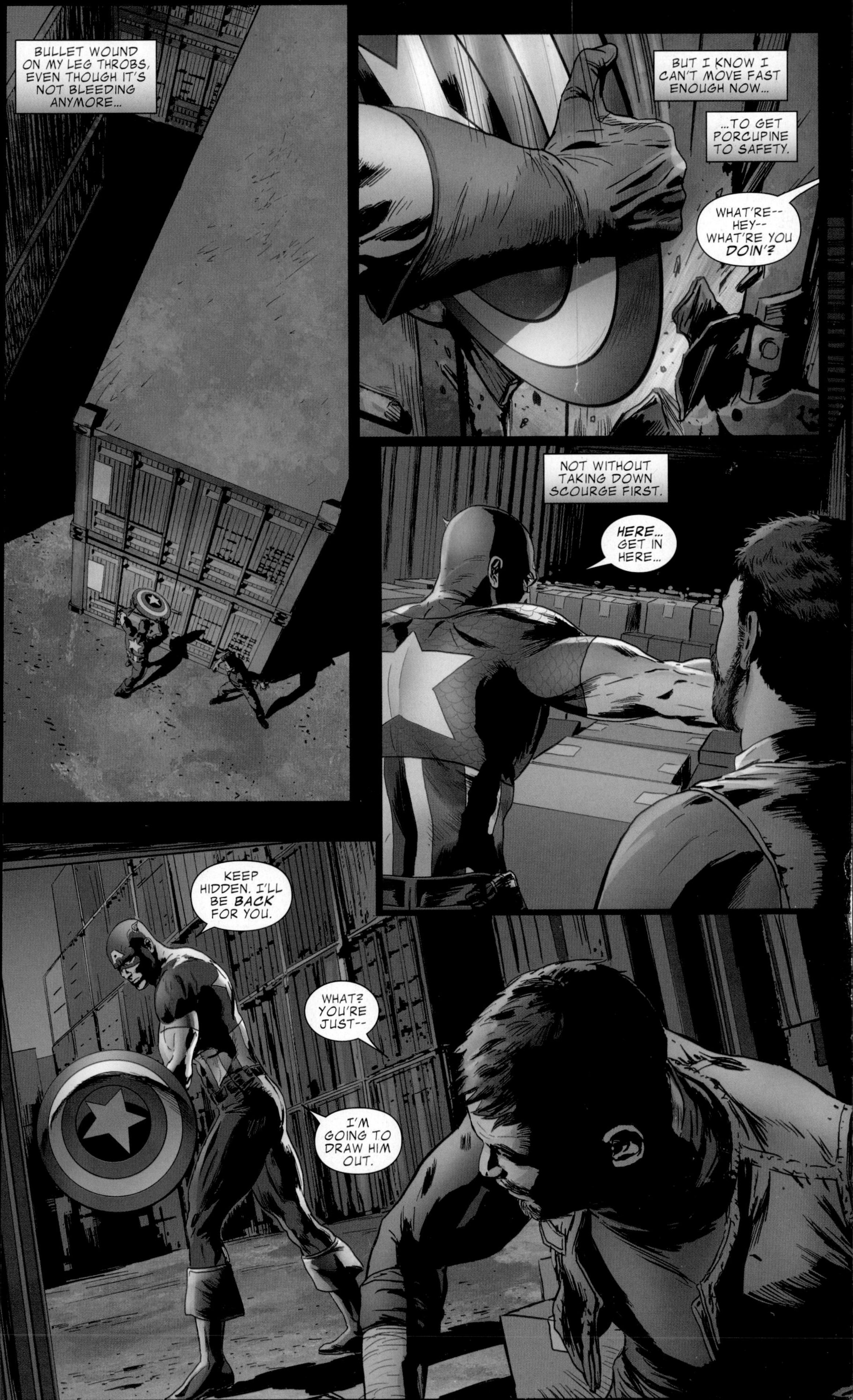
BULLET WOUND ON MY LEG THROBS, EVEN THOUGH IT'S NOT BLEEDING ANYMORE...
BUT I KNOW I CAN'T MOVE FAST ENOUGH NOW...
...TO GET PORCUPINE TO SAFETY.
WHAT'RE-- HEY-- WHAT'RE YOU DOIN'?
NOT WITHOUT TAKING DOWN SCOURGE FIRST.
HERE... GET IN HERE...
KEEP HIDDEN. I'LL BE BACK FOR YOU.
WHAT? YOU'RE JUST--
I'M GOING TO DRAW HIM OUT.

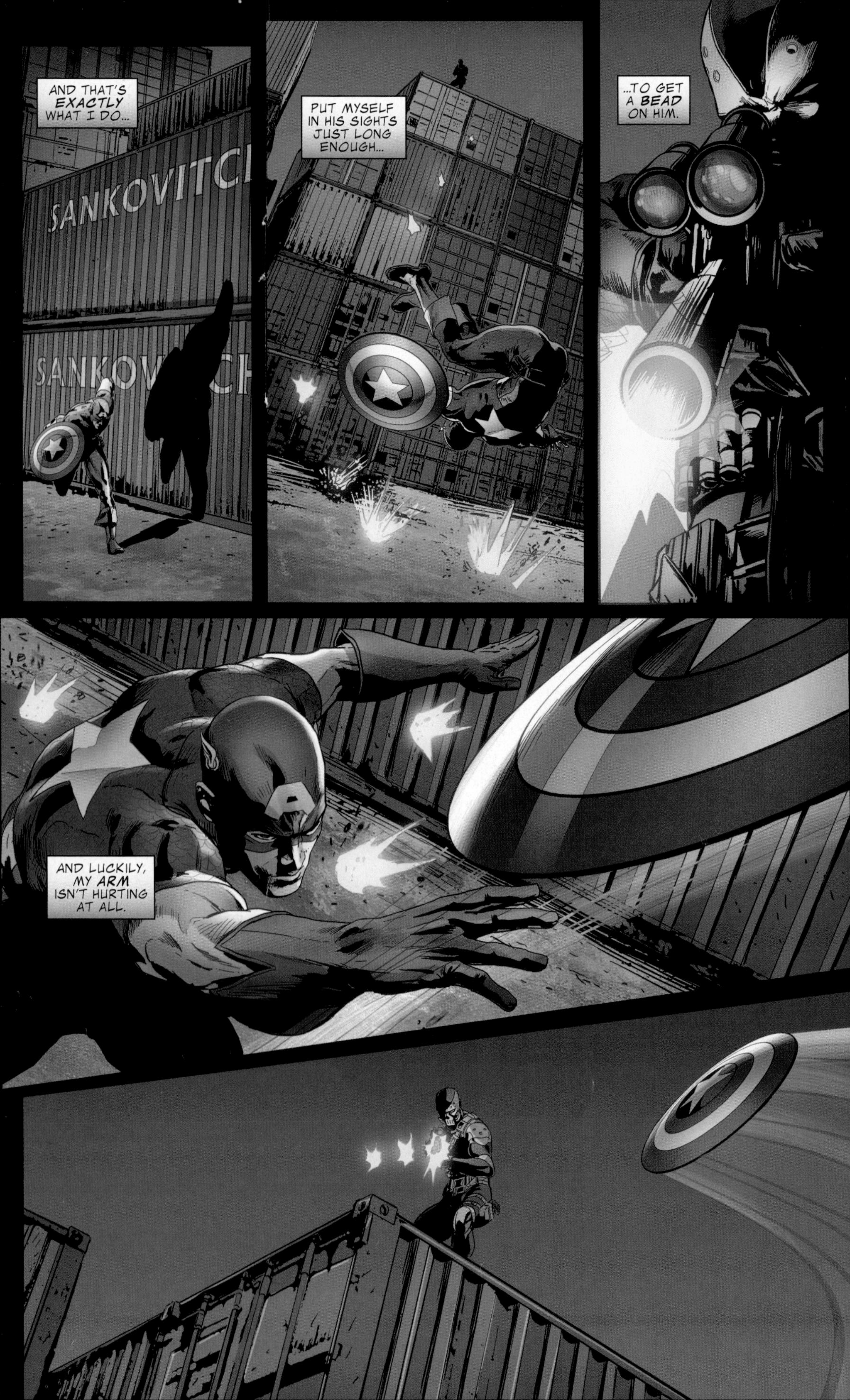
AND THAT'S EXACTLY WHAT I DO...
SANKOVITCH
SANKOVITCH
PUT MYSELF IN HIS SIGHTS JUST LONG ENOUGH...
...TO GET A BEAD ON HIM.
AND LUCKILY, MY ARM ISN'T HURTING AT ALL.

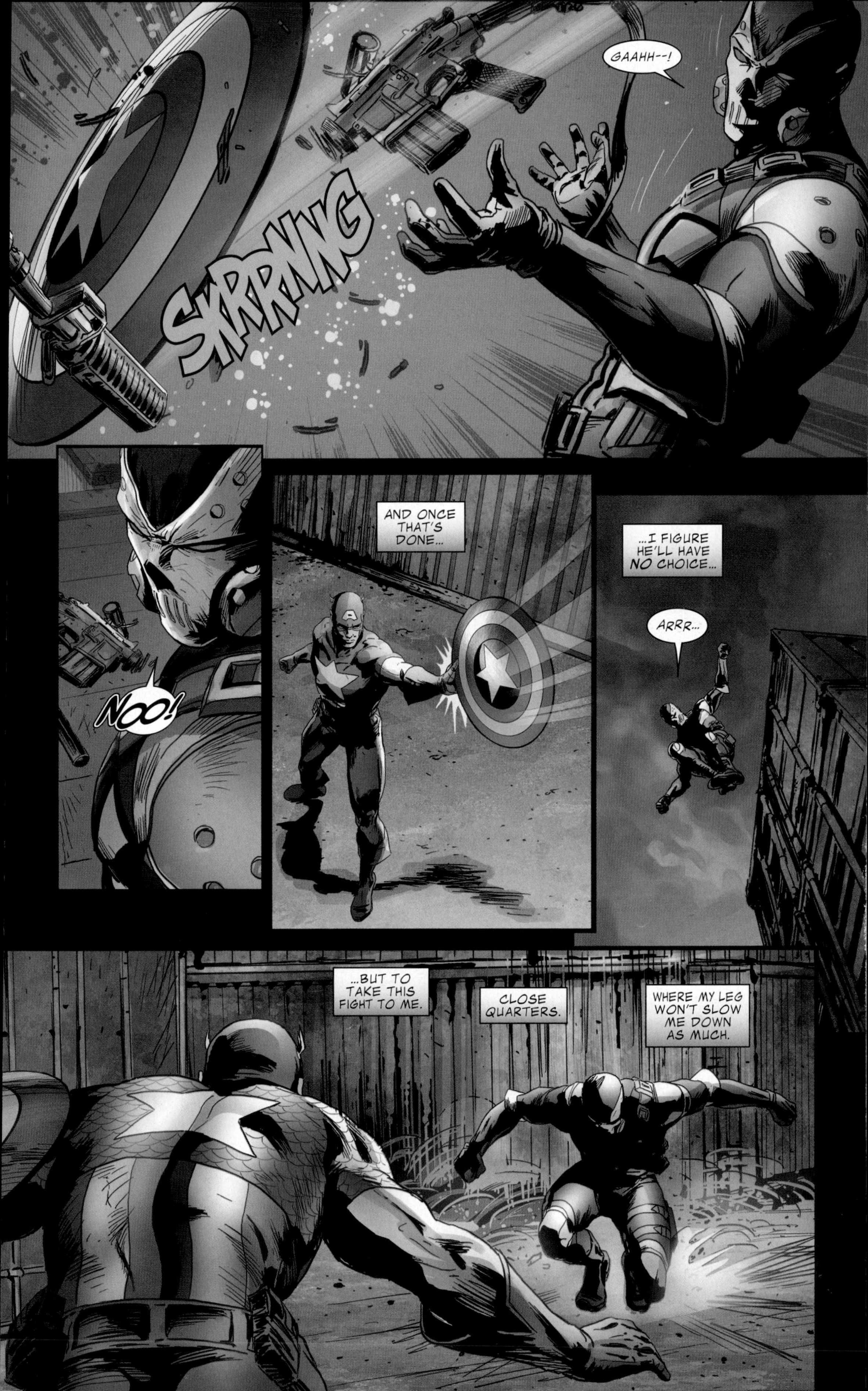
GAAHH--!
SKRRNNG
NOO!
AND ONCE THAT'S DONE...
...I FIGURE HE'LL HAVE NO CHOICE...
ARRR...
...BUT TO TAKE THIS FIGHT TO ME.
CLOSE QUARTERS.
WHERE MY LEG WON'T SLOW ME DOWN AS MUCH.

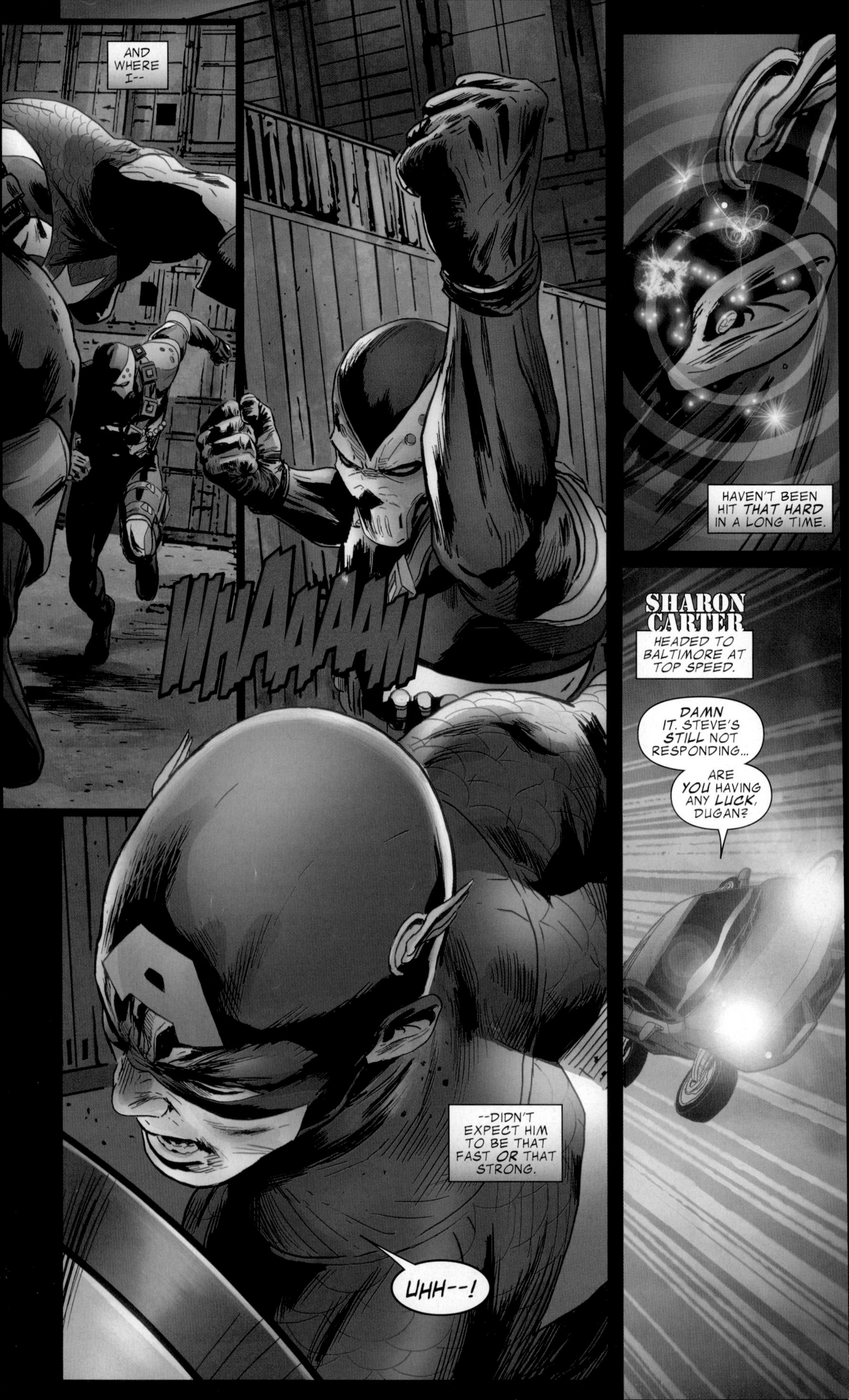

AND WHERE I--
WHAAAAM
HAVEN'T BEEN HIT THAT HARD IN A LONG TIME.
--DIDN'T EXPECT HIM TO BE THAT FAST OR THAT STRONG.
UHH--!
SHARON CARTER
HEADED TO BALTIMORE AT TOP SPEED.
DAMN IT. STEVE'S STILL NOT RESPONDING...
ARE YOU HAVING ANY LUCK, DUGAN?

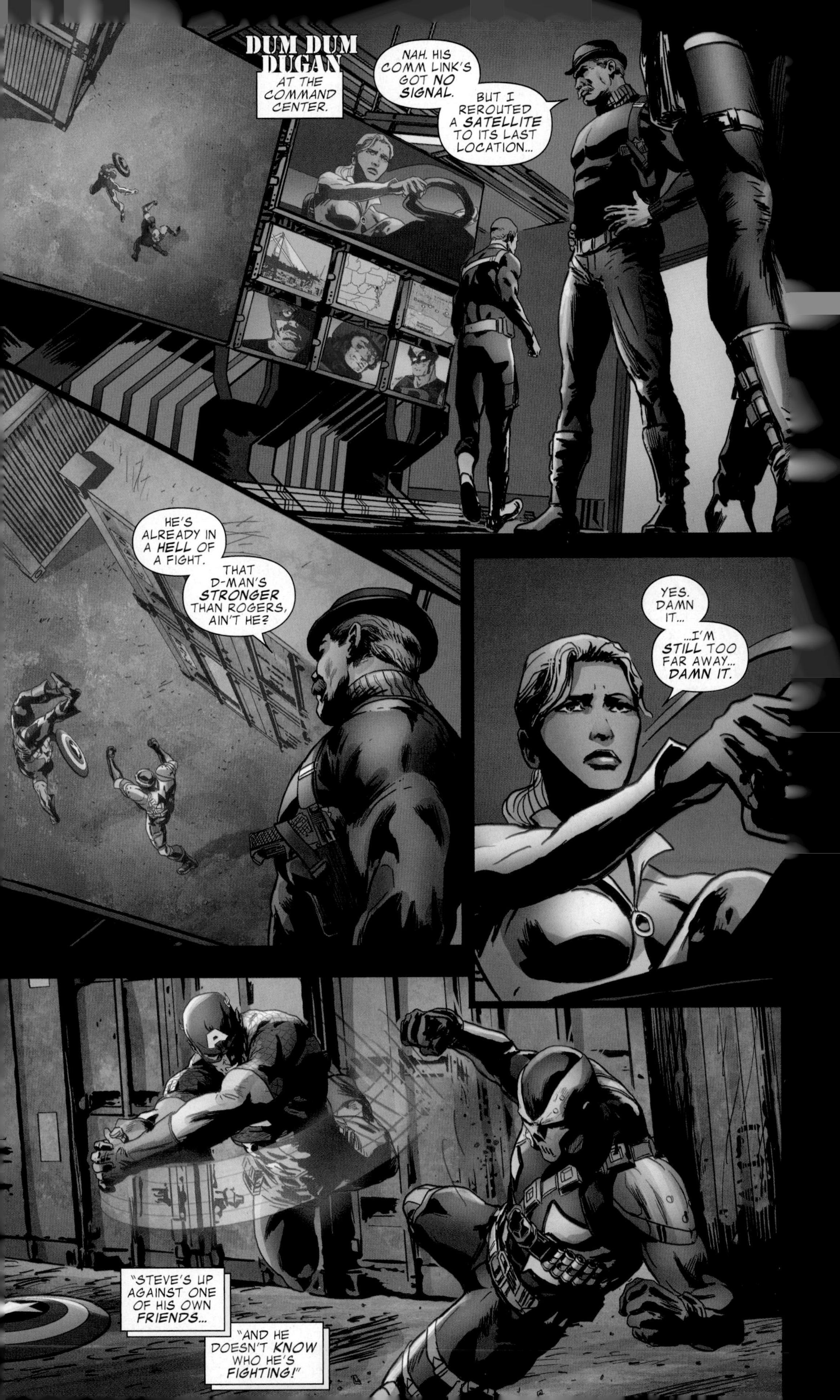
DUM DUM DUGAN
AT THE COMMAND CENTER.
NAH. HIS COMM LINK'S GOT NO SIGNAL.
BUT I REROUTED A SATELLITE TO ITS LAST LOCATION...
HE'S ALREADY IN A HELL OF A FIGHT.
THAT D-MAN'S STRONGER THAN ROGERS, AIN'T HE?
YES. DAMN IT...
...I'M STILL TOO FAR AWAY... DAMN IT.
"STEVE'S UP AGAINST ONE OF HIS OWN FRIENDS...
"AND HE DOESN'T KNOW WHO HE'S FIGHTING!"

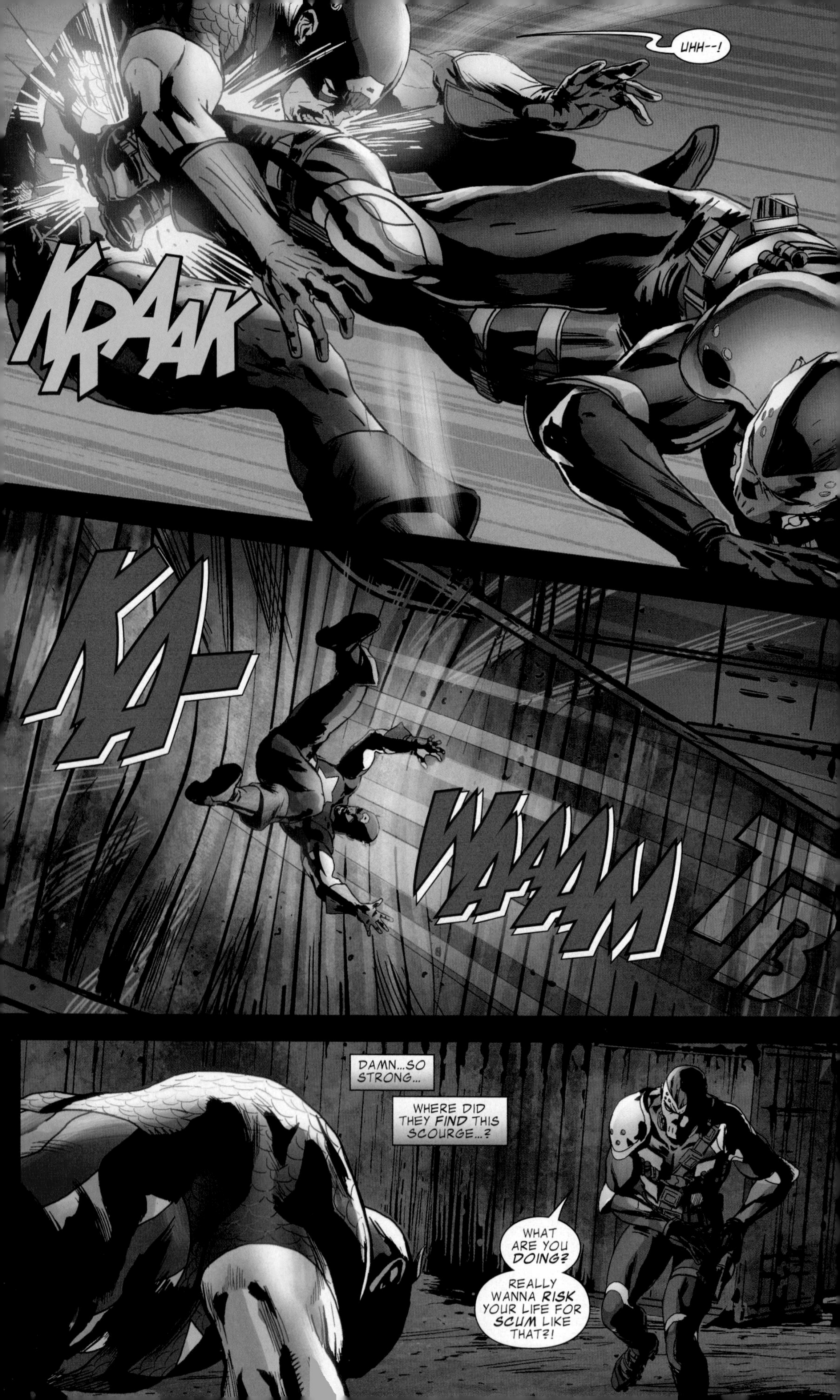
UHH--!
KRAAK
KA-
WAAM
DAMN...SO STRONG...
WHERE DID THEY FIND THIS SCOURGE...?
WHAT ARE YOU DOING?
REALLY WANNA RISK YOUR LIFE FOR SCUM LIKE THAT?!

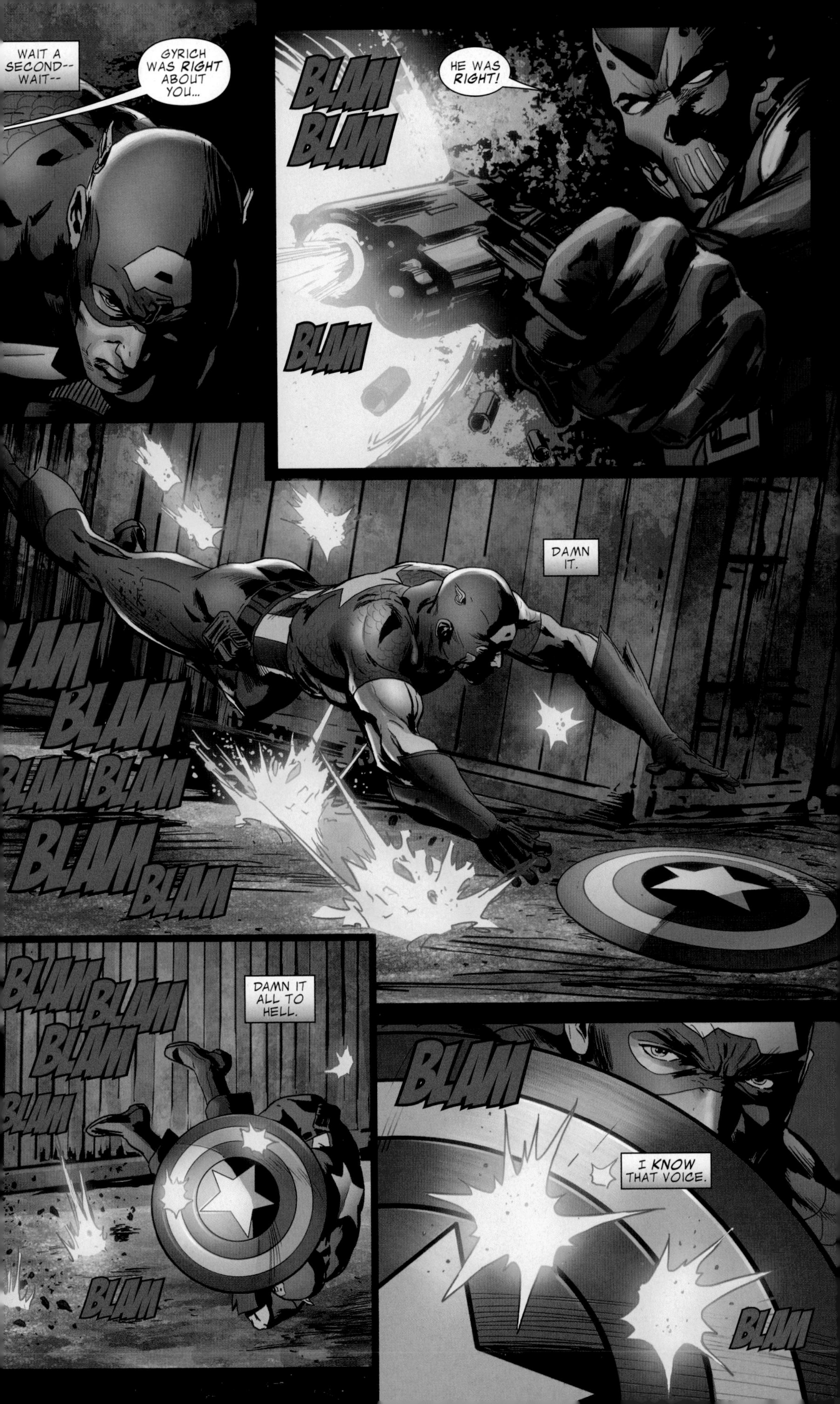

WAIT A SECOND-- WAIT--
GYRICH WAS RIGHT ABOUT YOU...
BLAM BLAM
BLAM
HE WAS RIGHT!
DAMN IT.
BLAM BLAM BLAM BLAM BLAM BLAM
DAMN IT ALL TO HELL.
BLAM BLAM BLAM BLAM
BLAM
BLAM
I KNOW THAT VOICE.
BLAM

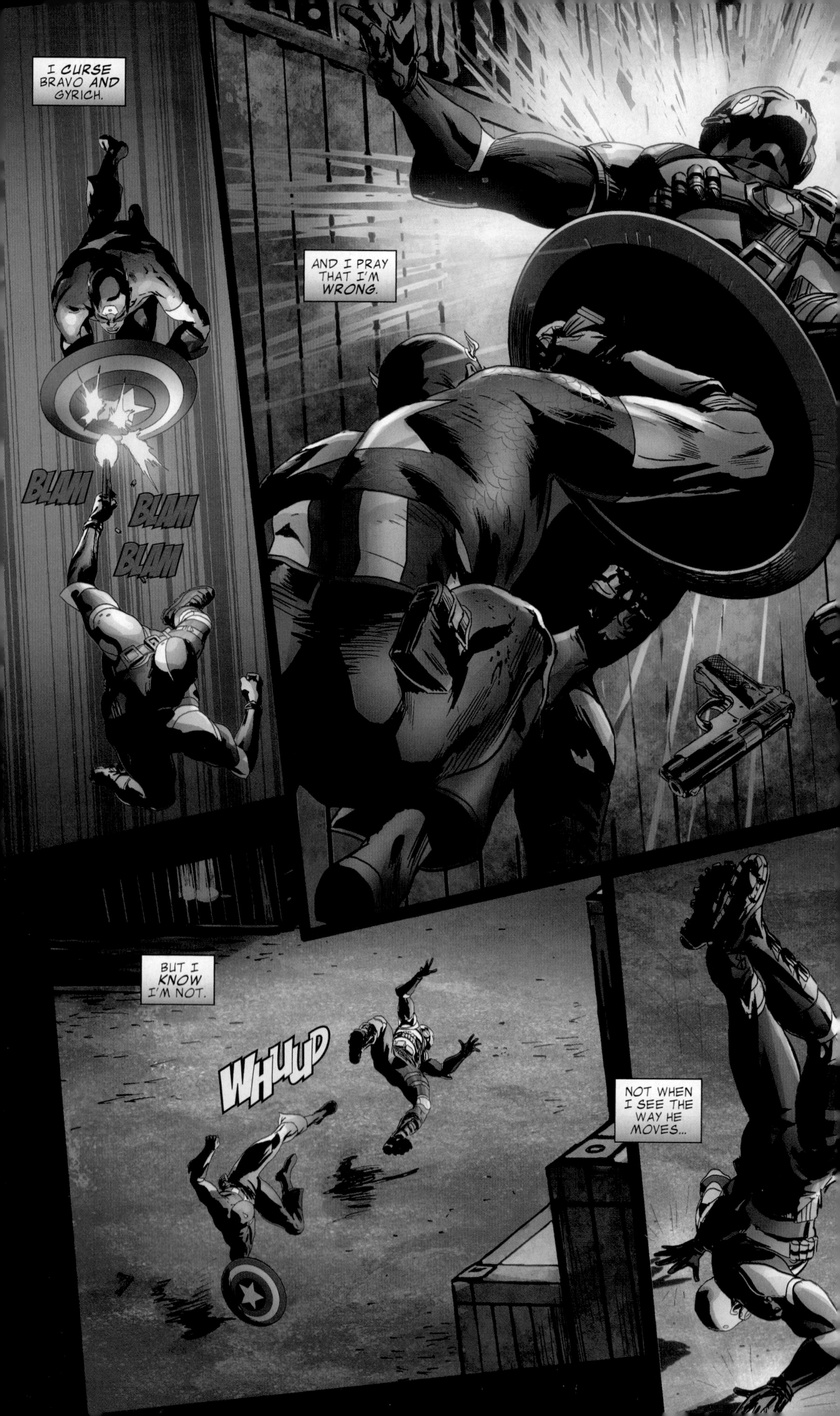
I CURSE BRAVO AND GYRICH.
BLAM
BLAM
BLAM
AND I PRAY THAT I'M WRONG.
BUT I KNOW I'M NOT.
WHUUD
NOT WHEN I SEE THE WAY HE MOVES...

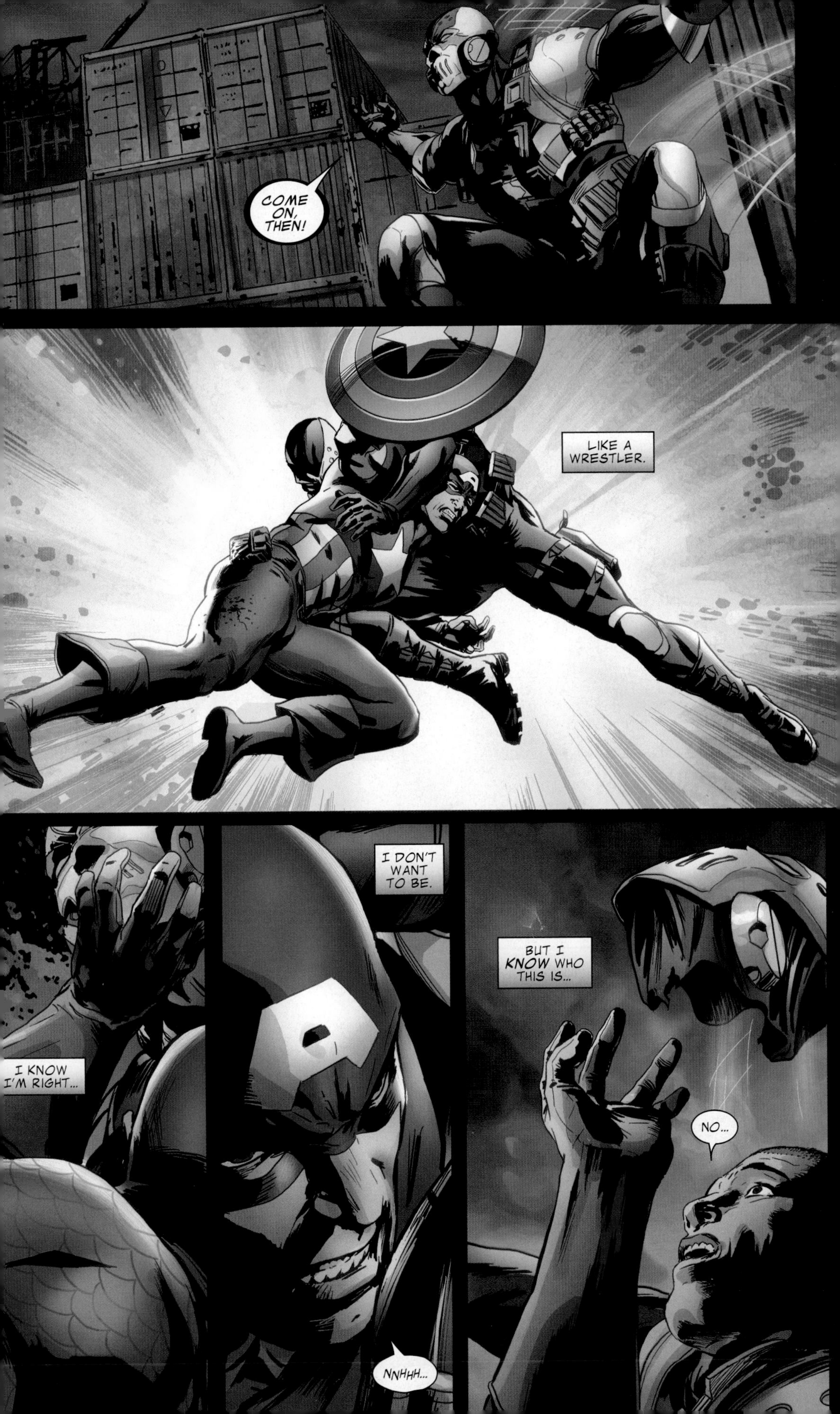
COME ON, THEN!
LIKE A WRESTLER.
I KNOW I'M RIGHT...
I DON'T WANT TO BE.
NNHHH...
BUT I KNOW WHO THIS IS...
NO...

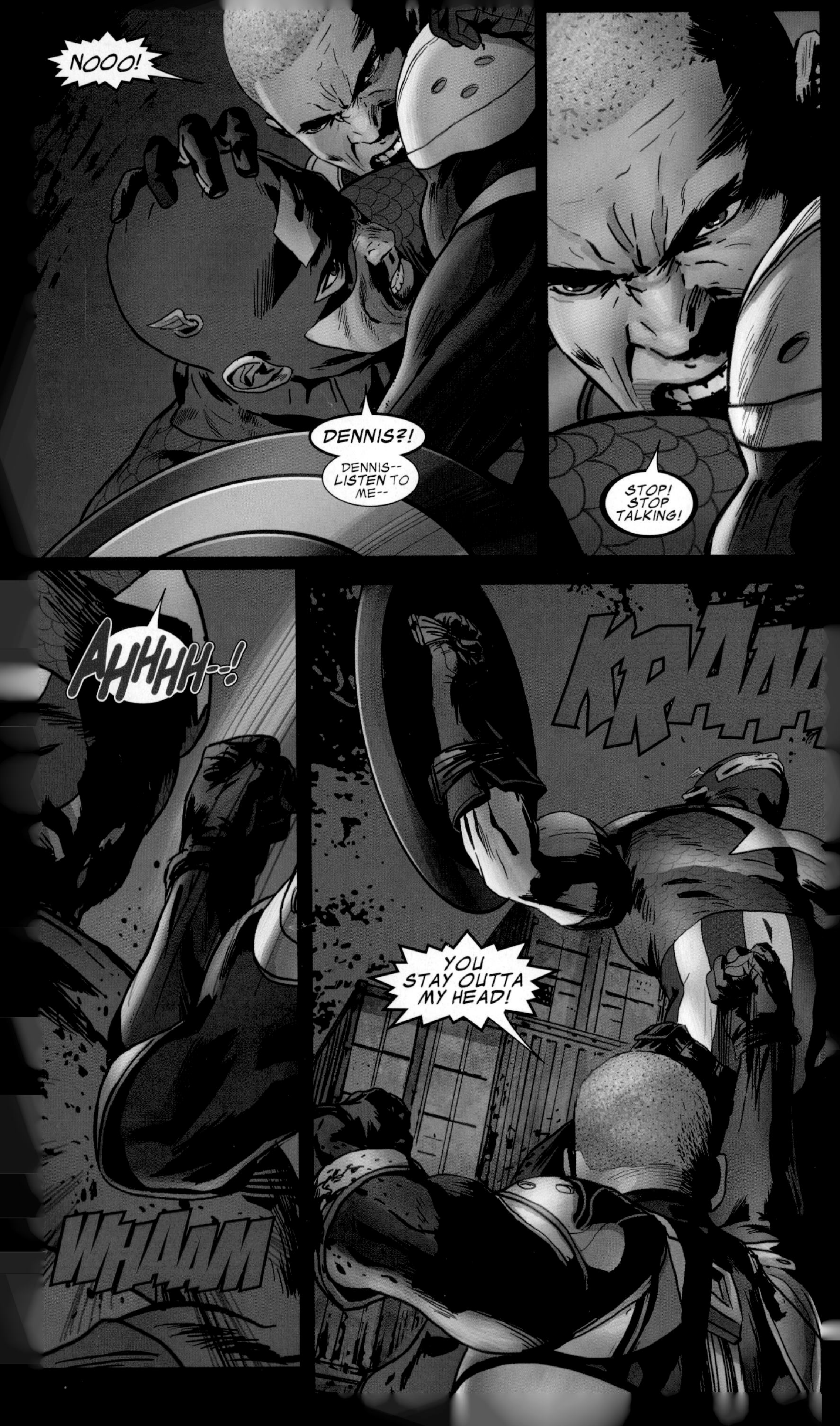
NOOO!
DENNIS?!
DENNIS-- LISTEN TO ME--
STOP! STOP TALKING!
AHHHH--!
WHAAM
KRAAM
YOU STAY OUTTA MY HEAD!

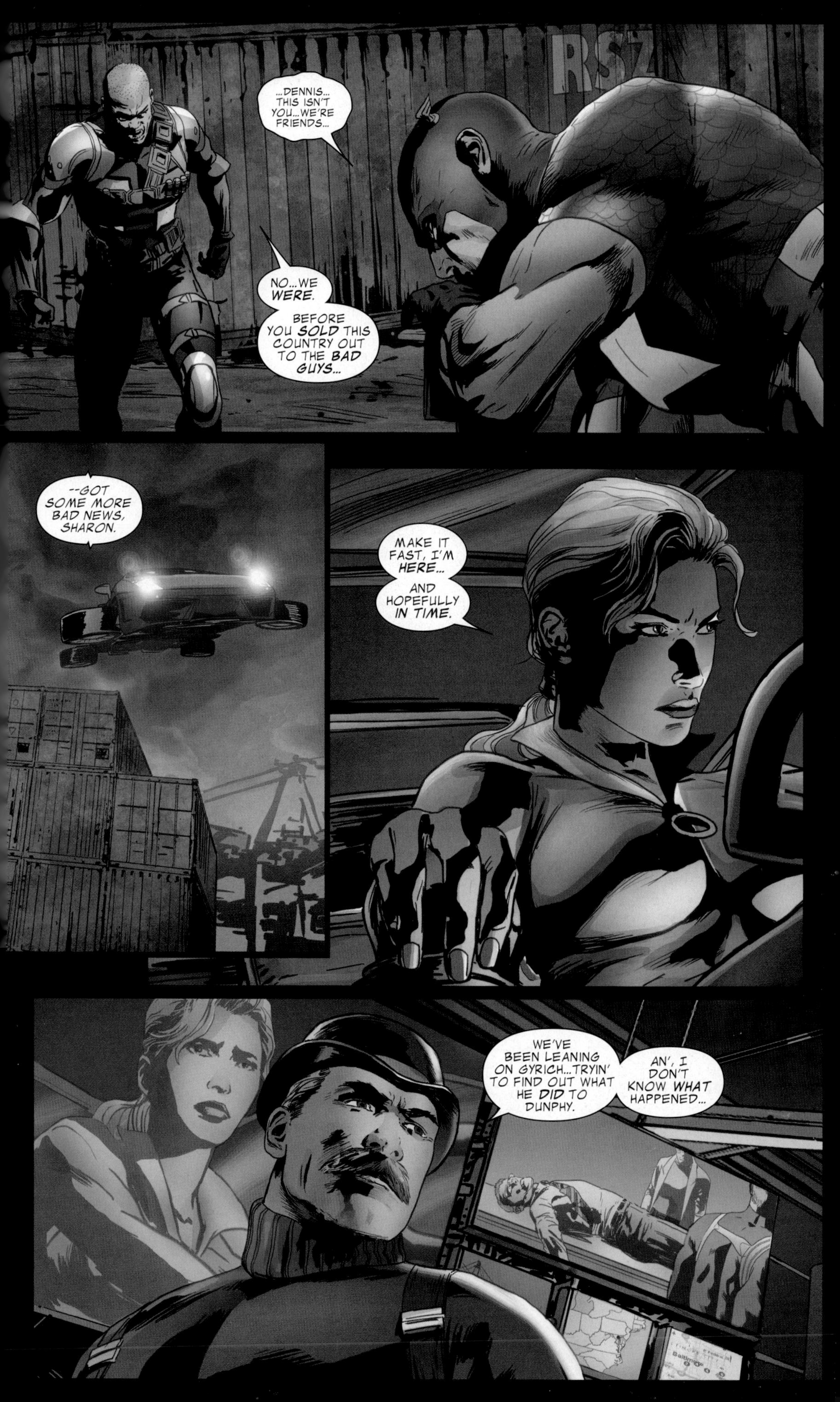
...DENNIS... THIS ISN'T YOU...WE'RE FRIENDS...
NO...WE WERE.
BEFORE YOU SOLD THIS COUNTRY OUT TO THE BAD GUYS...
--GOT SOME MORE BAD NEWS, SHARON.
MAKE IT FAST, I'M HERE...
AND HOPEFULLY IN TIME.
WE'VE BEEN LEANING ON GYRICH...TRYIN' TO FIND OUT WHAT HE DID TO DUNPHY.
AN', I DON'T KNOW WHAT HAPPENED...

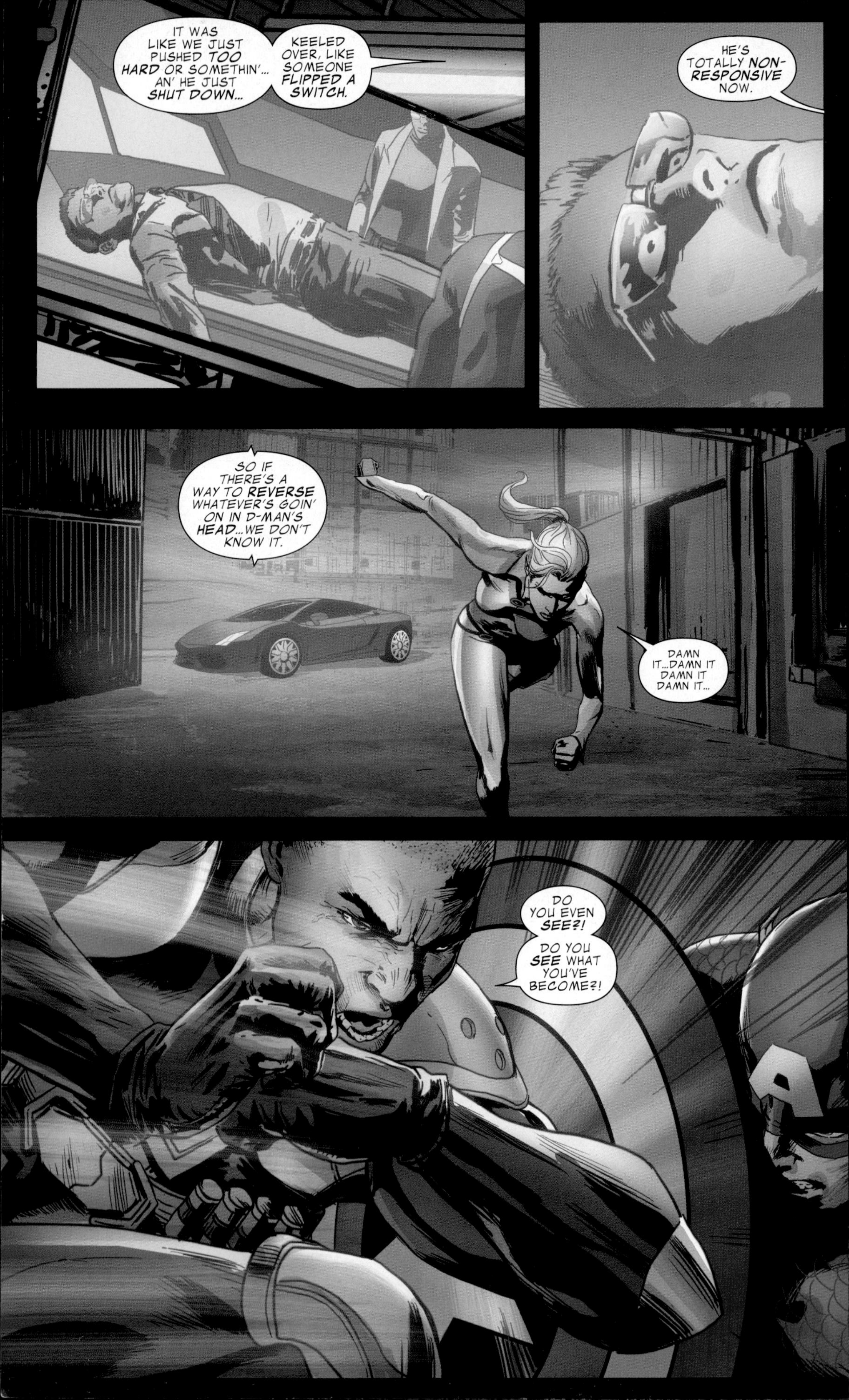
IT WAS LIKE WE JUST PUSHED TOO HARD OR SOMETHIN'... AN' HE JUST SHUT DOWN...
KEELED OVER, LIKE SOMEONE FLIPPED A SWITCH.
HE'S TOTALLY NON-RESPONSIVE NOW.
SO IF THERE'S A WAY TO REVERSE WHATEVER'S GOIN' ON IN D-MAN'S HEAD...WE DON'T KNOW IT.
DAMN IT...DAMN IT DAMN IT DAMN IT...
DO YOU EVEN SEE?!
DO YOU SEE WHAT YOU'VE BECOME?!

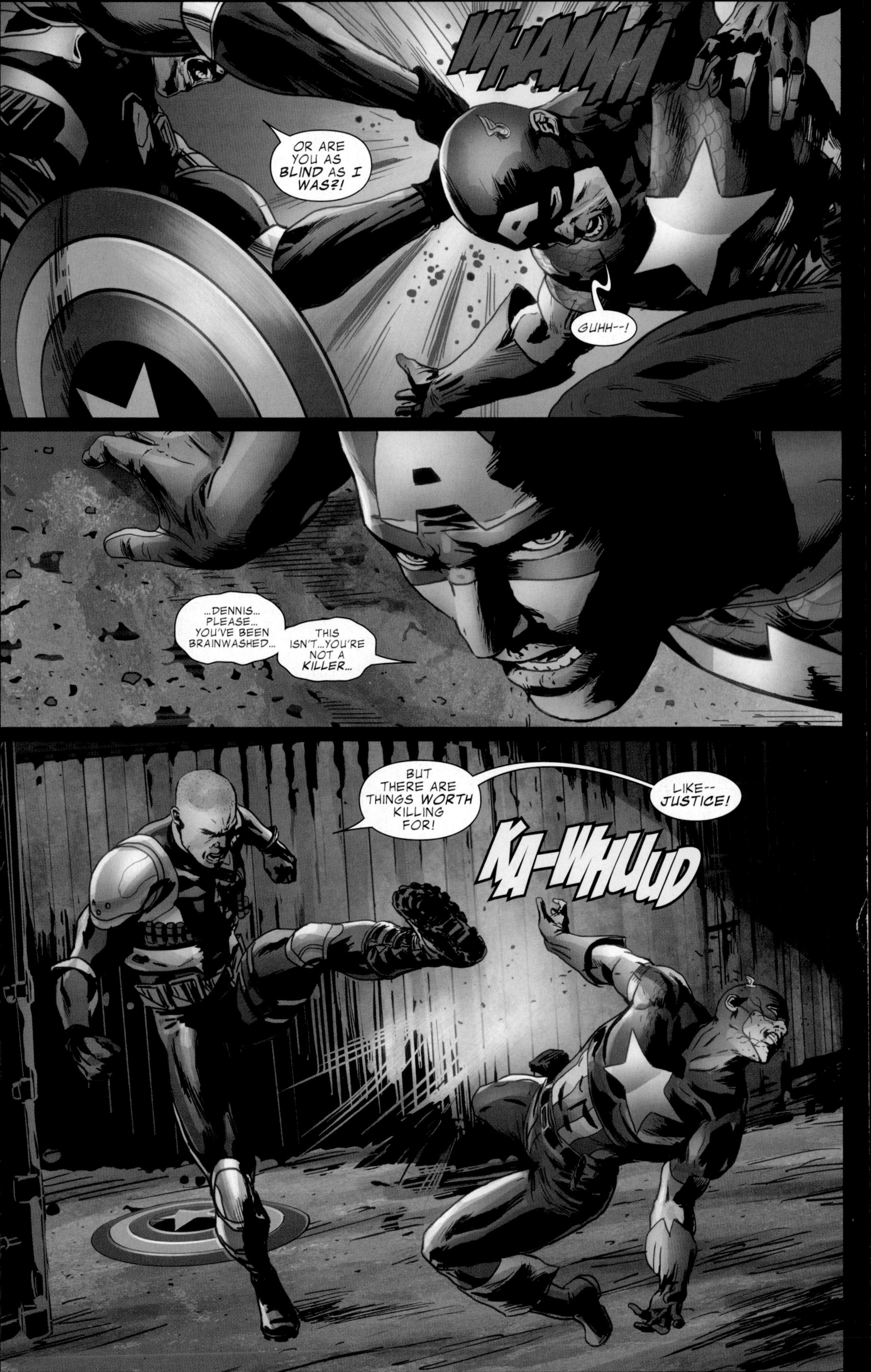
WHAMM
OR ARE YOU AS BLIND AS I WAS?!
GUHH--!
...DENNIS... PLEASE... YOU'VE BEEN BRAINWASHED...
THIS ISN'T...YOU'RE NOT A KILLER...
BUT THERE ARE THINGS WORTH KILLING FOR!
LIKE-- JUSTICE!
KA-WHUUD

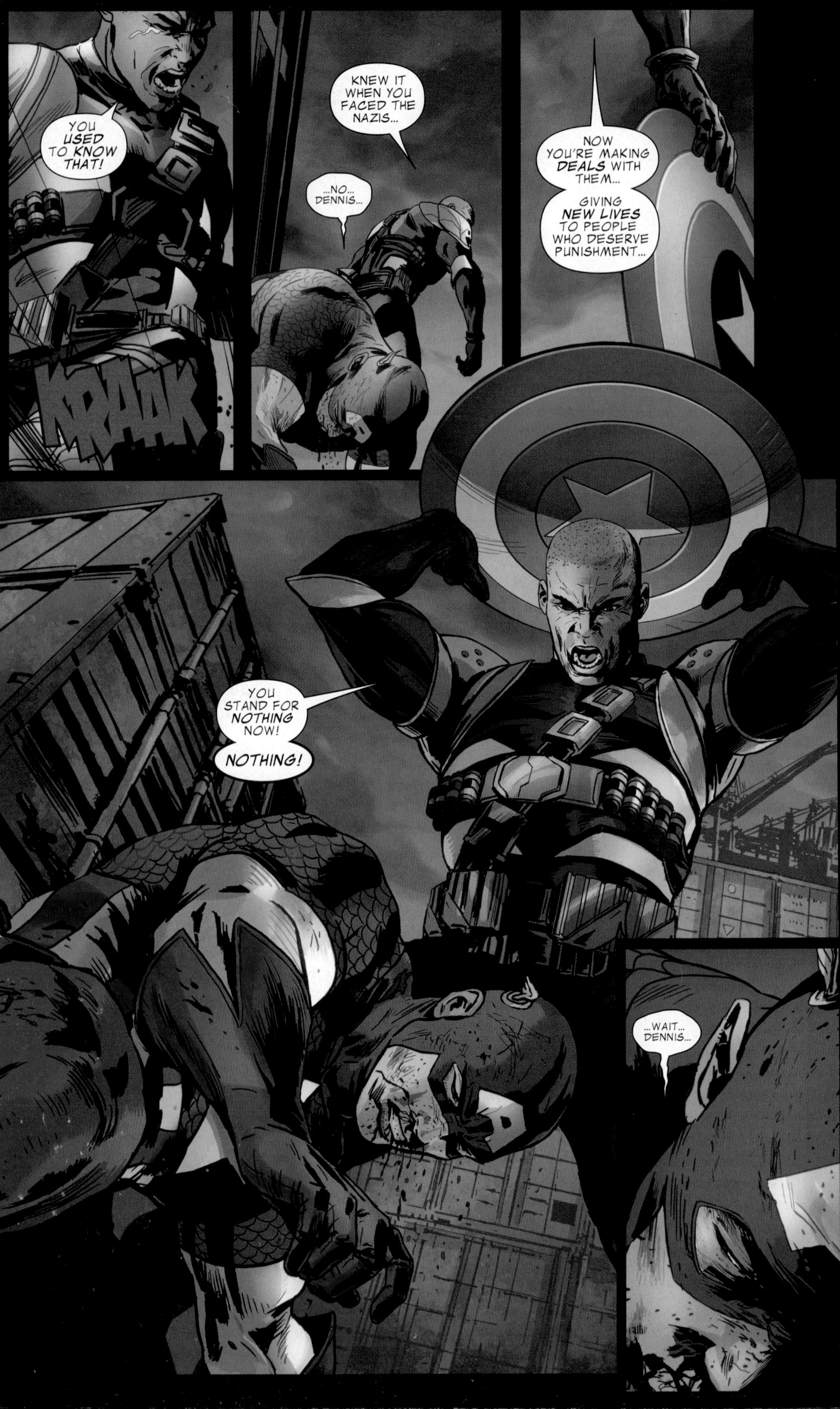

YOU USED TO KNOW THAT!
KRAAK
KNEW IT WHEN YOU FACED THE NAZIS...
...NO... DENNIS...
NOW YOU'RE MAKING DEALS WITH THEM...
GIVING NEW LIVES TO PEOPLE WHO DESERVE PUNISHMENT...
YOU STAND FOR NOTHING NOW!
NOTHING!
...WAIT... DENNIS...

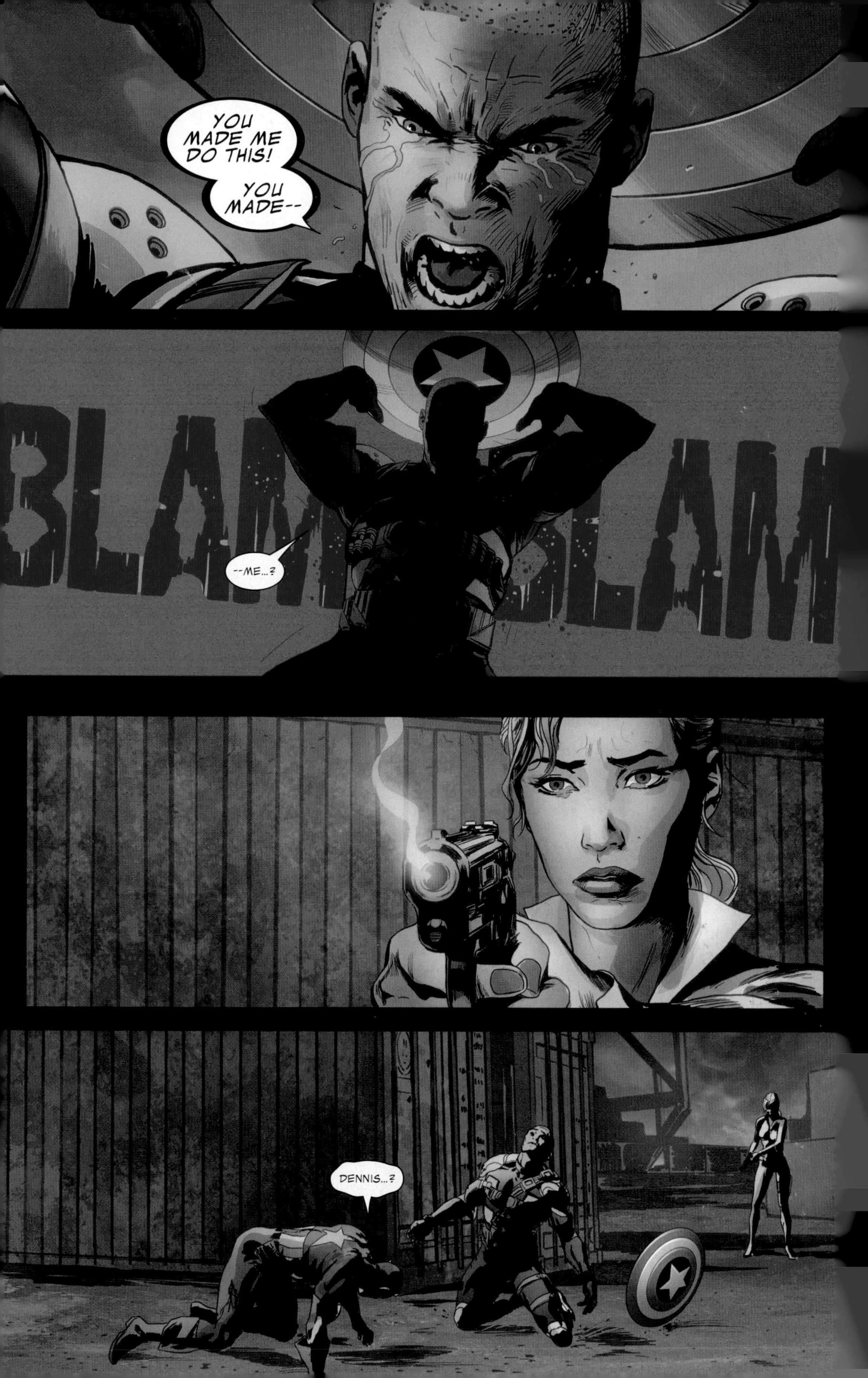
YOU MADE ME DO THIS!
YOU MADE--
BLAM
BLAM
--ME...?
DENNIS...?

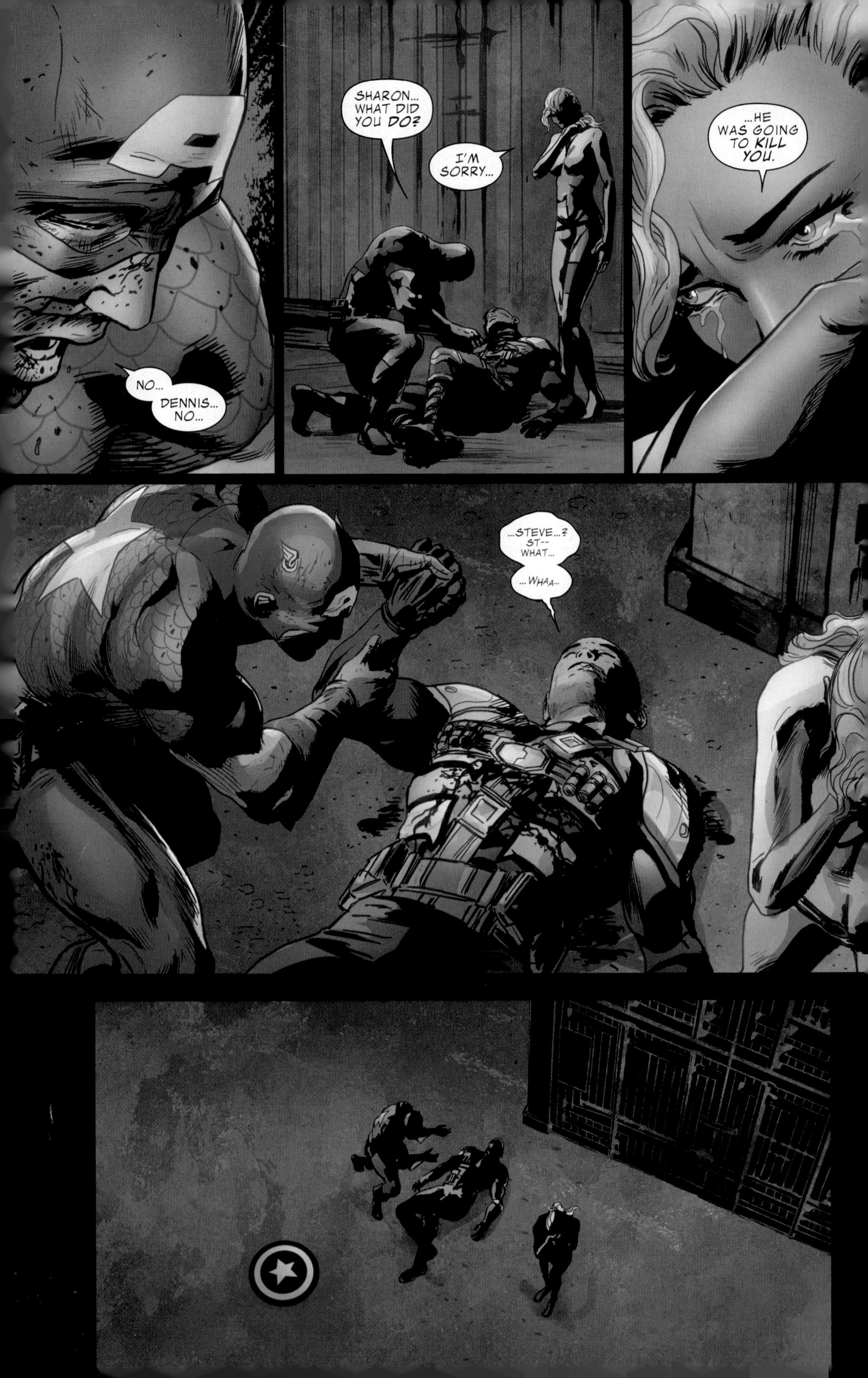
NO... DENNIS... NO...
SHARON... WHAT DID YOU DO?
I'M SORRY...
...HE WAS GOING TO KILL YOU.
...STEVE...? ST-- WHAT...
...WHAA...

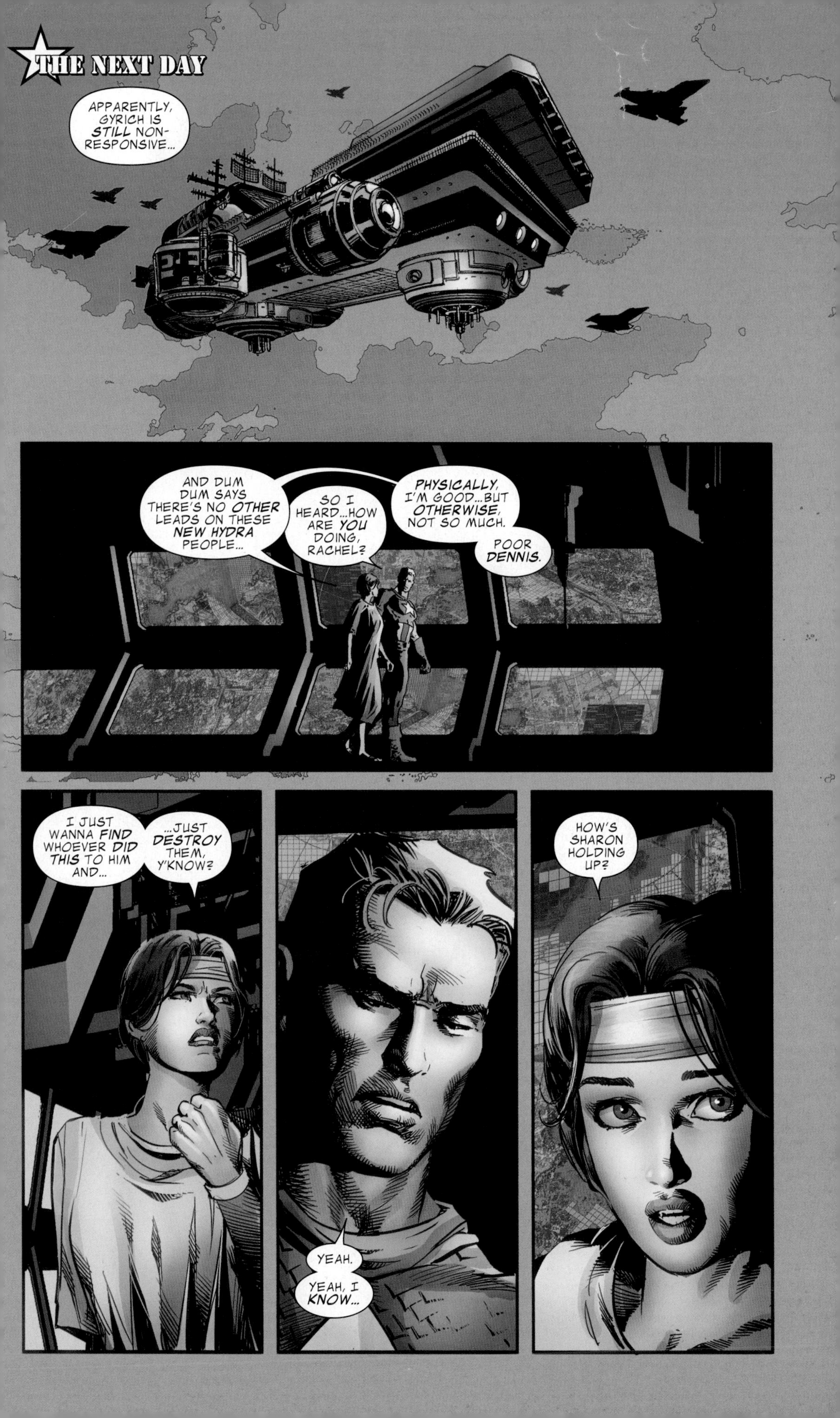
THE NEXT DAY
APPARENTLY, GYRICH IS STILL NON-RESPONSIVE...
AND DUM DUM SAYS THERE'S NO OTHER LEADS ON THESE NEW HYDRA PEOPLE...
SO I HEARD...HOW ARE YOU DOING, RACHEL?
PHYSICALLY, I'M GOOD...BUT OTHERWISE, NOT SO MUCH.
POOR DENNIS.
I JUST WANNA FIND WHOEVER DID THIS TO HIM AND...
...JUST DESTROY THEM, Y'KNOW?
YEAH.
YEAH, I KNOW...
HOW'S SHARON HOLDING UP?

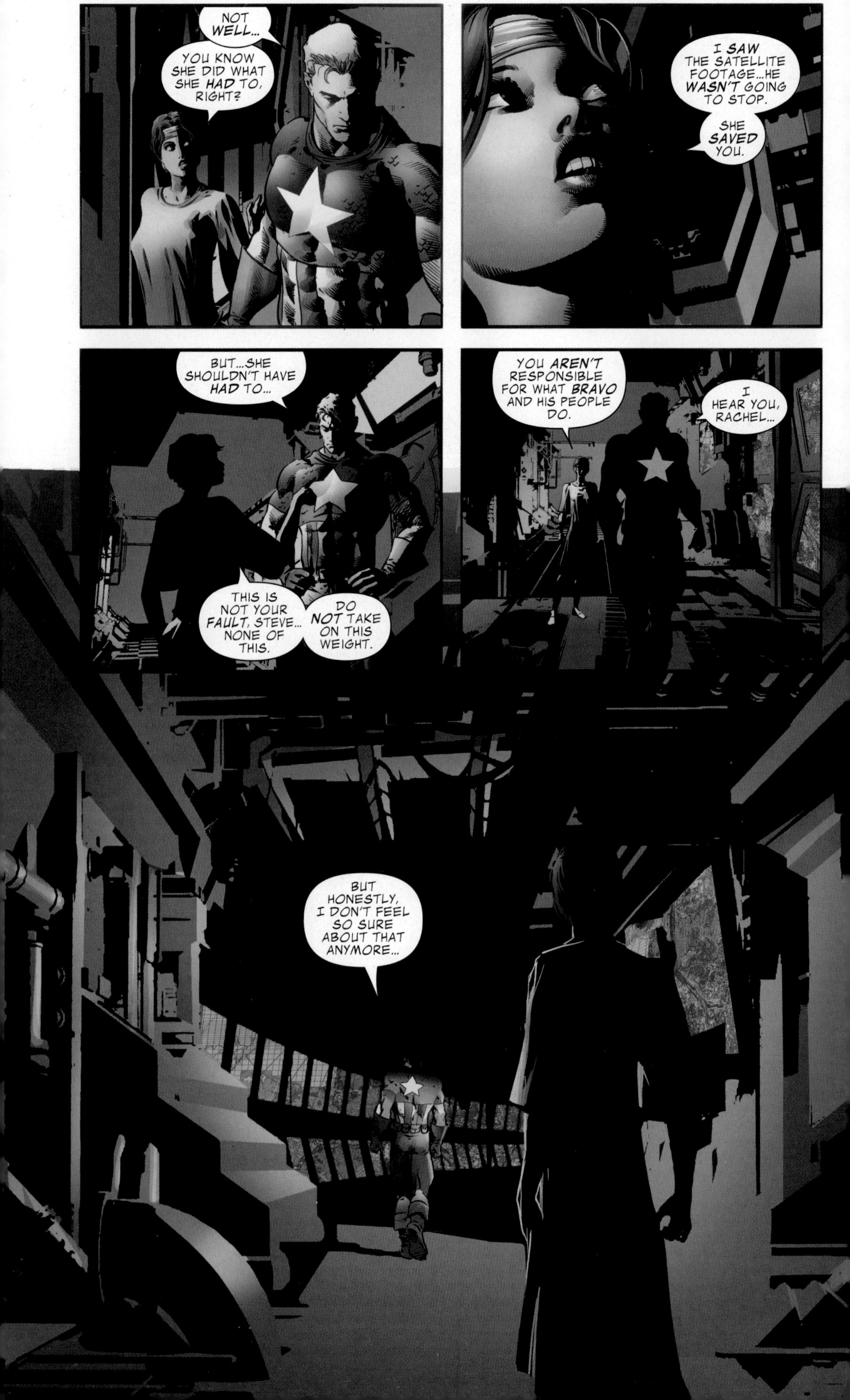
NOT WELL...
YOU KNOW SHE DID WHAT SHE HAD TO, RIGHT?
I SAW THE SATELLITE FOOTAGE...HE WASN'T GOING TO STOP.
SHE SAVED YOU.
BUT...SHE SHOULDN'T HAVE HAD TO...
THIS IS NOT YOUR FAULT, STEVE... NONE OF THIS.
DO NOT TAKE ON THIS WEIGHT.
YOU AREN'T RESPONSIBLE FOR WHAT BRAVO AND HIS PEOPLE DO.
I HEAR YOU, RACHEL...
BUT HONESTLY, I DON'T FEEL SO SURE ABOUT THAT ANYMORE...

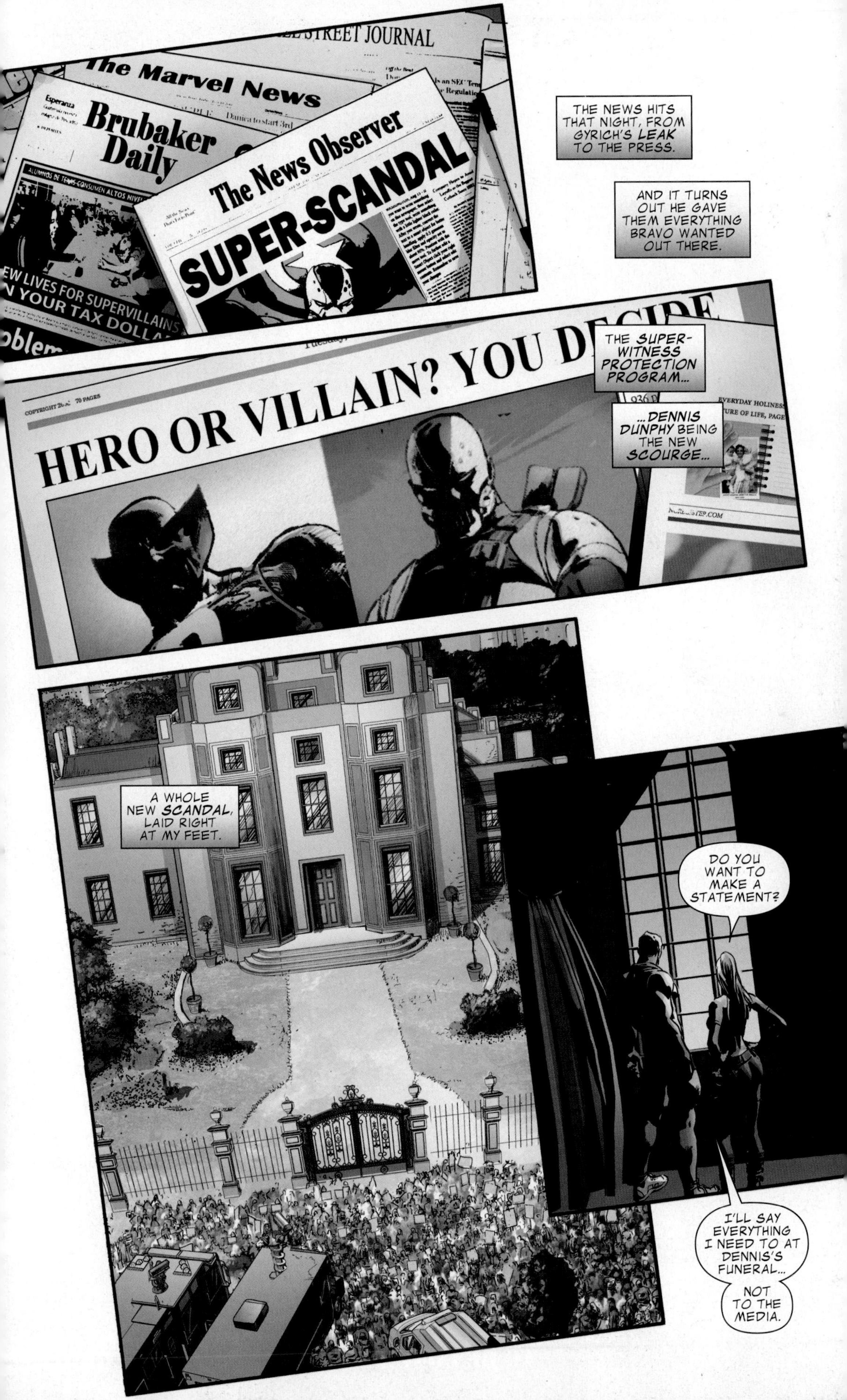

STREET JOURNAL
The Marvel News
Brubaker Daily
The News Observer
SUPER-SCANDAL
EW LIVES FOR SUPERVILLAINS
N YOUR TAX DOLLA
THE NEWS HITS THAT NIGHT, FROM GYRICH'S LEAK TO THE PRESS.
AND IT TURNS OUT HE GAVE THEM EVERYTHING BRAVO WANTED OUT THERE.
HERO OR VILLAIN? YOU DE
THE SUPER-WITNESS PROTECTION PROGRAM...
...DENNIS DUNPHY BEING THE NEW SCOURGE...
A WHOLE NEW SCANDAL, LAID RIGHT AT MY FEET.
DO YOU WANT TO MAKE A STATEMENT?
I'LL SAY EVERYTHING I NEED TO AT DENNIS'S FUNERAL...
NOT TO THE MEDIA.

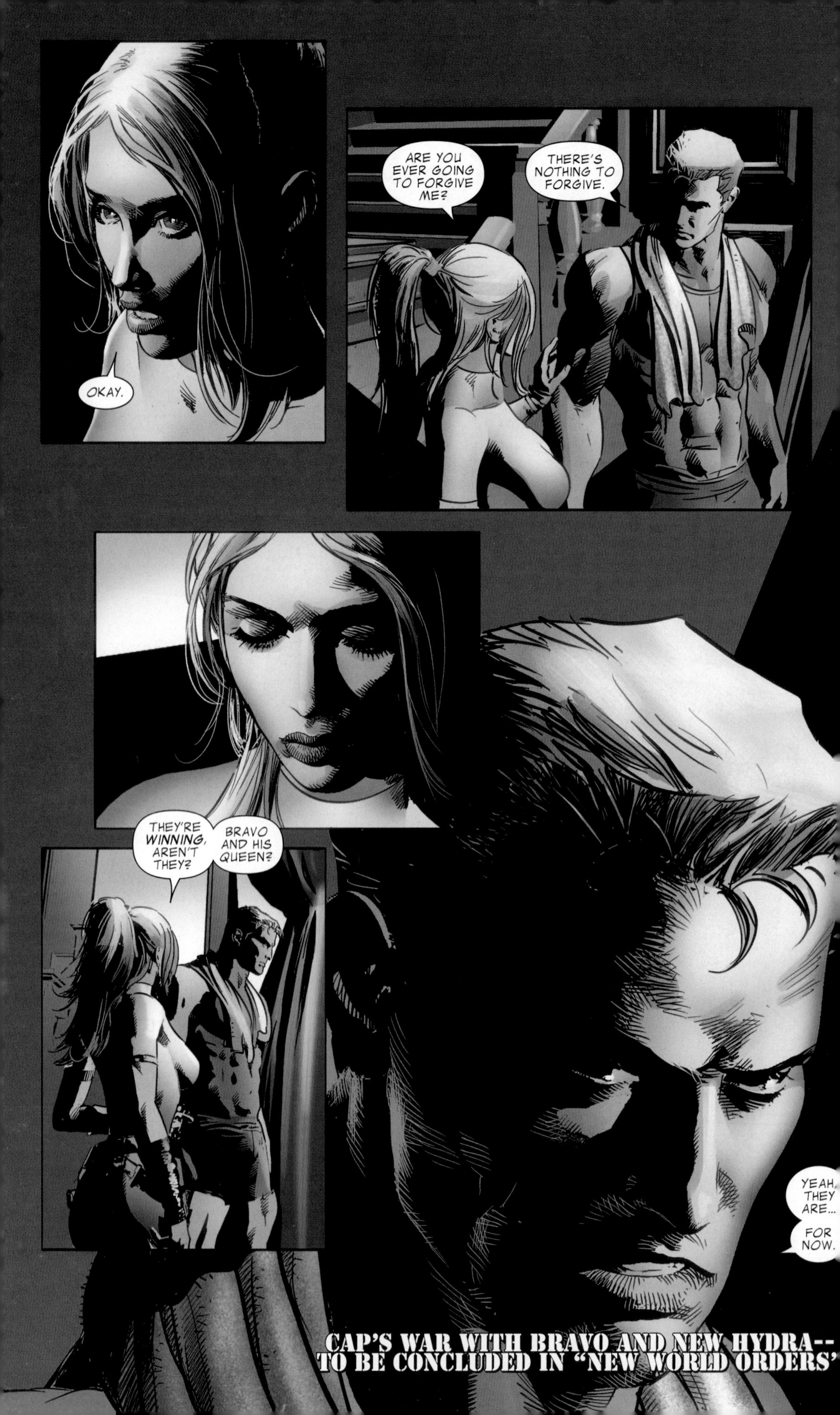
OKAY.
ARE YOU EVER GOING TO FORGIVE ME?
THERE'S NOTHING TO FORGIVE.
THEY'RE WINNING, AREN'T THEY?
BRAVO AND HIS QUEEN?
YEAH, THEY ARE...
FOR NOW.
CAP'S WAR WITH BRAVO AND NEW HYDRA--
TO BE CONCLUDED IN "NEW WORLD ORDERS"

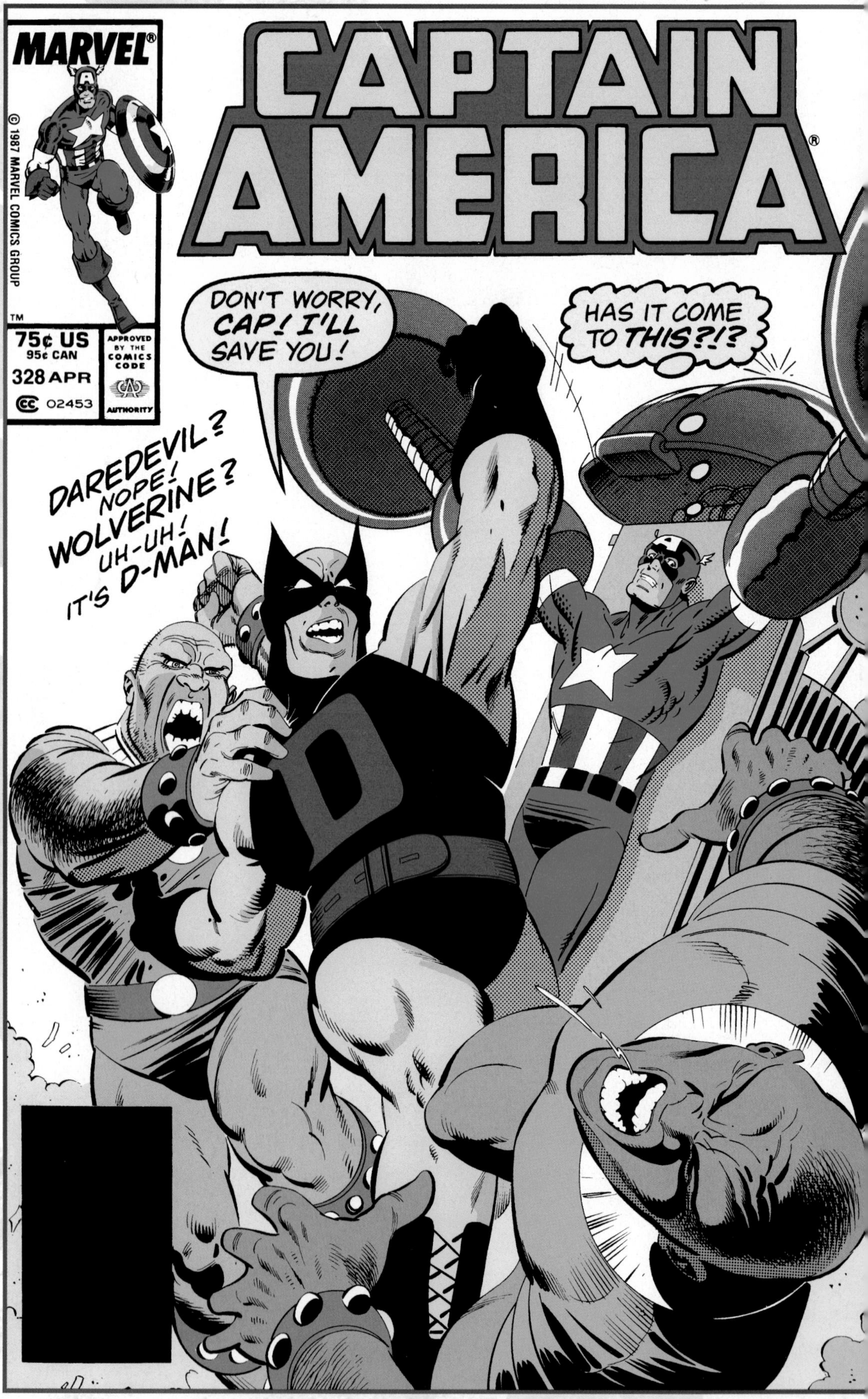
MARVEL®
CAPTAIN AMERICA®
© 1987 MARVEL COMICS GROUP
TM
75¢ US
95¢ CAN
328 APR
CC 02453
APPROVED BY THE COMICS CODE AUTHORITY
DON'T WORRY, CAP! I'LL SAVE YOU!
HAS IT COME TO THIS?!?
DAREDEVIL? NOPE! WOLVERINE? UH-UH! IT'S D-MAN!

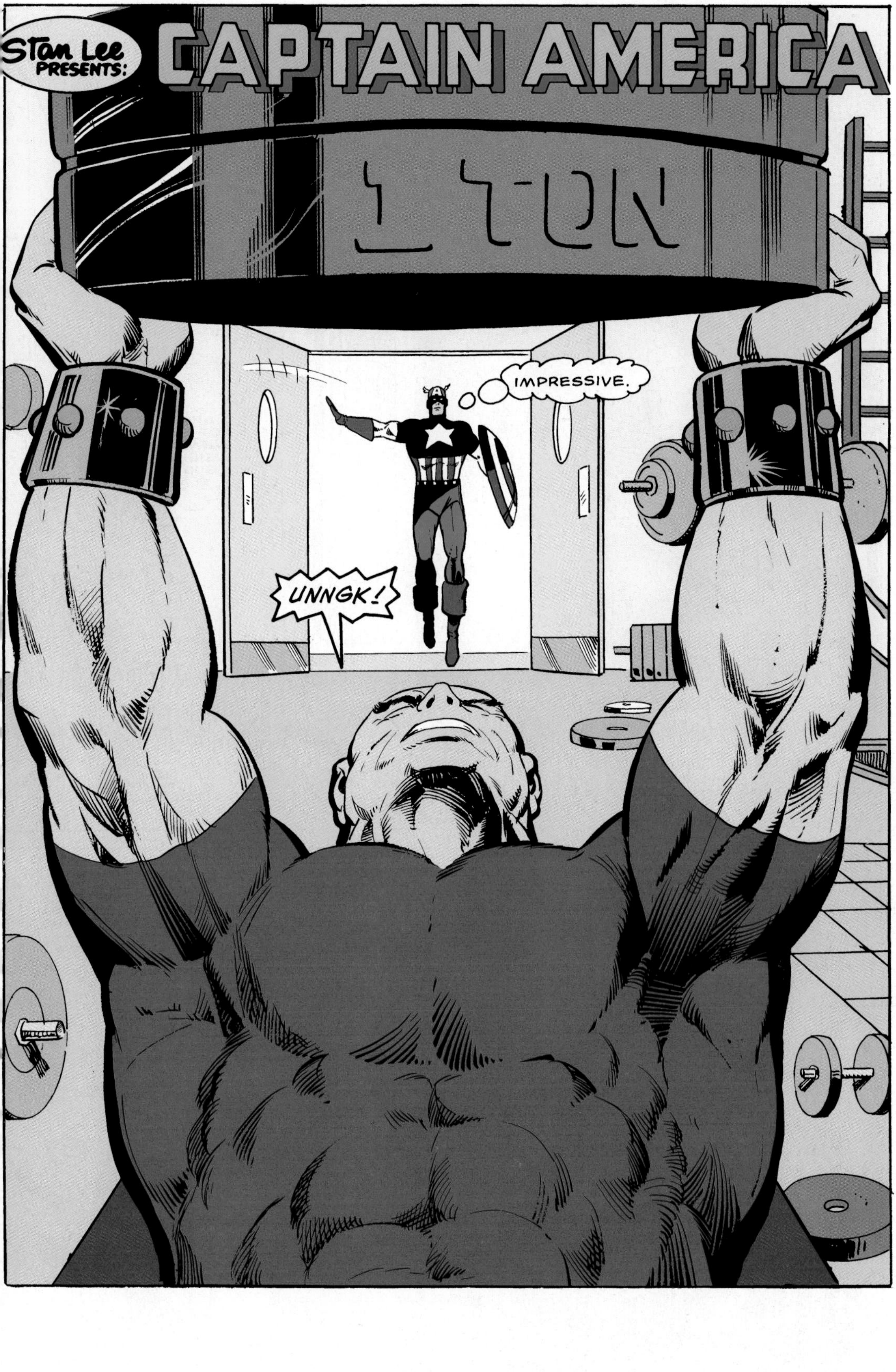

STAN LEE PRESENTS:
CAPTAIN AMERICA
1 TON
IMPRESSIVE.
UNNGK!

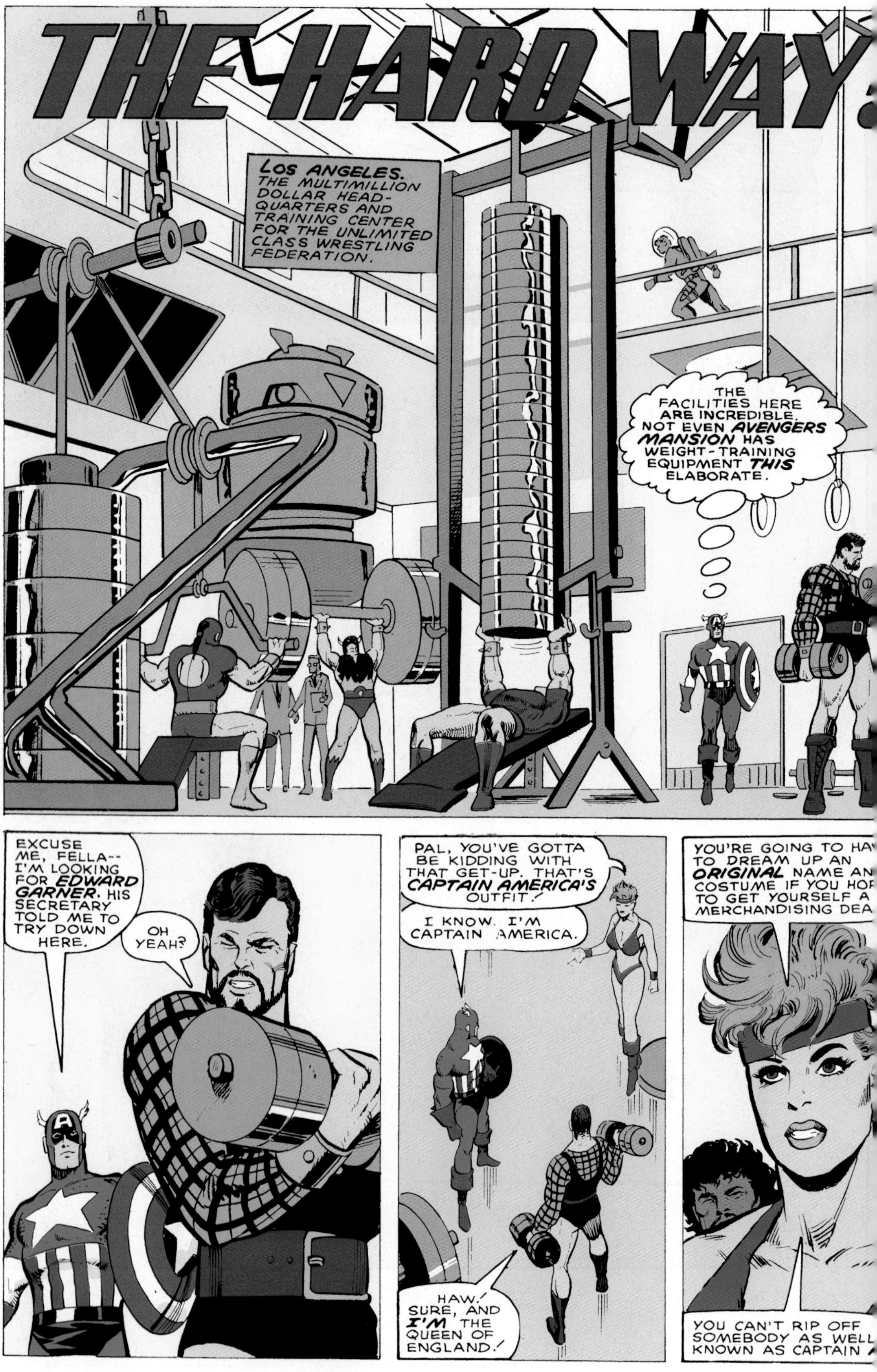

THE HARD WAY!
LOS ANGELES. THE MULTIMILLION DOLLAR HEAD-QUARTERS AND TRAINING CENTER FOR THE UNLIMITED CLASS WRESTLING FEDERATION.
THE FACILITIES HERE ARE INCREDIBLE. NOT EVEN AVENGERS MANSION HAS WEIGHT-TRAINING EQUIPMENT THIS ELABORATE.
EXCUSE ME, FELLA-- I'M LOOKING FOR EDWARD GARNER. HIS SECRETARY TOLD ME TO TRY DOWN HERE.
OH YEAH?
PAL, YOU'VE GOTTA BE KIDDING WITH THAT GET-UP. THAT'S CAPTAIN AMERICA'S OUTFIT!
I KNOW. I'M CAPTAIN AMERICA.
HAW! SURE, AND I'M THE QUEEN OF ENGLAND!
YOU'RE GOING TO HA
TO DREAM UP AN ORIGINAL NAME AN
COSTUME IF YOU HOP
TO GET YOURSELF A
MERCHANDISING DEA
YOU CAN'T RIP OFF
SOMEBODY AS WELL
KNOWN AS CAPTAIN

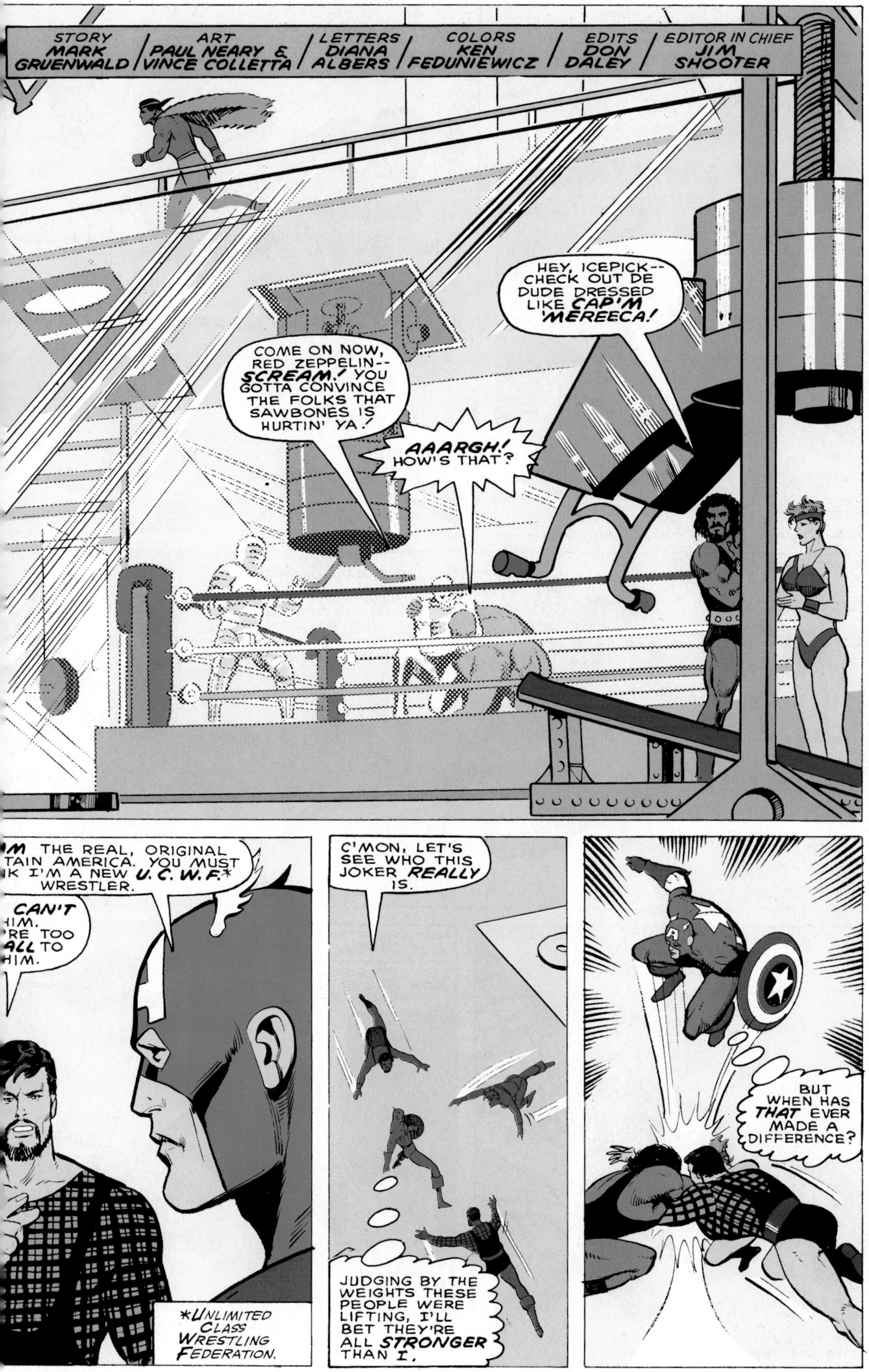

STORY MARK GRUENWALD / ART PAUL NEARY & VINCE COLLETTA / LETTERS DIANA ALBERS / COLORS KEN FEDUNIEWICZ / EDITS DON DALEY / EDITOR IN CHIEF JIM SHOOTER
HEY, ICEPICK-- CHECK OUT DE DUDE DRESSED LIKE CAP'M 'MEREECA!
COME ON NOW, RED ZEPPELIN-- SCREAM! YOU GOTTA CONVINCE THE FOLKS THAT SAWBONES IS HURTIN' YA!
AAAARGH! HOW'S THAT?
M THE REAL, ORIGINAL TAIN AMERICA. YOU MUST K I'M A NEW U.C.W.F.* WRESTLER.
CAN'T HIM. RE TOO ALL TO HIM.
*UNLIMITED CLASS WRESTLING FEDERATION.
C'MON, LET'S SEE WHO THIS JOKER REALLY IS.
JUDGING BY THE WEIGHTS THESE PEOPLE WERE LIFTING, I'LL BET THEY'RE ALL STRONGER THAN I.
BUT WHEN HAS THAT EVER MADE A DIFFERENCE?

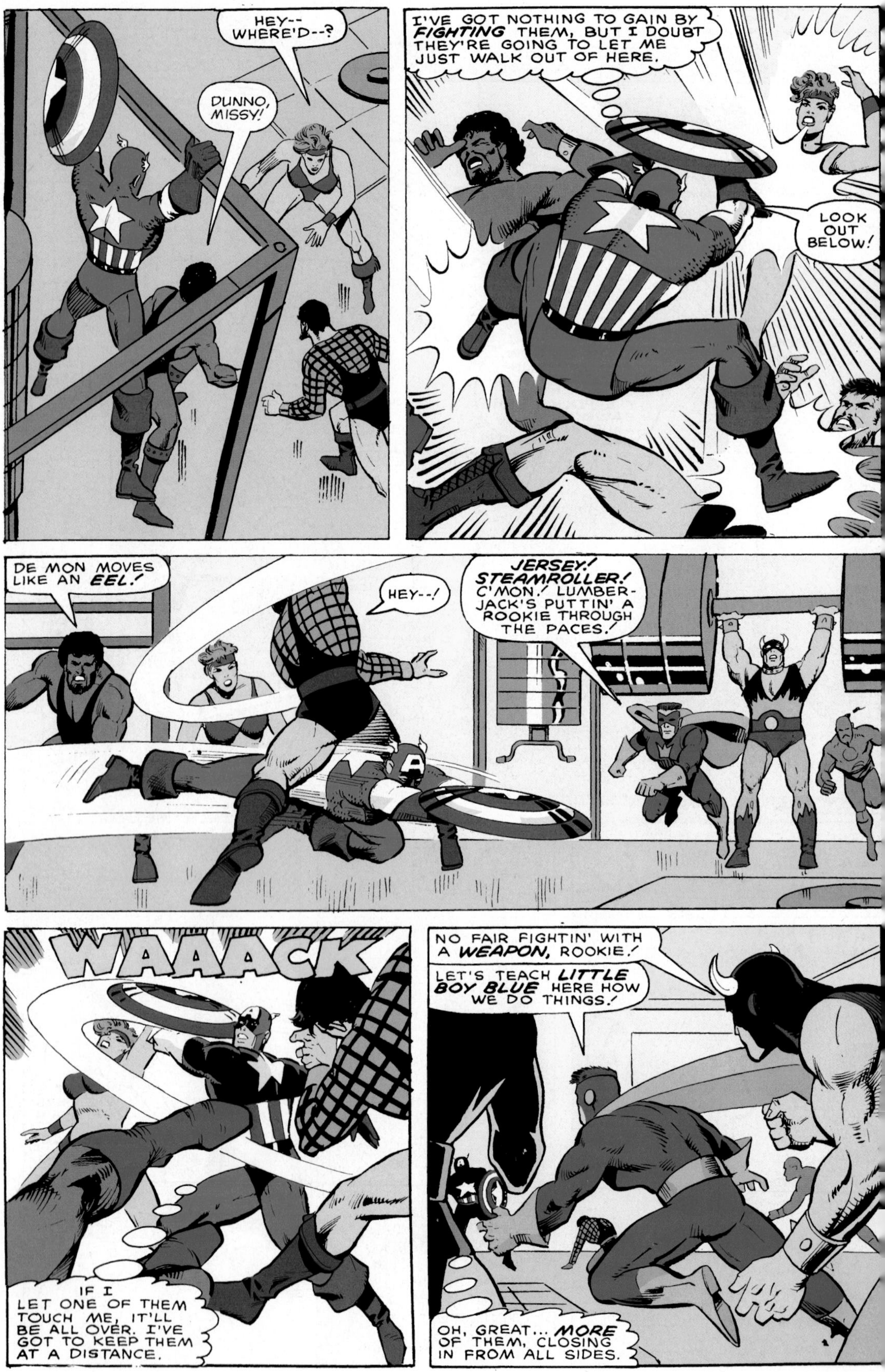
HEY-- WHERE'D--?
DUNNO, MISSY!
I'VE GOT NOTHING TO GAIN BY FIGHTING THEM, BUT I DOUBT THEY'RE GOING TO LET ME JUST WALK OUT OF HERE.
LOOK OUT BELOW!
DE MON MOVES LIKE AN EEL!
HEY--!
JERSEY! STEAMROLLER! C'MON! LUMBERJACK'S PUTTIN' A ROOKIE THROUGH THE PACES!
WAAACK
IF I LET ONE OF THEM TOUCH ME, IT'LL BE ALL OVER. I'VE GOT TO KEEP THEM AT A DISTANCE.
NO FAIR FIGHTIN' WITH A WEAPON, ROOKIE!
LET'S TEACH LITTLE BOY BLUE HERE HOW WE DO THINGS!
OH, GREAT... MORE OF THEM, CLOSING IN FROM ALL SIDES.

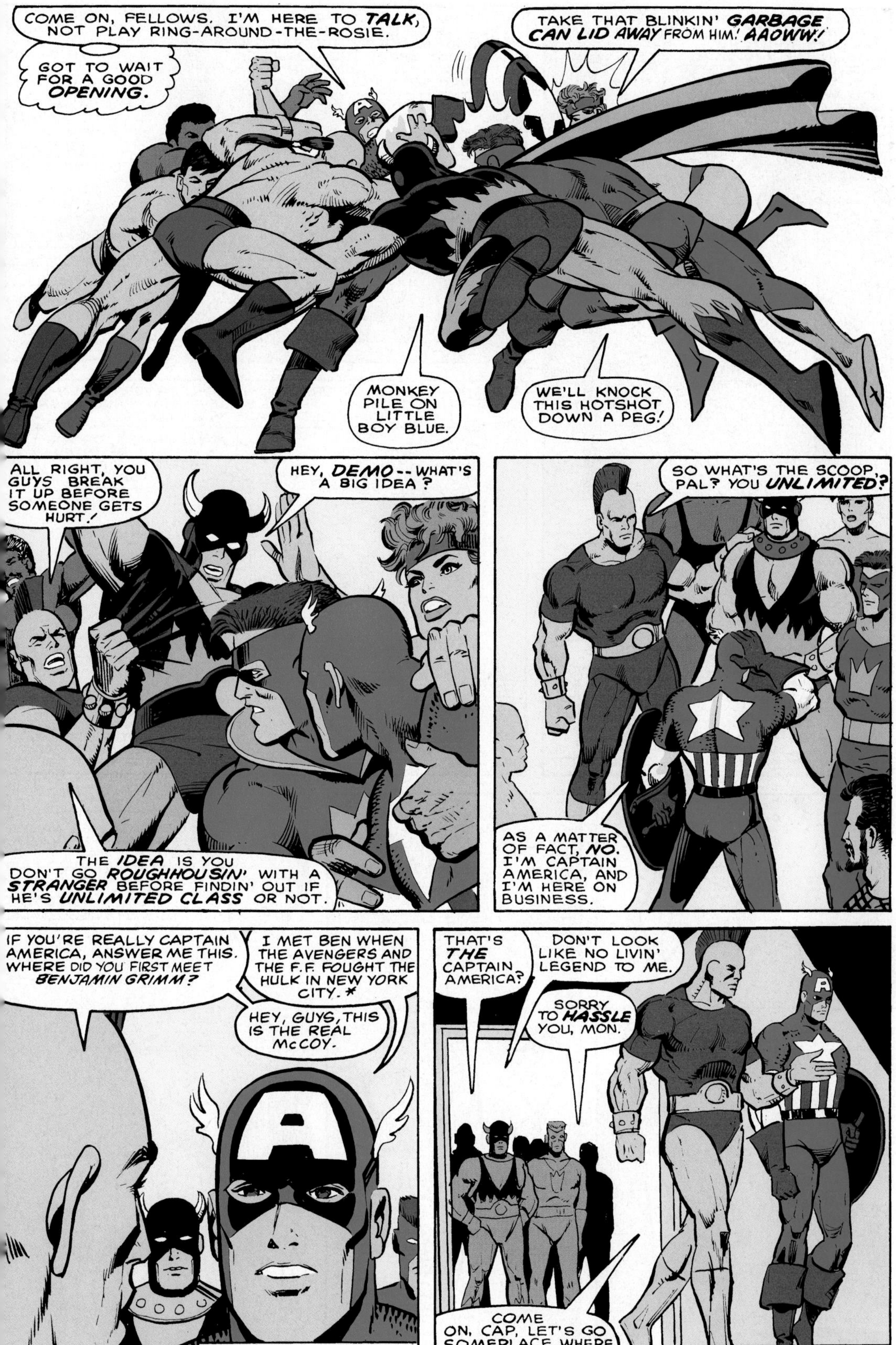
COME ON, FELLOWS. I'M HERE TO TALK, NOT PLAY RING-AROUND-THE-ROSIE.
GOT TO WAIT FOR A GOOD OPENING.
TAKE THAT BLINKIN' GARBAGE CAN LID AWAY FROM HIM! AAOWW!
MONKEY PILE ON LITTLE BOY BLUE.
WE'LL KNOCK THIS HOTSHOT DOWN A PEG!
ALL RIGHT, YOU GUYS BREAK IT UP BEFORE SOMEONE GETS HURT!
HEY, DEMO -- WHAT'S A BIG IDEA?
THE IDEA IS YOU DON'T GO ROUGHHOUSIN' WITH A STRANGER BEFORE FINDIN' OUT IF HE'S UNLIMITED CLASS OR NOT.
SO WHAT'S THE SCOOP, PAL? YOU UNLIMITED?
AS A MATTER OF FACT, NO. I'M CAPTAIN AMERICA, AND I'M HERE ON BUSINESS.
IF YOU'RE REALLY CAPTAIN AMERICA, ANSWER ME THIS. WHERE DID YOU FIRST MEET BENJAMIN GRIMM?
I MET BEN WHEN THE AVENGERS AND THE F.F. FOUGHT THE HULK IN NEW YORK CITY. *
HEY, GUYS, THIS IS THE REAL McCOY.
* SPECIFICALLY ON EAST 63RD ST. IN FF #26.
THAT'S THE CAPTAIN AMERICA?
DON'T LOOK LIKE NO LIVIN' LEGEND TO ME.
SORRY TO HASSLE YOU, MON.
COME ON, CAP, LET'S GO SOMEPLACE WHERE WE CAN HEAR OURSELVES TALK.

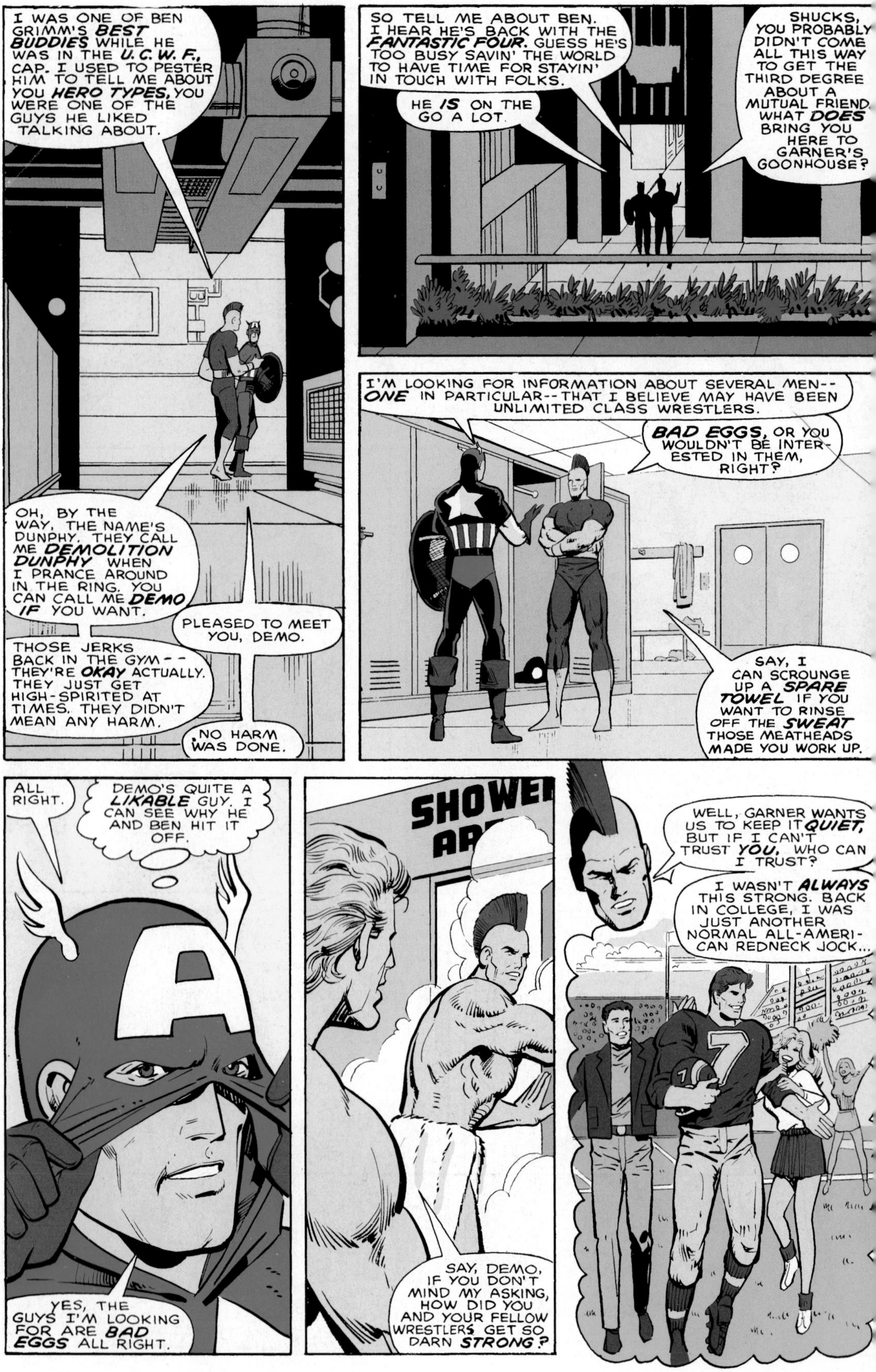

I WAS ONE OF BEN GRIMM'S BEST BUDDIES WHILE HE WAS IN THE U.C.W.F., CAP. I USED TO PESTER HIM TO TELL ME ABOUT YOU HERO TYPES. YOU WERE ONE OF THE GUYS HE LIKED TALKING ABOUT.
OH, BY THE WAY, THE NAME'S DUNPHY. THEY CALL ME DEMOLITION DUNPHY WHEN I PRANCE AROUND IN THE RING. YOU CAN CALL ME DEMO IF YOU WANT.
PLEASED TO MEET YOU, DEMO.
THOSE JERKS BACK IN THE GYM--THEY'RE OKAY ACTUALLY. THEY JUST GET HIGH-SPIRITED AT TIMES. THEY DIDN'T MEAN ANY HARM.
NO HARM WAS DONE.
SO TELL ME ABOUT BEN. I HEAR HE'S BACK WITH THE FANTASTIC FOUR. GUESS HE'S TOO BUSY SAVIN' THE WORLD TO HAVE TIME FOR STAYIN' IN TOUCH WITH FOLKS.
HE IS ON THE GO A LOT.
SHUCKS, YOU PROBABLY DIDN'T COME ALL THIS WAY TO GET THE THIRD DEGREE ABOUT A MUTUAL FRIEND. WHAT DOES BRING YOU HERE TO GARNER'S GOONHOUSE?
I'M LOOKING FOR INFORMATION ABOUT SEVERAL MEN--ONE IN PARTICULAR--THAT I BELIEVE MAY HAVE BEEN UNLIMITED CLASS WRESTLERS.
BAD EGGS, OR YOU WOULDN'T BE INTERESTED IN THEM, RIGHT?
SAY, I CAN SCROUNGE UP A SPARE TOWEL IF YOU WANT TO RINSE OFF THE SWEAT THOSE MEATHEADS MADE YOU WORK UP.
ALL RIGHT.
DEMO'S QUITE A LIKABLE GUY. I CAN SEE WHY HE AND BEN HIT IT OFF.
YES, THE GUYS I'M LOOKING FOR ARE BAD EGGS ALL RIGHT.
SHOWER AR
SAY, DEMO, IF YOU DON'T MIND MY ASKING, HOW DID YOU AND YOUR FELLOW WRESTLERS GET SO DARN STRONG?
WELL, GARNER WANTS US TO KEEP IT QUIET, BUT IF I CAN'T TRUST YOU, WHO CAN I TRUST?
I WASN'T ALWAYS THIS STRONG. BACK IN COLLEGE, I WAS JUST ANOTHER NORMAL ALL-AMERICAN REDNECK JOCK...

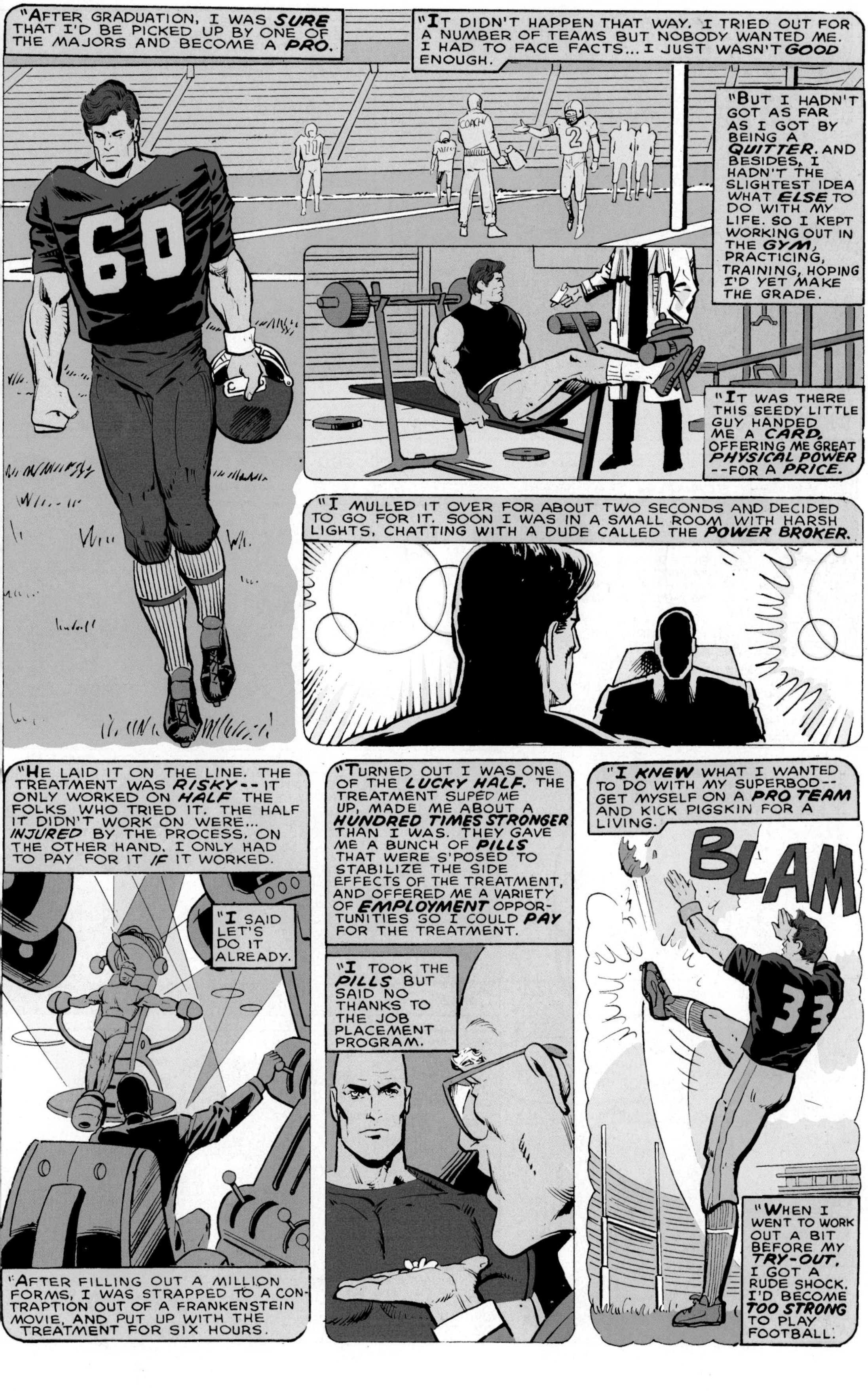
"AFTER GRADUATION, I WAS SURE THAT I'D BE PICKED UP BY ONE OF THE MAJORS AND BECOME A PRO.
"IT DIDN'T HAPPEN THAT WAY. I TRIED OUT FOR A NUMBER OF TEAMS BUT NOBODY WANTED ME. I HAD TO FACE FACTS... I JUST WASN'T GOOD ENOUGH.
COACH
"BUT I HADN'T GOT AS FAR AS I GOT BY BEING A QUITTER. AND BESIDES, I HADN'T THE SLIGHTEST IDEA WHAT ELSE TO DO WITH MY LIFE. SO I KEPT WORKING OUT IN THE GYM, PRACTICING, TRAINING, HOPING I'D YET MAKE THE GRADE.
"IT WAS THERE THIS SEEDY LITTLE GUY HANDED ME A CARD, OFFERING ME GREAT PHYSICAL POWER --FOR A PRICE.
"I MULLED IT OVER FOR ABOUT TWO SECONDS AND DECIDED TO GO FOR IT. SOON I WAS IN A SMALL ROOM WITH HARSH LIGHTS, CHATTING WITH A DUDE CALLED THE POWER BROKER.
"HE LAID IT ON THE LINE. THE TREATMENT WAS RISKY -- IT ONLY WORKED ON HALF THE FOLKS WHO TRIED IT. THE HALF IT DIDN'T WORK ON WERE... INJURED BY THE PROCESS. ON THE OTHER HAND, I ONLY HAD TO PAY FOR IT IF IT WORKED.
"I SAID LET'S DO IT ALREADY.
"AFTER FILLING OUT A MILLION FORMS, I WAS STRAPPED TO A CONTRAPTION OUT OF A FRANKENSTEIN MOVIE, AND PUT UP WITH THE TREATMENT FOR SIX HOURS.
"TURNED OUT I WAS ONE OF THE LUCKY HALF. THE TREATMENT SUPED ME UP, MADE ME ABOUT A HUNDRED TIMES STRONGER THAN I WAS. THEY GAVE ME A BUNCH OF PILLS THAT WERE S'POSED TO STABILIZE THE SIDE EFFECTS OF THE TREATMENT, AND OFFERED ME A VARIETY OF EMPLOYMENT OPPORTUNITIES SO I COULD PAY FOR THE TREATMENT.
"I TOOK THE PILLS BUT SAID NO THANKS TO THE JOB PLACEMENT PROGRAM.
"I KNEW WHAT I WANTED TO DO WITH MY SUPERBOD-- GET MYSELF ON A PRO TEAM AND KICK PIGSKIN FOR A LIVING.
BLAM
"WHEN I WENT TO WORK OUT A BIT BEFORE MY TRY-OUT, I GOT A RUDE SHOCK. I'D BECOME TOO STRONG TO PLAY FOOTBALL.

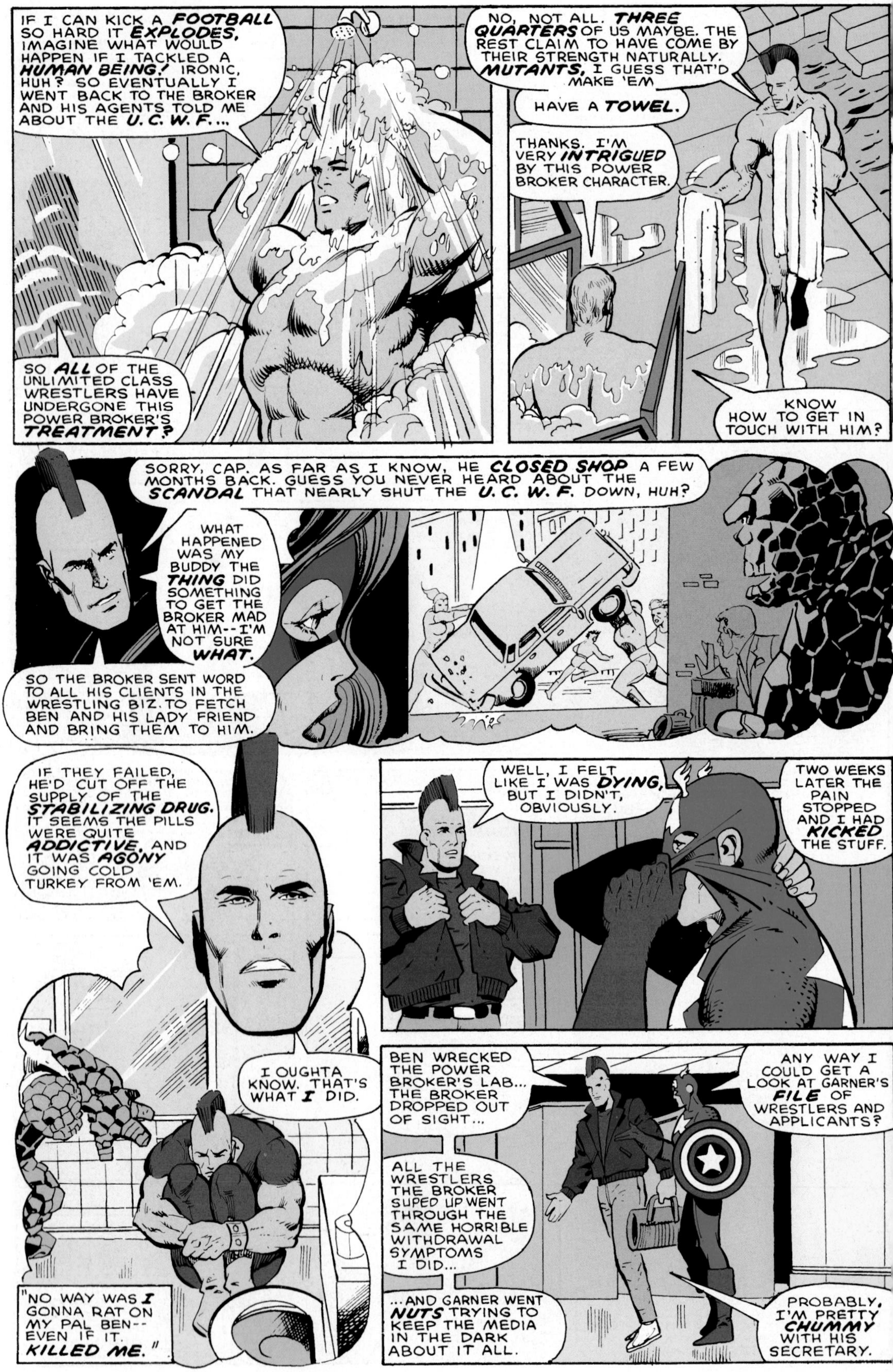
IF I CAN KICK A FOOTBALL SO HARD IT EXPLODES, IMAGINE WHAT WOULD HAPPEN IF I TACKLED A HUMAN BEING! IRONIC, HUH? SO EVENTUALLY I WENT BACK TO THE BROKER AND HIS AGENTS TOLD ME ABOUT THE U.C.W.F....
SO ALL OF THE UNLIMITED CLASS WRESTLERS HAVE UNDERGONE THIS POWER BROKER'S TREATMENT?
NO, NOT ALL. THREE QUARTERS OF US MAYBE. THE REST CLAIM TO HAVE COME BY THEIR STRENGTH NATURALLY. MUTANTS, I GUESS THAT'D MAKE 'EM
HAVE A TOWEL.
THANKS. I'M VERY INTRIGUED BY THIS POWER BROKER CHARACTER.
KNOW HOW TO GET IN TOUCH WITH HIM?
SORRY, CAP. AS FAR AS I KNOW, HE CLOSED SHOP A FEW MONTHS BACK. GUESS YOU NEVER HEARD ABOUT THE SCANDAL THAT NEARLY SHUT THE U.C.W.F. DOWN, HUH?
WHAT HAPPENED WAS MY BUDDY THE THING DID SOMETHING TO GET THE BROKER MAD AT HIM--I'M NOT SURE WHAT.
SO THE BROKER SENT WORD TO ALL HIS CLIENTS IN THE WRESTLING BIZ TO FETCH BEN AND HIS LADY FRIEND AND BRING THEM TO HIM.
IF THEY FAILED, HE'D CUT OFF THE SUPPLY OF THE STABILIZING DRUG. IT SEEMS THE PILLS WERE QUITE ADDICTIVE, AND IT WAS AGONY GOING COLD TURKEY FROM 'EM.
I OUGHTA KNOW. THAT'S WHAT I DID.
"NO WAY WAS I GONNA RAT ON MY PAL BEN-- EVEN IF IT KILLED ME."
WELL, I FELT LIKE I WAS DYING, BUT I DIDN'T, OBVIOUSLY.
TWO WEEKS LATER THE PAIN STOPPED AND I HAD KICKED THE STUFF.
BEN WRECKED THE POWER BROKER'S LAB... THE BROKER DROPPED OUT OF SIGHT...
ALL THE WRESTLERS THE BROKER SUPED UP WENT THROUGH THE SAME HORRIBLE WITHDRAWAL SYMPTOMS I DID...
...AND GARNER WENT NUTS TRYING TO KEEP THE MEDIA IN THE DARK ABOUT IT ALL.
ANY WAY I COULD GET A LOOK AT GARNER'S FILE OF WRESTLERS AND APPLICANTS?
PROBABLY. I'M PRETTY CHUMMY WITH HIS SECRETARY.

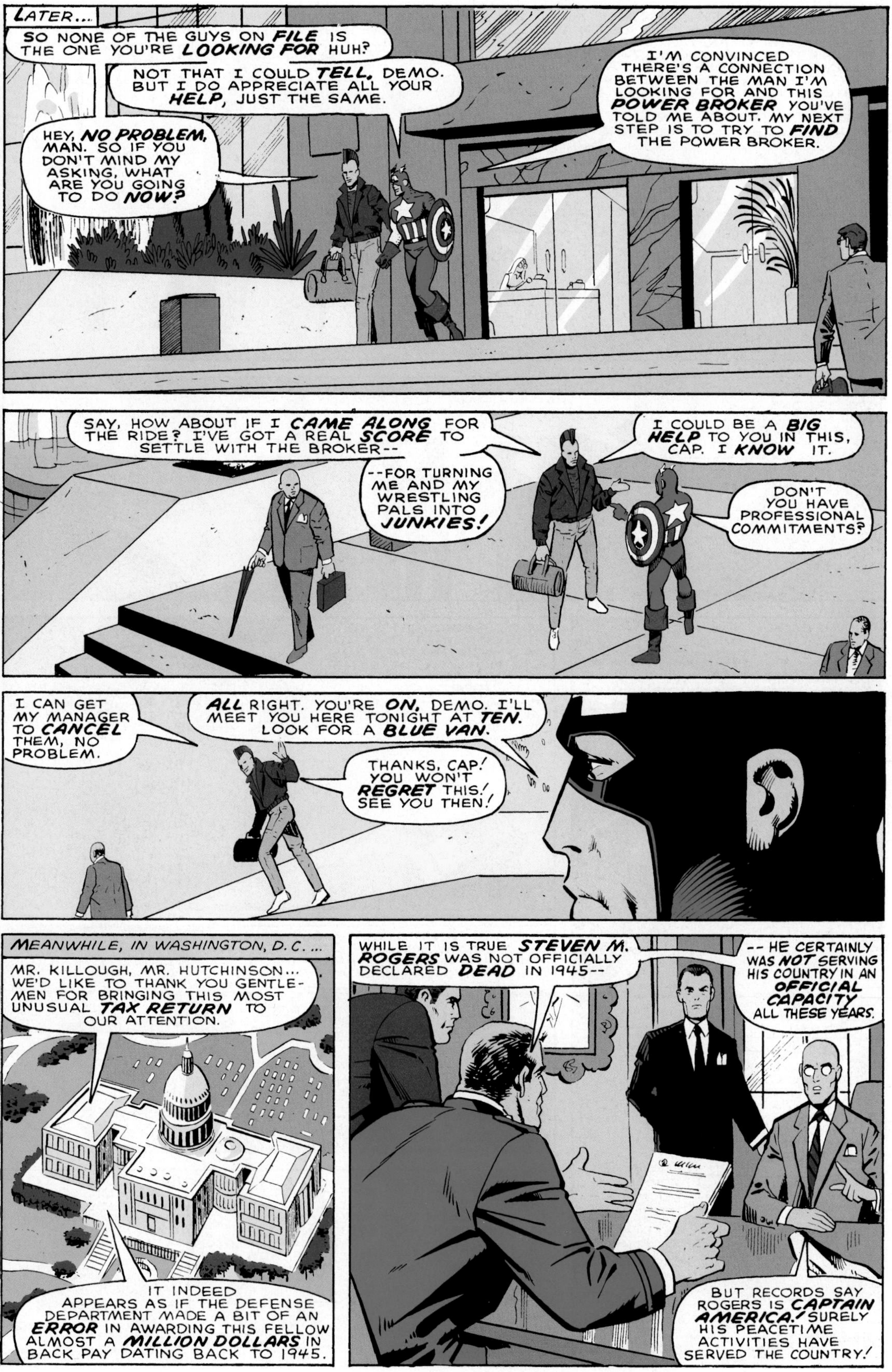
LATER...
SO NONE OF THE GUYS ON FILE IS THE ONE YOU'RE LOOKING FOR HUH?
NOT THAT I COULD TELL, DEMO. BUT I DO APPRECIATE ALL YOUR HELP, JUST THE SAME.
I'M CONVINCED THERE'S A CONNECTION BETWEEN THE MAN I'M LOOKING FOR AND THIS POWER BROKER YOU'VE TOLD ME ABOUT. MY NEXT STEP IS TO TRY TO FIND THE POWER BROKER.
HEY, NO PROBLEM, MAN. SO IF YOU DON'T MIND MY ASKING, WHAT ARE YOU GOING TO DO NOW?
SAY, HOW ABOUT IF I CAME ALONG FOR THE RIDE? I'VE GOT A REAL SCORE TO SETTLE WITH THE BROKER--
--FOR TURNING ME AND MY WRESTLING PALS INTO JUNKIES!
I COULD BE A BIG HELP TO YOU IN THIS, CAP. I KNOW IT.
DON'T YOU HAVE PROFESSIONAL COMMITMENTS?
I CAN GET MY MANAGER TO CANCEL THEM, NO PROBLEM.
ALL RIGHT. YOU'RE ON, DEMO. I'LL MEET YOU HERE TONIGHT AT TEN. LOOK FOR A BLUE VAN.
THANKS, CAP! YOU WON'T REGRET THIS! SEE YOU THEN!
MEANWHILE, IN WASHINGTON, D.C. ...
MR. KILLOUGH, MR. HUTCHINSON... WE'D LIKE TO THANK YOU GENTLEMEN FOR BRINGING THIS MOST UNUSUAL TAX RETURN TO OUR ATTENTION.
IT INDEED APPEARS AS IF THE DEFENSE DEPARTMENT MADE A BIT OF AN ERROR IN AWARDING THIS FELLOW ALMOST A MILLION DOLLARS IN BACK PAY DATING BACK TO 1945.
WHILE IT IS TRUE STEVEN M. ROGERS WAS NOT OFFICIALLY DECLARED DEAD IN 1945--
--HE CERTAINLY WAS NOT SERVING HIS COUNTRY IN AN OFFICIAL CAPACITY ALL THESE YEARS.
BUT RECORDS SAY ROGERS IS CAPTAIN AMERICA! SURELY HIS PEACETIME ACTIVITIES HAVE SERVED THE COUNTRY!

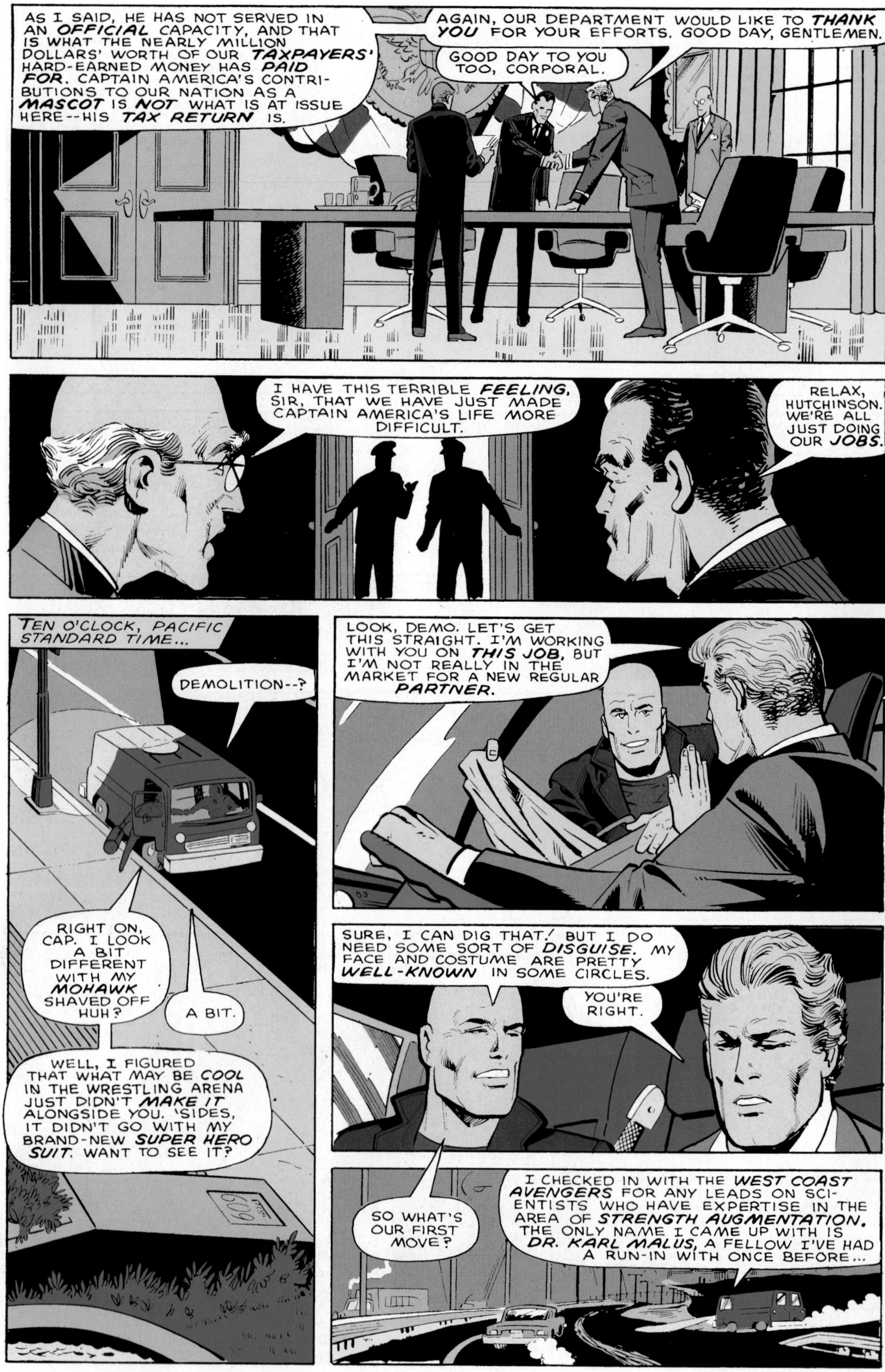

AS I SAID, HE HAS NOT SERVED IN AN OFFICIAL CAPACITY, AND THAT IS WHAT THE NEARLY MILLION DOLLARS' WORTH OF OUR TAXPAYERS' HARD-EARNED MONEY HAS PAID FOR. CAPTAIN AMERICA'S CONTRIBUTIONS TO OUR NATION AS A MASCOT IS NOT WHAT IS AT ISSUE HERE--HIS TAX RETURN IS.
AGAIN, OUR DEPARTMENT WOULD LIKE TO THANK YOU FOR YOUR EFFORTS. GOOD DAY, GENTLEMEN.
GOOD DAY TO YOU TOO, CORPORAL.
I HAVE THIS TERRIBLE FEELING, SIR, THAT WE HAVE JUST MADE CAPTAIN AMERICA'S LIFE MORE DIFFICULT.
RELAX, HUTCHINSON. WE'RE ALL JUST DOING OUR JOBS.
TEN O'CLOCK, PACIFIC STANDARD TIME...
DEMOLITION--?
RIGHT ON, CAP. I LOOK A BIT DIFFERENT WITH MY MOHAWK SHAVED OFF HUH?
A BIT.
WELL, I FIGURED THAT WHAT MAY BE COOL IN THE WRESTLING ARENA JUST DIDN'T MAKE IT ALONGSIDE YOU. 'SIDES, IT DIDN'T GO WITH MY BRAND-NEW SUPER HERO SUIT. WANT TO SEE IT?
LOOK, DEMO. LET'S GET THIS STRAIGHT. I'M WORKING WITH YOU ON THIS JOB, BUT I'M NOT REALLY IN THE MARKET FOR A NEW REGULAR PARTNER.
SURE, I CAN DIG THAT! BUT I DO NEED SOME SORT OF DISGUISE. MY FACE AND COSTUME ARE PRETTY WELL-KNOWN IN SOME CIRCLES.
YOU'RE RIGHT.
SO WHAT'S OUR FIRST MOVE?
I CHECKED IN WITH THE WEST COAST AVENGERS FOR ANY LEADS ON SCIENTISTS WHO HAVE EXPERTISE IN THE AREA OF STRENGTH AUGMENTATION. THE ONLY NAME I CAME UP WITH IS DR. KARL MALUS, A FELLOW I'VE HAD A RUN-IN WITH ONCE BEFORE...

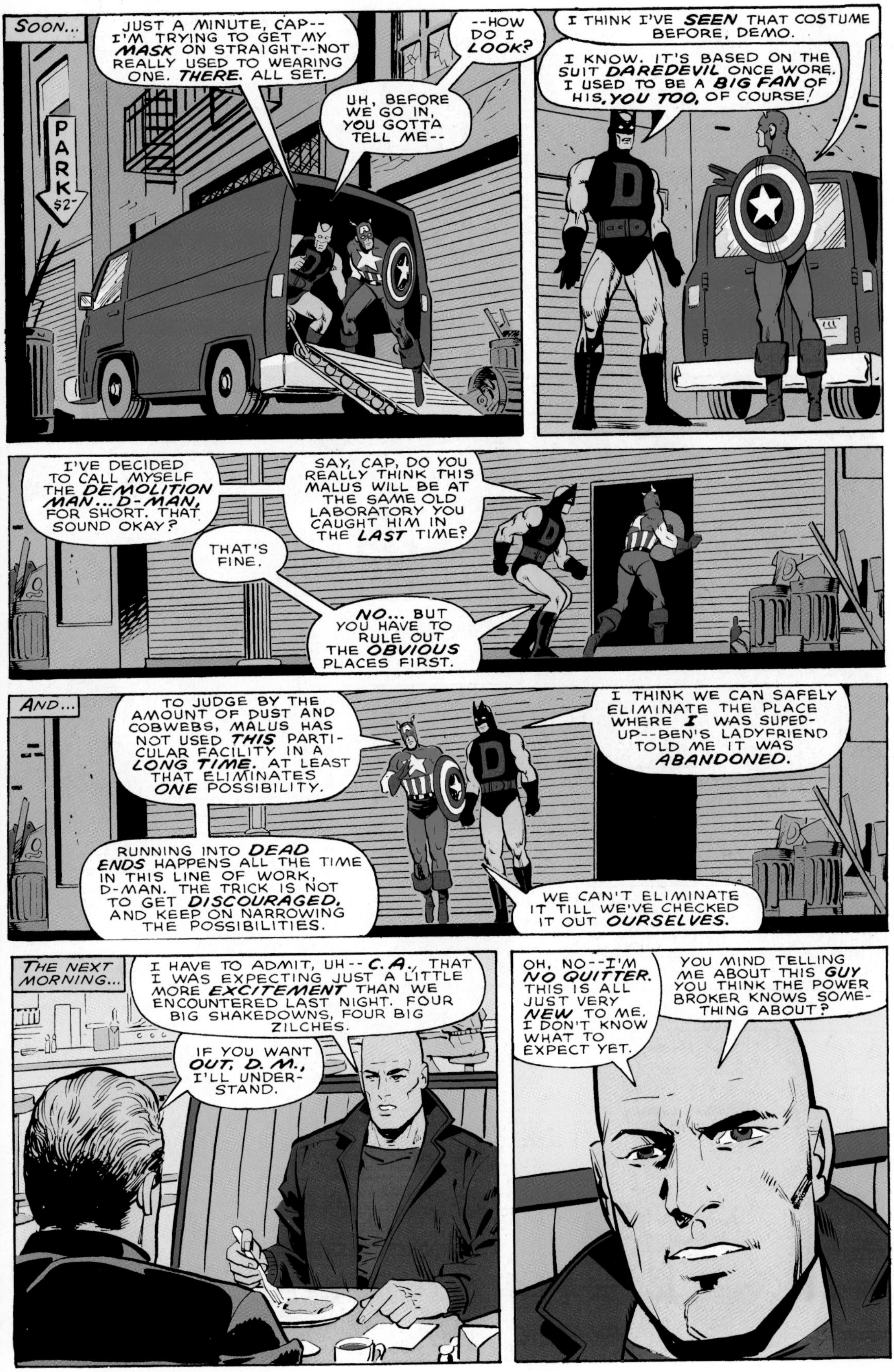
SOON...
JUST A MINUTE, CAP-- I'M TRYING TO GET MY MASK ON STRAIGHT--NOT REALLY USED TO WEARING ONE. THERE. ALL SET.
UH, BEFORE WE GO IN, YOU GOTTA TELL ME--
--HOW DO I LOOK?
PARK $2
I THINK I'VE SEEN THAT COSTUME BEFORE, DEMO.
I KNOW. IT'S BASED ON THE SUIT DAREDEVIL ONCE WORE. I USED TO BE A BIG FAN OF HIS, YOU TOO, OF COURSE!
I'VE DECIDED TO CALL MYSELF THE DEMOLITION MAN...D-MAN, FOR SHORT. THAT SOUND OKAY?
THAT'S FINE.
SAY, CAP, DO YOU REALLY THINK THIS MALUS WILL BE AT THE SAME OLD LABORATORY YOU CAUGHT HIM IN THE LAST TIME?
NO... BUT YOU HAVE TO RULE OUT THE OBVIOUS PLACES FIRST.
AND...
TO JUDGE BY THE AMOUNT OF DUST AND COBWEBS, MALUS HAS NOT USED THIS PARTICULAR FACILITY IN A LONG TIME. AT LEAST THAT ELIMINATES ONE POSSIBILITY.
I THINK WE CAN SAFELY ELIMINATE THE PLACE WHERE I WAS SUPED-UP--BEN'S LADYFRIEND TOLD ME IT WAS ABANDONED.
RUNNING INTO DEAD ENDS HAPPENS ALL THE TIME IN THIS LINE OF WORK, D-MAN. THE TRICK IS NOT TO GET DISCOURAGED, AND KEEP ON NARROWING THE POSSIBILITIES.
WE CAN'T ELIMINATE IT TILL WE'VE CHECKED IT OUT OURSELVES.
THE NEXT MORNING...
I HAVE TO ADMIT, UH-- C.A., THAT I WAS EXPECTING JUST A LITTLE MORE EXCITEMENT THAN WE ENCOUNTERED LAST NIGHT. FOUR BIG SHAKEDOWNS, FOUR BIG ZILCHES.
IF YOU WANT OUT, D.M., I'LL UNDERSTAND.
OH, NO--I'M NO QUITTER. THIS IS ALL JUST VERY NEW TO ME. I DON'T KNOW WHAT TO EXPECT YET.
YOU MIND TELLING ME ABOUT THIS GUY YOU THINK THE POWER BROKER KNOWS SOMETHING ABOUT?

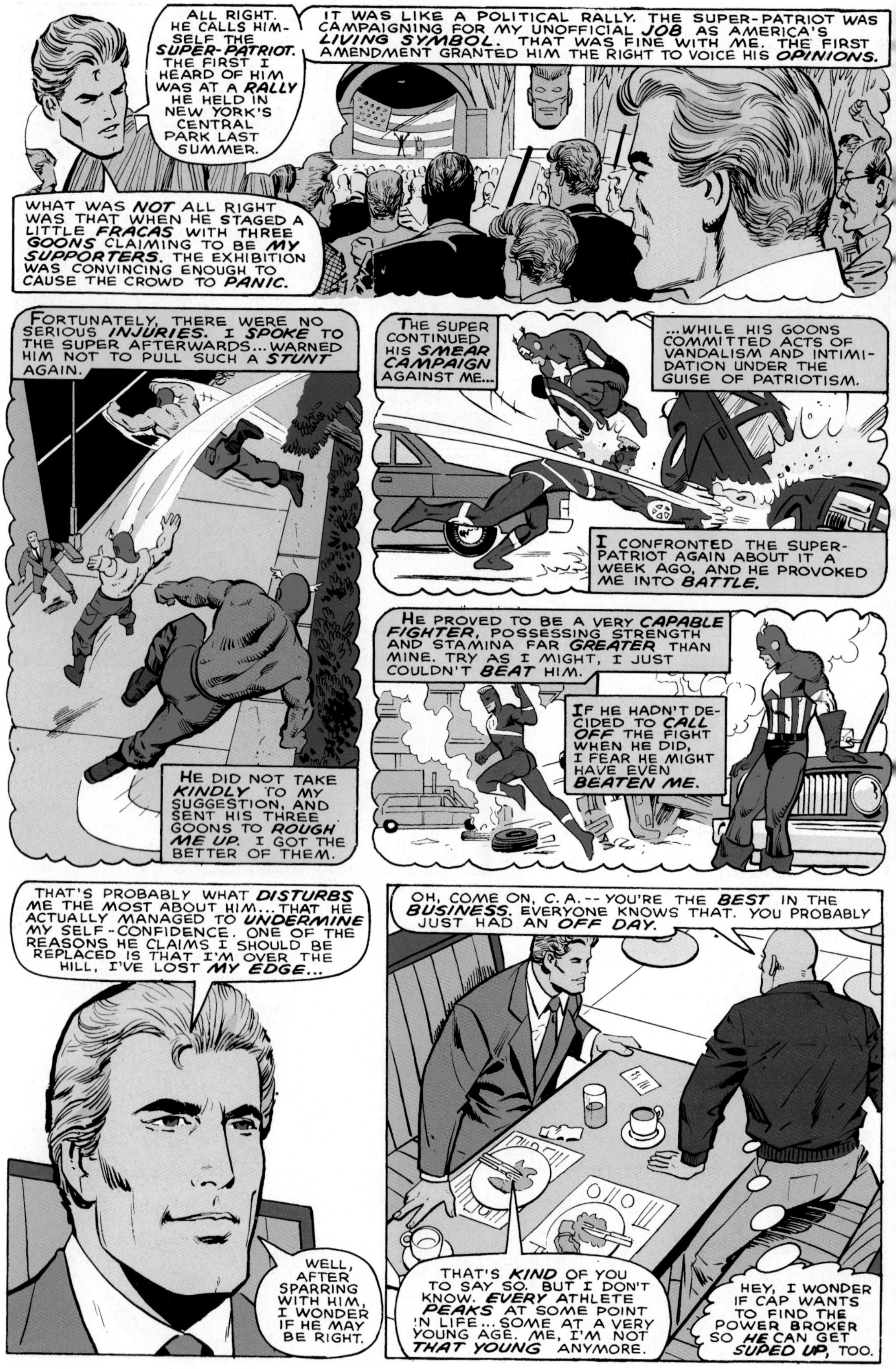
ALL RIGHT. HE CALLS HIMSELF THE SUPER-PATRIOT. THE FIRST I HEARD OF HIM WAS AT A RALLY HE HELD IN NEW YORK'S CENTRAL PARK LAST SUMMER.
IT WAS LIKE A POLITICAL RALLY. THE SUPER-PATRIOT WAS CAMPAIGNING FOR MY UNOFFICIAL JOB AS AMERICA'S LIVING SYMBOL. THAT WAS FINE WITH ME. THE FIRST AMENDMENT GRANTED HIM THE RIGHT TO VOICE HIS OPINIONS.
WHAT WAS NOT ALL RIGHT WAS THAT WHEN HE STAGED A LITTLE FRACAS WITH THREE GOONS CLAIMING TO BE MY SUPPORTERS. THE EXHIBITION WAS CONVINCING ENOUGH TO CAUSE THE CROWD TO PANIC.
FORTUNATELY, THERE WERE NO SERIOUS INJURIES. I SPOKE TO THE SUPER AFTERWARDS... WARNED HIM NOT TO PULL SUCH A STUNT AGAIN.
HE DID NOT TAKE KINDLY TO MY SUGGESTION, AND SENT HIS THREE GOONS TO ROUGH ME UP. I GOT THE BETTER OF THEM.
THE SUPER CONTINUED HIS SMEAR CAMPAIGN AGAINST ME...
...WHILE HIS GOONS COMMITTED ACTS OF VANDALISM AND INTIMIDATION UNDER THE GUISE OF PATRIOTISM.
I CONFRONTED THE SUPER-PATRIOT AGAIN ABOUT IT A WEEK AGO, AND HE PROVOKED ME INTO BATTLE.
HE PROVED TO BE A VERY CAPABLE FIGHTER, POSSESSING STRENGTH AND STAMINA FAR GREATER THAN MINE. TRY AS I MIGHT, I JUST COULDN'T BEAT HIM.
IF HE HADN'T DECIDED TO CALL OFF THE FIGHT WHEN HE DID, I FEAR HE MIGHT HAVE EVEN BEATEN ME.
THAT'S PROBABLY WHAT DISTURBS ME THE MOST ABOUT HIM... THAT HE ACTUALLY MANAGED TO UNDERMINE MY SELF-CONFIDENCE. ONE OF THE REASONS HE CLAIMS I SHOULD BE REPLACED IS THAT I'M OVER THE HILL, I'VE LOST MY EDGE...
WELL, AFTER SPARRING WITH HIM, I WONDER IF HE MAY BE RIGHT.
OH, COME ON, C. A.-- YOU'RE THE BEST IN THE BUSINESS. EVERYONE KNOWS THAT. YOU PROBABLY JUST HAD AN OFF DAY.
THAT'S KIND OF YOU TO SAY SO. BUT I DON'T KNOW. EVERY ATHLETE PEAKS AT SOME POINT IN LIFE... SOME AT A VERY YOUNG AGE. ME, I'M NOT THAT YOUNG ANYMORE.
HEY, I WONDER IF CAP WANTS TO FIND THE POWER BROKER SO HE CAN GET SUPED UP, TOO.

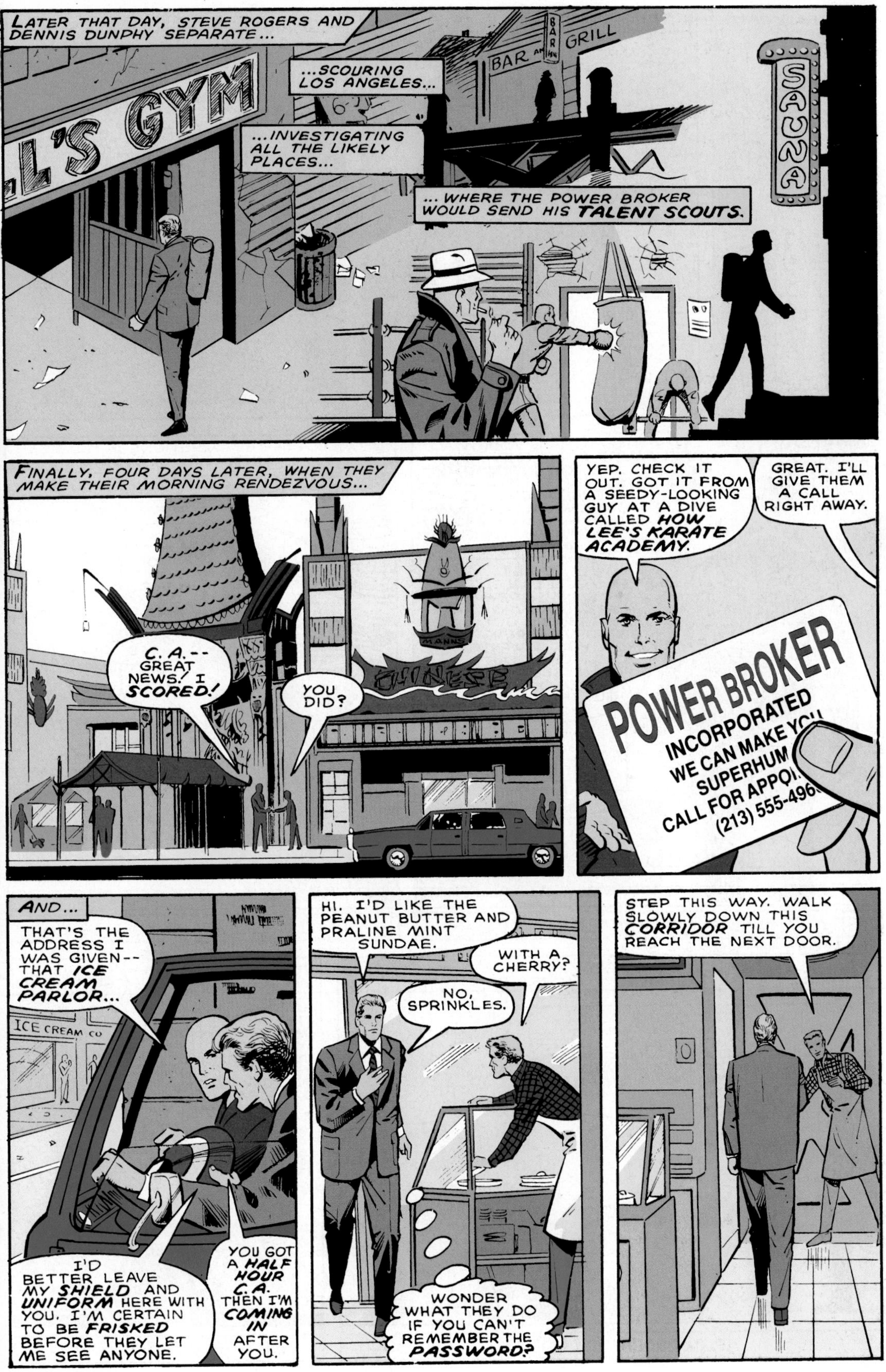

LATER THAT DAY, STEVE ROGERS AND DENNIS DUNPHY SEPARATE...
...SCOURING LOS ANGELES...
...INVESTIGATING ALL THE LIKELY PLACES...
...WHERE THE POWER BROKER WOULD SEND HIS TALENT SCOUTS.
L'S GYM
BAR AND GRILL
SAUNA
FINALLY, FOUR DAYS LATER, WHEN THEY MAKE THEIR MORNING RENDEZVOUS...
C.A.-- GREAT NEWS! I SCORED!
YOU DID?
YEP. CHECK IT OUT. GOT IT FROM A SEEDY-LOOKING GUY AT A DIVE CALLED HOW LEE'S KARATE ACADEMY.
GREAT. I'LL GIVE THEM A CALL RIGHT AWAY.
POWER BROKER
INCORPORATED
WE CAN MAKE YOU
SUPERHUM
CALL FOR APPOI
(213) 555-496
AND...
THAT'S THE ADDRESS I WAS GIVEN-- THAT ICE CREAM PARLOR...
ICE CREAM CO
I'D BETTER LEAVE MY SHIELD AND UNIFORM HERE WITH YOU. I'M CERTAIN TO BE FRISKED BEFORE THEY LET ME SEE ANYONE.
YOU GOT A HALF HOUR C.A. THEN I'M COMING IN AFTER YOU.
HI. I'D LIKE THE PEANUT BUTTER AND PRALINE MINT SUNDAE.
WITH A CHERRY?
NO, SPRINKLES.
WONDER WHAT THEY DO IF YOU CAN'T REMEMBER THE PASSWORD?
STEP THIS WAY. WALK SLOWLY DOWN THIS CORRIDOR TILL YOU REACH THE NEXT DOOR.

THIS HALLWAY'S PROBABLY STUDDED WITH VARIOUS *SCANNING DEVICES.*

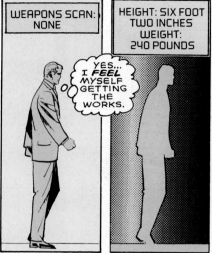

WEAPONS SCAN: NONE

YES... I *FEEL* MYSELF GETTING THE WORKS.

HEIGHT: SIX FOOT TWO INCHES WEIGHT: 240 POUNDS

RESPIRATION RATE: 8PM PERCENTAGE BODY FAT TO WEIGHT: 2%

SURE HOPE I CAN GET SOME *INFORMATION* OUT OF HIM BEFORE MY COVER IS PENETRATED.

LIKENESS SEARCH: NOT ON FILE

FINALLY...

IT'S NICE TO SEE YOU, *MR. STEVENS.* I COMMEND YOUR ABILITY TO FOLLOW INSTRUCTIONS.

NOW COULD YOU TELL ME IN YOUR OWN WORDS *WHY* YOU'D LIKE TO UNDERGO MY STRENGTH-AUGMENTATION PROGRAM?

WELL, I MET THIS GUY, CALLED HIMSELF *SUPER-PATRIOT,* WHO BRAGGED HE GOT SUPED-UP STRENGTH FROM *YOU.* I WANTED TO CHECK IT OUT FOR MYSELF. YOU *HEARD* OF THE GUY, HAVEN'T YOU?

TRUTH PROBABILITY INDEX: 7.8

I WILL ASK THE QUESTIONS IF YOU DON'T MIND, MR. STEVENS.

WHAT WOULD YOU *DO* WITH SUPERHUMAN STRENGTH IF YOU HAD IT?

OH, I DON'T KNOW. *MAKE MONEY* OR *GET FAMOUS* LIKE SUPER-PATRIOT DID.

TRUTH PROBABILITY INDEX: 3.3

YOU ARE NOT TELLING THE *TRUTH,* MR. STEVENS. SPEAK *TRULY* OR YOU WILL BE CATEGORICALLY DENIED THE OPPORTUNITY TO--

OKAY, *OKAY--* LOOK, I WANT TO FIND OUT MORE ABOUT THE *SUPER-PATRIOT--* HE GAVE ME A HARD TIME, MADE ME LOOK LIKE A *CHUMP.* I WANT TO GET HIM BACK.

TRUTH PROBABILITY INDEX: 9.5

I'M SORRY, MR. STEVENS BUT WE RESPECT THE *CONFI-DENTIALITY* OF ALL OUR CLIENTS. ARE YOU A *POLICE OFFICER?*

NO, I--

THIS IS GETTING ME NOWHERE.

TRUTH PROBABILITY INDEX: 5.1

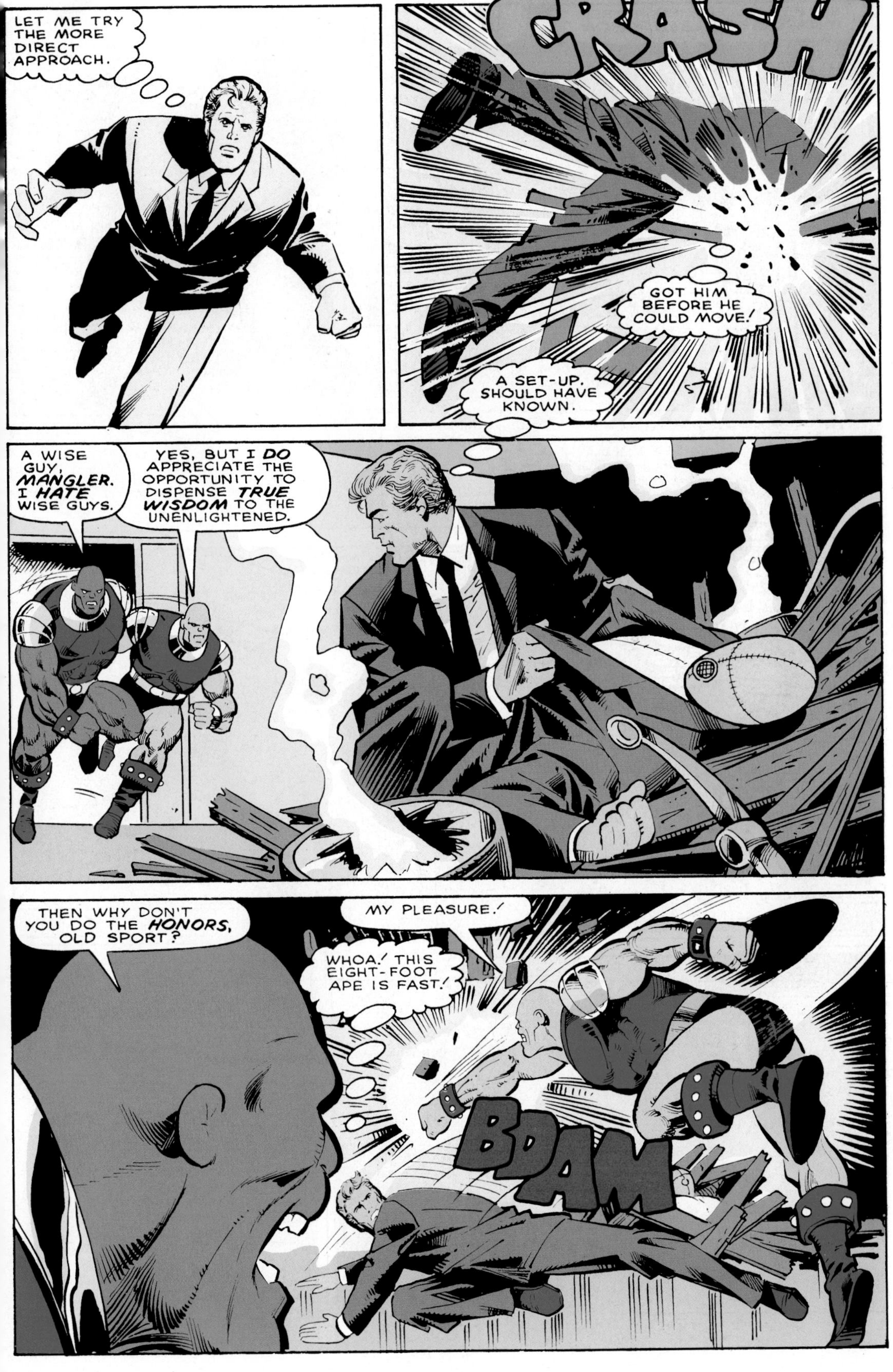

LET ME TRY THE MORE DIRECT APPROACH.
CRASH
GOT HIM BEFORE HE COULD MOVE!
A SET-UP. SHOULD HAVE KNOWN.
A WISE GUY, MANGLER. I HATE WISE GUYS.
YES, BUT I DO APPRECIATE THE OPPORTUNITY TO DISPENSE TRUE WISDOM TO THE UNENLIGHTENED.
THEN WHY DON'T YOU DO THE HONORS, OLD SPORT?
MY PLEASURE!
WHOA! THIS EIGHT-FOOT APE IS FAST!
BDAM

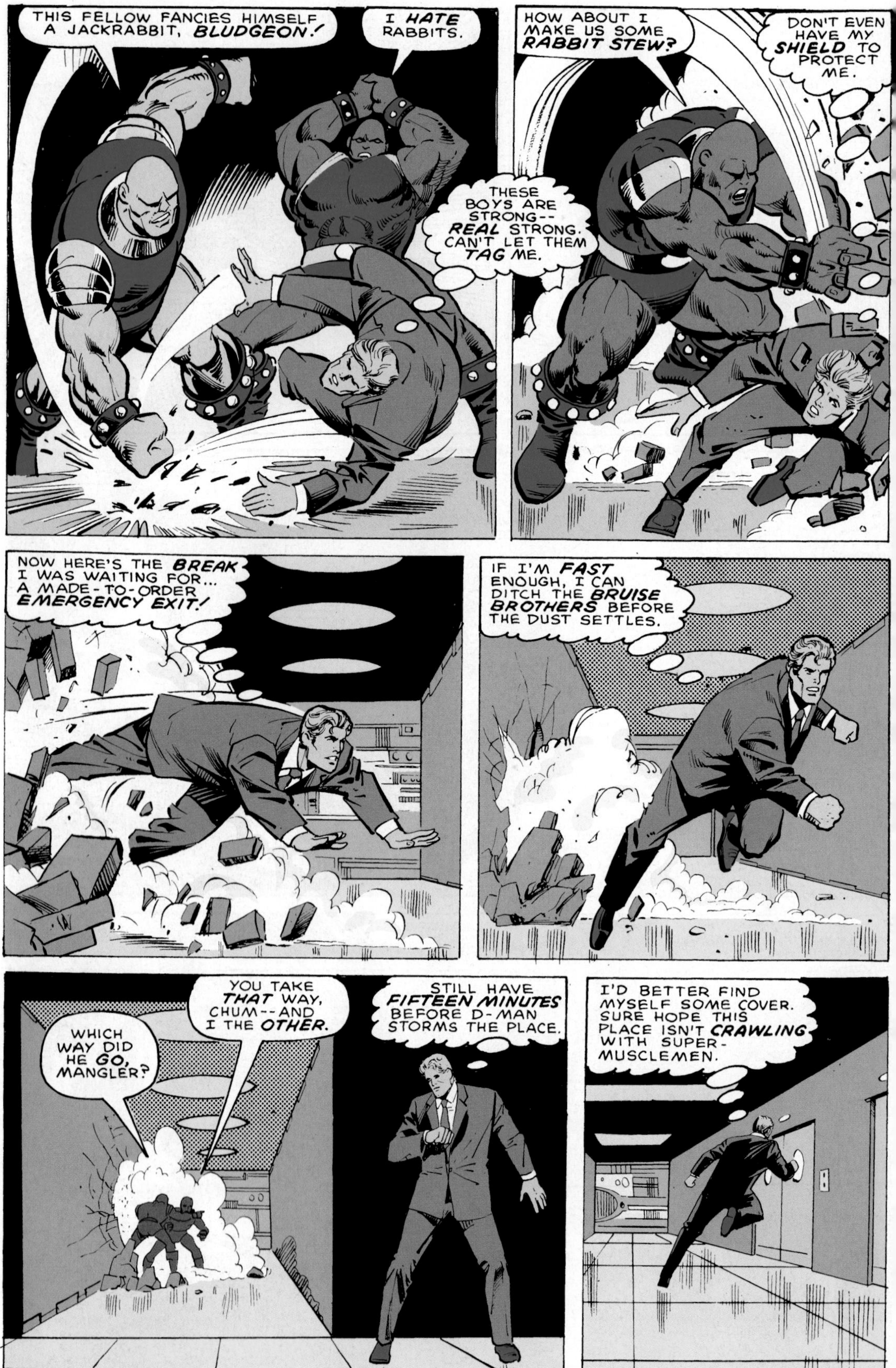
THIS FELLOW FANCIES HIMSELF A JACKRABBIT, BLUDGEON!
I HATE RABBITS.
THESE BOYS ARE STRONG-- REAL STRONG. CAN'T LET THEM TAG ME.
HOW ABOUT I MAKE US SOME RABBIT STEW?
DON'T EVEN HAVE MY SHIELD TO PROTECT ME.
NOW HERE'S THE BREAK I WAS WAITING FOR... A MADE-TO-ORDER EMERGENCY EXIT!
IF I'M FAST ENOUGH, I CAN DITCH THE BRUISE BROTHERS BEFORE THE DUST SETTLES.
WHICH WAY DID HE GO, MANGLER?
YOU TAKE THAT WAY, CHUM--AND I THE OTHER.
STILL HAVE FIFTEEN MINUTES BEFORE D-MAN STORMS THE PLACE.
I'D BETTER FIND MYSELF SOME COVER. SURE HOPE THIS PLACE ISN'T CRAWLING WITH SUPER-MUSCLEMEN.

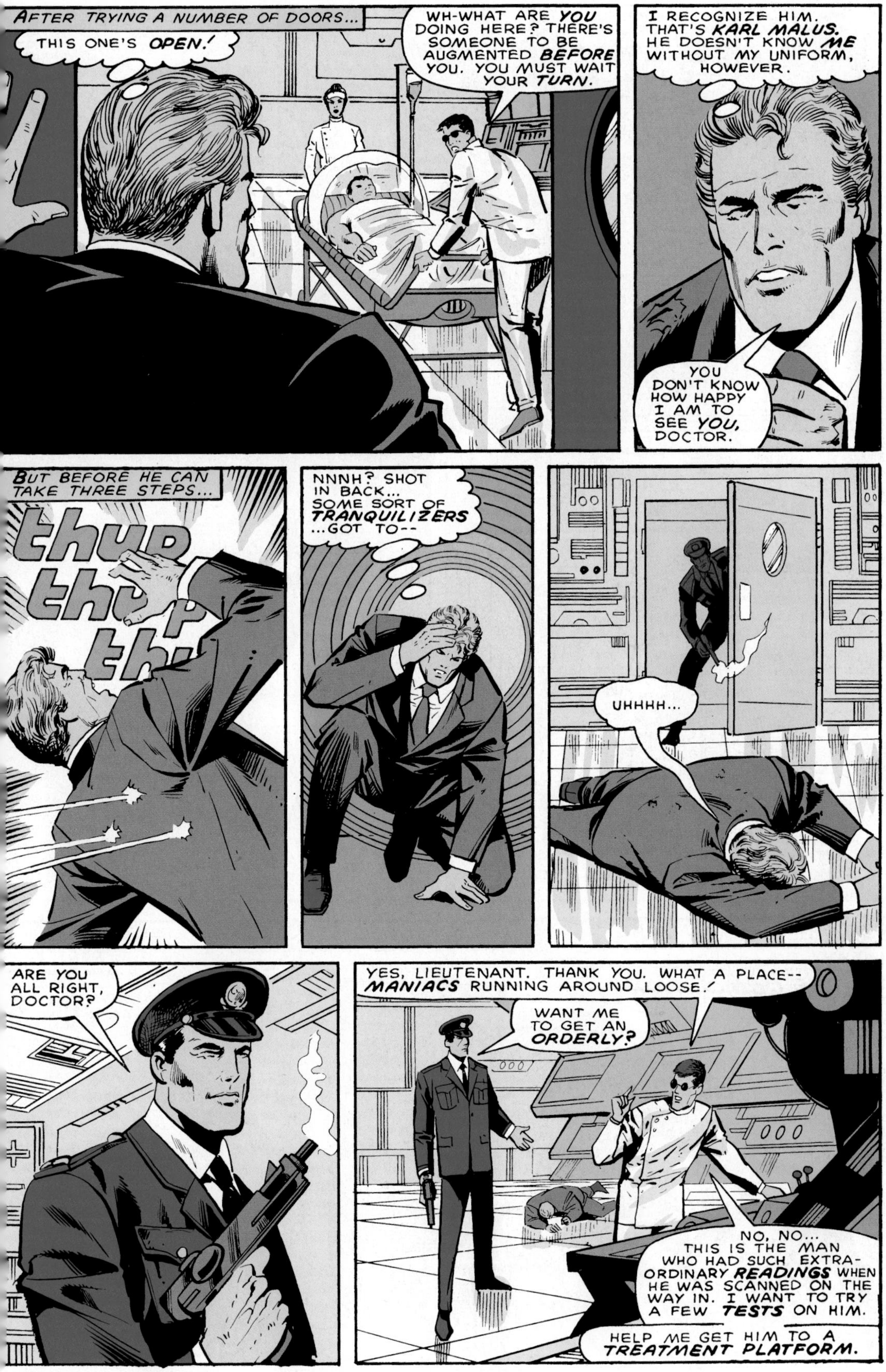
AFTER TRYING A NUMBER OF DOORS...
THIS ONE'S OPEN!
WH-WHAT ARE YOU DOING HERE? THERE'S SOMEONE TO BE AUGMENTED BEFORE YOU. YOU MUST WAIT YOUR TURN.
I RECOGNIZE HIM. THAT'S KARL MALUS. HE DOESN'T KNOW ME WITHOUT MY UNIFORM, HOWEVER.
YOU DON'T KNOW HOW HAPPY I AM TO SEE YOU, DOCTOR.
BUT BEFORE HE CAN TAKE THREE STEPS...
thup thup th
NNNH? SHOT IN BACK... SOME SORT OF TRANQUILIZERS ...GOT TO--
UHHHH...
ARE YOU ALL RIGHT, DOCTOR?
YES, LIEUTENANT. THANK YOU. WHAT A PLACE-- MANIACS RUNNING AROUND LOOSE!
WANT ME TO GET AN ORDERLY?
NO, NO... THIS IS THE MAN WHO HAD SUCH EXTRA-ORDINARY READINGS WHEN HE WAS SCANNED ON THE WAY IN. I WANT TO TRY A FEW TESTS ON HIM.
HELP ME GET HIM TO A TREATMENT PLATFORM.

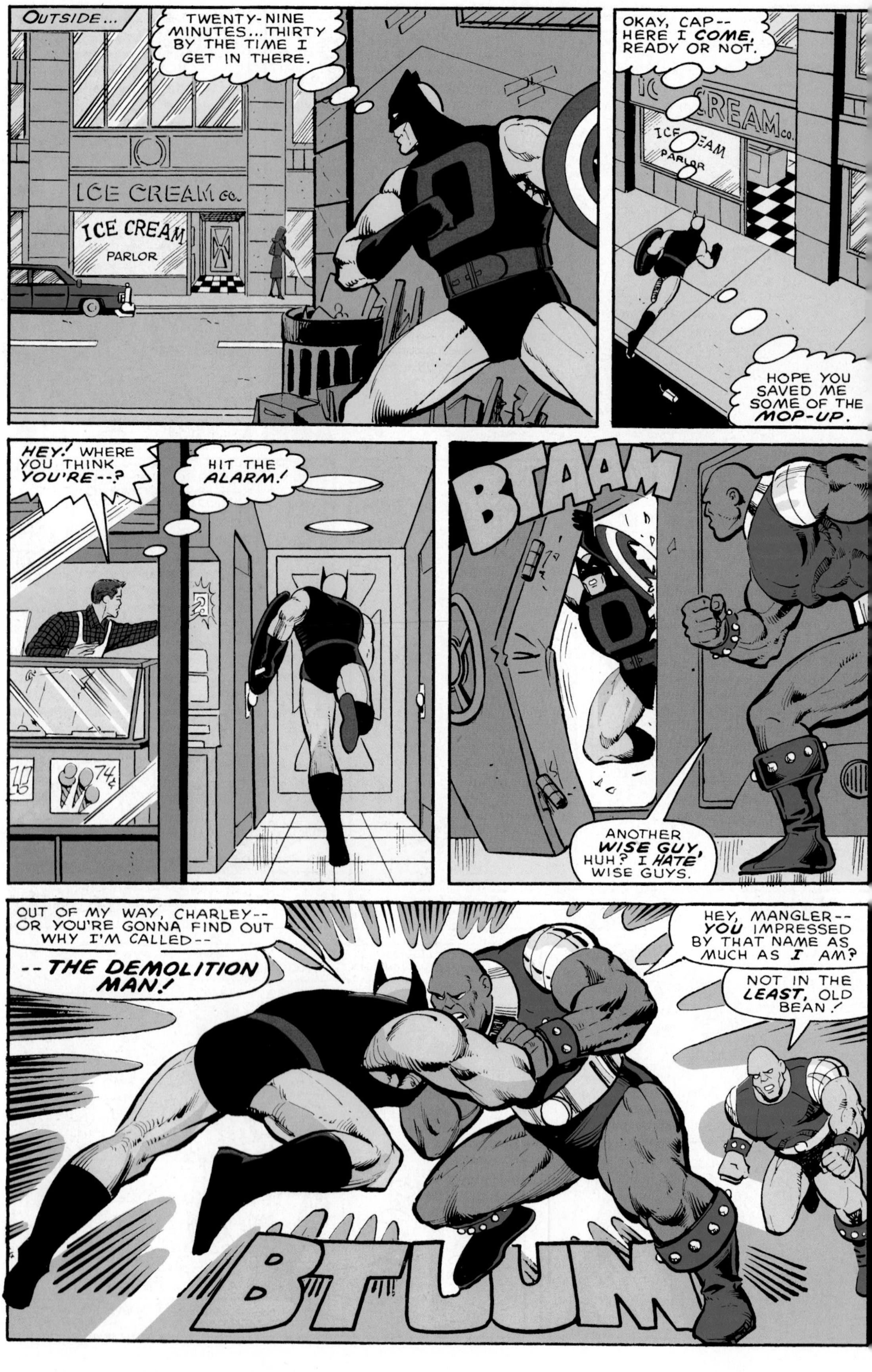
OUTSIDE...
TWENTY-NINE MINUTES... THIRTY BY THE TIME I GET IN THERE.
ICE CREAM CO.
ICE CREAM PARLOR
OKAY, CAP-- HERE I COME, READY OR NOT.
HOPE YOU SAVED ME SOME OF THE MOP-UP.
HEY! WHERE YOU THINK YOU'RE--?
HIT THE ALARM!
BTAAM
ANOTHER WISE GUY, HUH? I HATE WISE GUYS.
OUT OF MY WAY, CHARLEY-- OR YOU'RE GONNA FIND OUT WHY I'M CALLED--
--THE DEMOLITION MAN!
HEY, MANGLER-- YOU IMPRESSED BY THAT NAME AS MUCH AS I AM?
NOT IN THE LEAST, OLD BEAN!
BTUUM

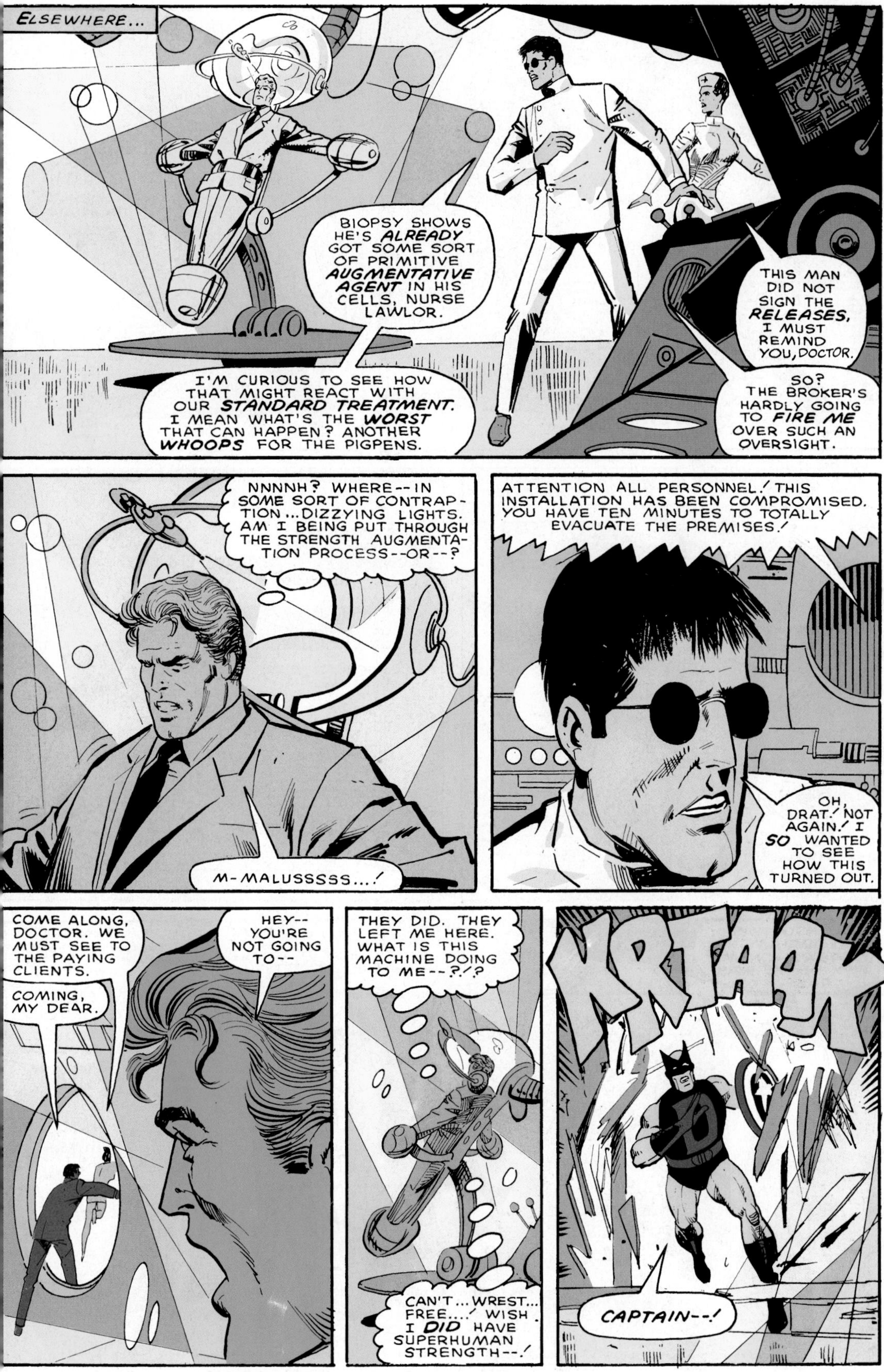
ELSEWHERE...
BIOPSY SHOWS HE'S ALREADY GOT SOME SORT OF PRIMITIVE AUGMENTATIVE AGENT IN HIS CELLS, NURSE LAWLOR.
I'M CURIOUS TO SEE HOW THAT MIGHT REACT WITH OUR STANDARD TREATMENT. I MEAN WHAT'S THE WORST THAT CAN HAPPEN? ANOTHER WHOOPS FOR THE PIGPENS.
THIS MAN DID NOT SIGN THE RELEASES, I MUST REMIND YOU, DOCTOR.
SO? THE BROKER'S HARDLY GOING TO FIRE ME OVER SUCH AN OVERSIGHT.
NNNNH? WHERE--IN SOME SORT OF CONTRAPTION...DIZZYING LIGHTS. AM I BEING PUT THROUGH THE STRENGTH AUGMENTATION PROCESS--OR--?
M-MALUSSSSS...!
ATTENTION ALL PERSONNEL! THIS INSTALLATION HAS BEEN COMPROMISED. YOU HAVE TEN MINUTES TO TOTALLY EVACUATE THE PREMISES!
OH, DRAT! NOT AGAIN! I SO WANTED TO SEE HOW THIS TURNED OUT.
COME ALONG, DOCTOR. WE MUST SEE TO THE PAYING CLIENTS.
COMING, MY DEAR.
HEY-- YOU'RE NOT GOING TO--
THEY DID. THEY LEFT ME HERE. WHAT IS THIS MACHINE DOING TO ME--?!?
CAN'T...WREST... FREE...! WISH I DID HAVE SUPERHUMAN STRENGTH--!
KRTAAK
CAPTAIN--!

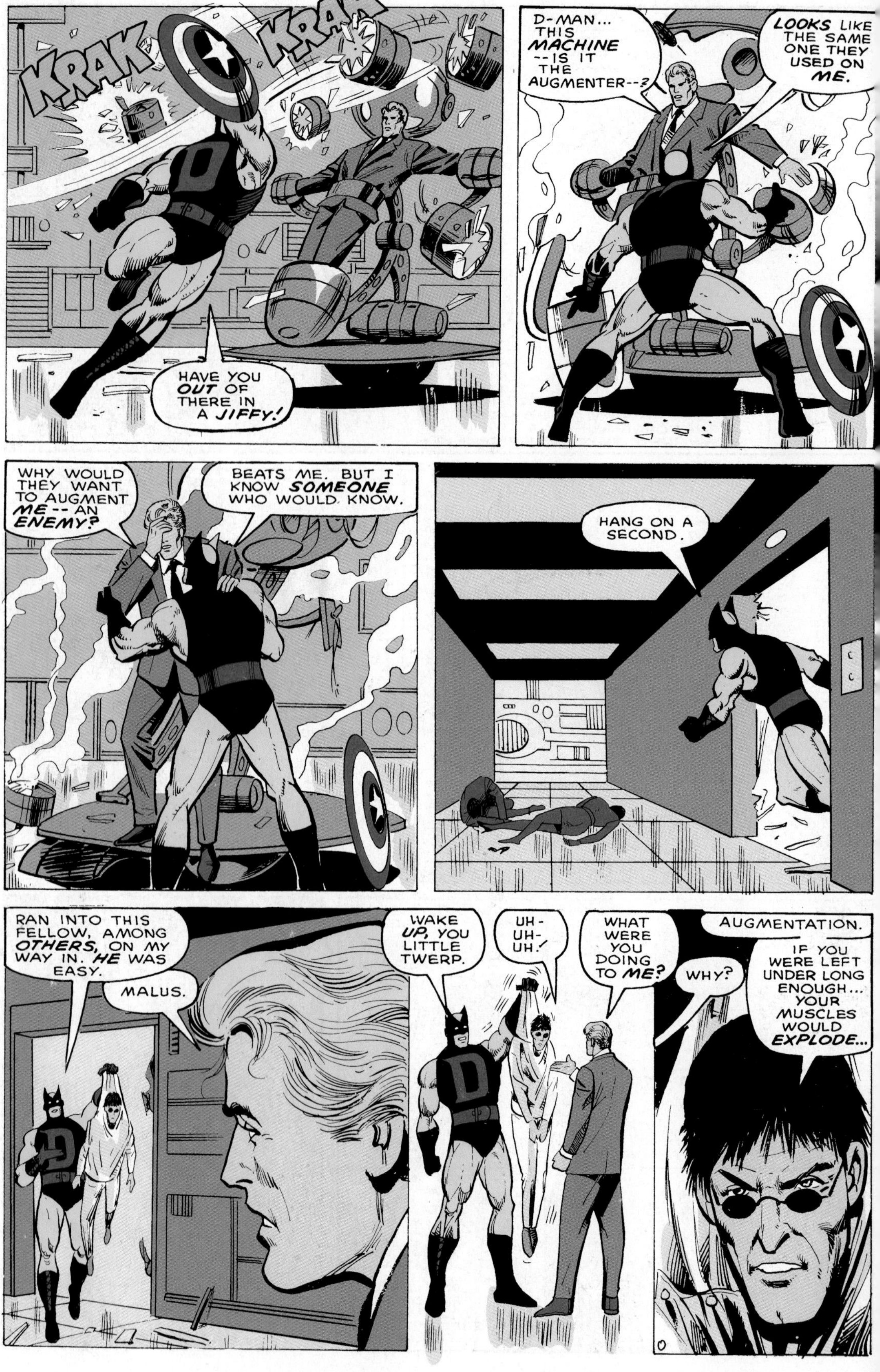
KRAK
KRAK
HAVE YOU OUT OF THERE IN A JIFFY!
D-MAN... THIS MACHINE --IS IT THE AUGMENTER--?
LOOKS LIKE THE SAME ONE THEY USED ON ME.
WHY WOULD THEY WANT TO AUGMENT ME -- AN ENEMY?
BEATS ME. BUT I KNOW SOMEONE WHO WOULD KNOW.
HANG ON A SECOND.
RAN INTO THIS FELLOW, AMONG OTHERS, ON MY WAY IN. HE WAS EASY.
MALUS.
WAKE UP, YOU LITTLE TWERP.
UH- UH- UH!
WHAT WERE YOU DOING TO ME?
WHY?
AUGMENTATION.
IF YOU WERE LEFT UNDER LONG ENOUGH... YOUR MUSCLES WOULD EXPLODE...

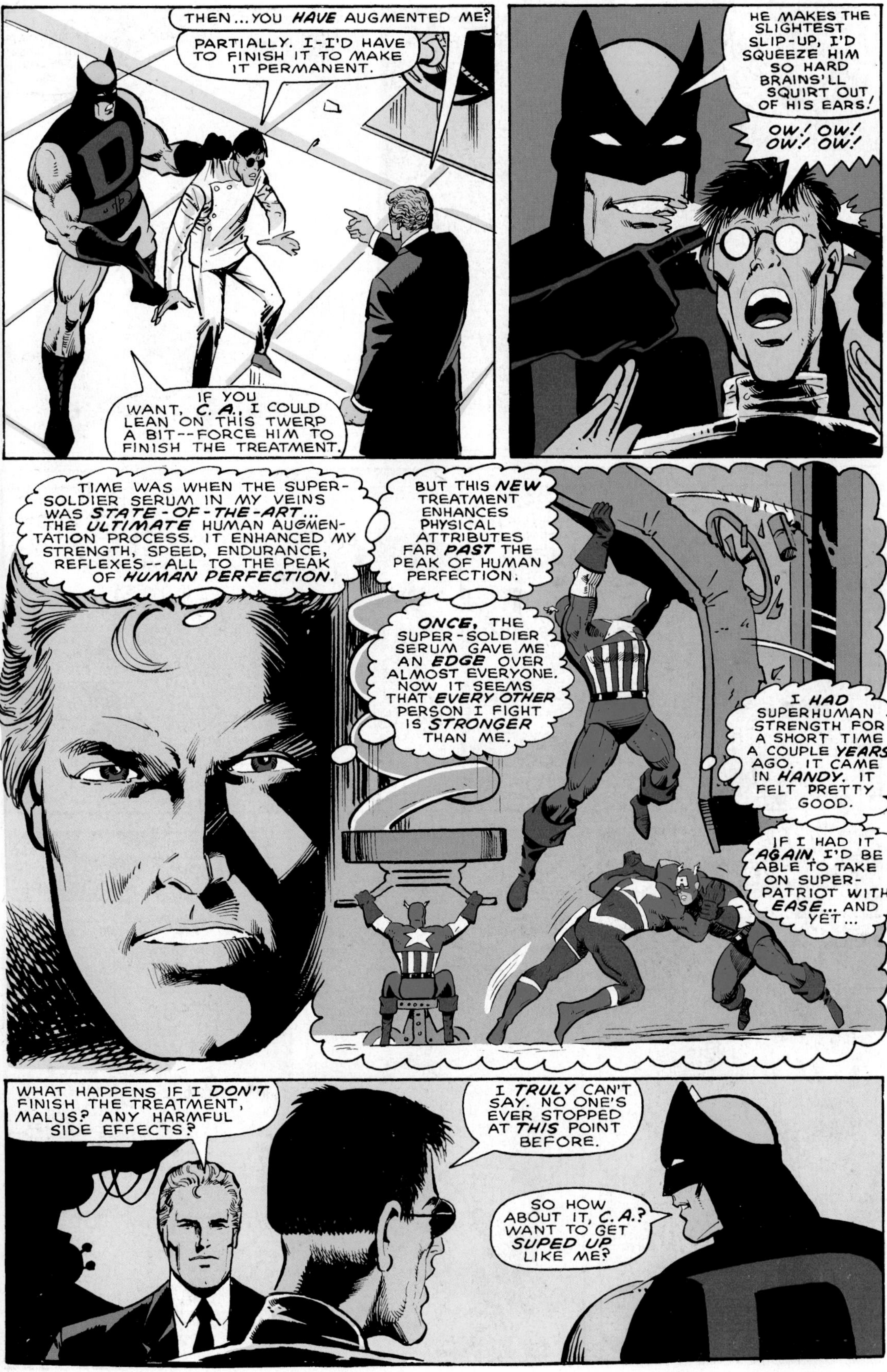
THEN... YOU HAVE AUGMENTED ME?
PARTIALLY. I-I'D HAVE TO FINISH IT TO MAKE IT PERMANENT.
IF YOU WANT, C.A., I COULD LEAN ON THIS TWERP A BIT--FORCE HIM TO FINISH THE TREATMENT.
HE MAKES THE SLIGHTEST SLIP-UP, I'D SQUEEZE HIM SO HARD BRAINS'LL SQUIRT OUT OF HIS EARS!
OW! OW! OW! OW!
TIME WAS WHEN THE SUPER-SOLDIER SERUM IN MY VEINS WAS STATE-OF-THE-ART... THE ULTIMATE HUMAN AUGMENTATION PROCESS. IT ENHANCED MY STRENGTH, SPEED, ENDURANCE, REFLEXES--ALL TO THE PEAK OF HUMAN PERFECTION.
BUT THIS NEW TREATMENT ENHANCES PHYSICAL ATTRIBUTES FAR PAST THE PEAK OF HUMAN PERFECTION.
ONCE, THE SUPER-SOLDIER SERUM GAVE ME AN EDGE OVER ALMOST EVERYONE. NOW IT SEEMS THAT EVERY OTHER PERSON I FIGHT IS STRONGER THAN ME.
I HAD SUPERHUMAN STRENGTH FOR A SHORT TIME A COUPLE YEARS AGO. IT CAME IN HANDY. IT FELT PRETTY GOOD.
IF I HAD IT AGAIN, I'D BE ABLE TO TAKE ON SUPER-PATRIOT WITH EASE... AND YET...
WHAT HAPPENS IF I DON'T FINISH THE TREATMENT, MALUS? ANY HARMFUL SIDE EFFECTS?
I TRULY CAN'T SAY. NO ONE'S EVER STOPPED AT THIS POINT BEFORE.
SO HOW ABOUT IT, C.A.? WANT TO GET SUPED UP LIKE ME?

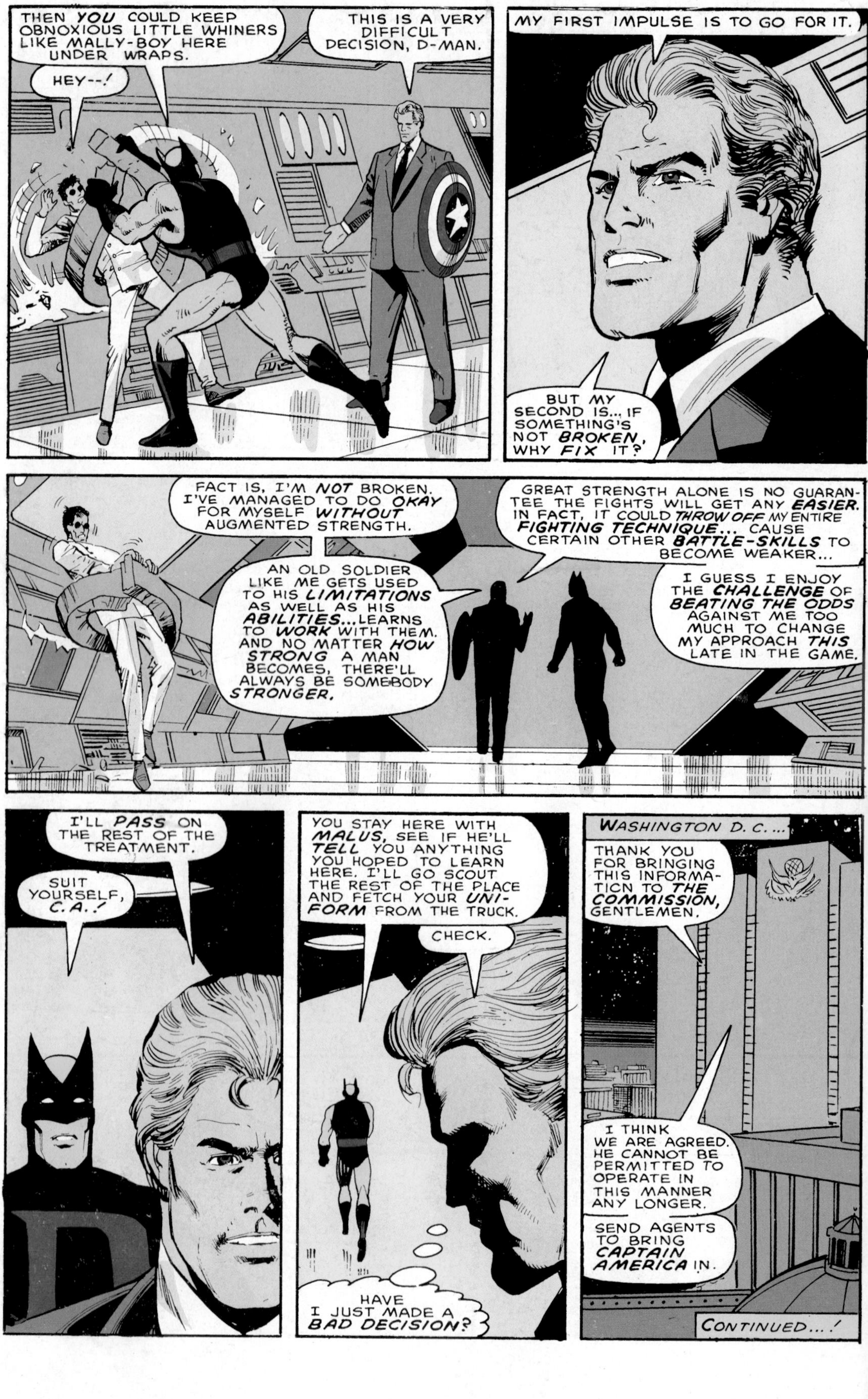
THEN YOU COULD KEEP OBNOXIOUS LITTLE WHINERS LIKE MALLY-BOY HERE UNDER WRAPS.
HEY--!
THIS IS A VERY DIFFICULT DECISION, D-MAN.
MY FIRST IMPULSE IS TO GO FOR IT.
BUT MY SECOND IS... IF SOMETHING'S NOT BROKEN, WHY FIX IT?
FACT IS, I'M NOT BROKEN. I'VE MANAGED TO DO OKAY FOR MYSELF WITHOUT AUGMENTED STRENGTH.
AN OLD SOLDIER LIKE ME GETS USED TO HIS LIMITATIONS AS WELL AS HIS ABILITIES... LEARNS TO WORK WITH THEM. AND NO MATTER HOW STRONG A MAN BECOMES, THERE'LL ALWAYS BE SOMEBODY STRONGER.
GREAT STRENGTH ALONE IS NO GUARANTEE THE FIGHTS WILL GET ANY EASIER. IN FACT, IT COULD THROW OFF MY ENTIRE FIGHTING TECHNIQUE... CAUSE CERTAIN OTHER BATTLE-SKILLS TO BECOME WEAKER...
I GUESS I ENJOY THE CHALLENGE OF BEATING THE ODDS AGAINST ME TOO MUCH TO CHANGE MY APPROACH THIS LATE IN THE GAME.
I'LL PASS ON THE REST OF THE TREATMENT.
SUIT YOURSELF, C.A.!
YOU STAY HERE WITH MALUS, SEE IF HE'LL TELL YOU ANYTHING YOU HOPED TO LEARN HERE. I'LL GO SCOUT THE REST OF THE PLACE AND FETCH YOUR UNIFORM FROM THE TRUCK.
CHECK.
HAVE I JUST MADE A BAD DECISION?
WASHINGTON D.C. ...
THANK YOU FOR BRINGING THIS INFORMATION TO THE COMMISSION, GENTLEMEN.
I THINK WE ARE AGREED. HE CANNOT BE PERMITTED TO OPERATE IN THIS MANNER ANY LONGER.
SEND AGENTS TO BRING CAPTAIN AMERICA IN.
CONTINUED...!